Philip Sidney

AN APOLOGY FOR POETRY

Philip Sidney

AN APOLOGY FOR POETRY

[Edited with Complete Introduction, Biography, Author's Background, Complete Text, Select Criticism and Bibliography]

Aditya Nandwani
B.A. English (Hons), Delhi University;
M.A. (English), IGNOU; Print Journalism (English) YMCA

ANMOL PUBLICATIONS PVT. LTD.
NEW DELHI - 110 002 (INDIA)

ANMOL PUBLICATIONS PVT. LTD.

H.O.: 4374/4B, Ansari Road, Darya Ganj,
New Delhi-110 002 (India)
Ph.: 23278000, 23261597

B.O.: No. 1015, Ist Main Road, BSK IIIrd Stage
IIIrd Phase, IIIrd Block
Bangalore - 560 085 (India)
Visit us at: www.anmolpublications.com

An Apology for Poetry

First Published, 2009

PRINTED IN INDIA

Printed at Balaji Offset Press, Delhi.

Contents

Preface

Sir Philip Sydney was born in November 30, 1554 and died on October 17, 1586. He is one of the most popular figures of Elizabethan Age. He was known as a poet, soldier and courtier. He was the eldest son of Sir Henry Sidney and Lady Mary Dudley. He did is education at Shrewsbury School and Christ Chuch, Oxford.

A few of the major works are Astrophel and Stella -The Countess of Pembroke's Arcadia, 'Defense of Poetry etc. Astrophil and Stella was created in 1580 and was the first popular English sonnet sequences.

Author

Chapter 1

Introduction

Sir Philip Sidney wrote An Apology for Poetry (or, The Defence of Poetry) in 1581, and published it in 1595. Sidney wrote the Apology before 1583. It is generally believed that he was at least partly motivated by Stephen Gosson, a former playwright who dedicated his attack on the English stage, The School of Abuse, to Sidney in 1579, but Sidney primarily addresses more general objections to poetry, such as those of Plato. In his essay, Sidney integrates a number of classical and Italian precepts on fiction. The essence of his defence is that poetry, by combining the liveliness of history with the ethical focus of philosophy, is more effective than either history or philosophy in rousing its readers to virtue. The work also offers important comments on Edmund Spenser and the Elizabethan stage.

Influence

Sir Philip Sidney's influence can be seen throughout the subsequent history of English literary criticism. One of the most important examples is in the work of the poet and critic, Percy Bysshe Shelley. Shelley's modern argument for poetry is cast in a Romantic strain in his critical work titled A Defence of Poetry. In 1858, William Stigant, a Cambridge-educated translator, poet and essayist, writes in his essay "Sir Philip Sidney"[1] that Shelley's "beautifully written Defence of Poetry" is a work which "analyses the very inner essence of poetry and the reason of its existence, - its development from, and operation on, the mind of man". Shelley writes in Defence that while "ethical science arranges the elements which poetry has created," and leads to a moral civil life, poetry acts in a way that "awakens and enlarges the mind itself by rendering it the receptacle of a thousand unapprehended combinations of thought".

Sidney's influence on future writers could also be analyzed from the standpoint of his handling of the utilitarian viewpoint. The utilitarian view of rhetoric can be traced from Sophists, Joseph Justus Scaliger, Petrus Ramus and humanists to Sidney. For instance, Sidney, following Aristotle, writes that praxis (human action) is tantamount to gnosis (knowledge). Men drawn to music, astronomy, philosophy and so forth all direct themselves to "the highest end of the mistress knowledge, by the Greeks called architectonike" (literarlly, "of or for a master builder")," which stands, according to Sidney, "in the knowledge of a man's self, in the ethic and political consideration, with the end of well doing and not of well knowing only". Sidney's programme of literary reform concerns the connection between art and virtue.

One of the themes of the Apology is the insufficiency of simply presenting virtue as a precept; the poet must move men to virtuous action. Poetry can lead to virtuous action. Action relates to experience.

From Sidney, the utilitarian view of rhetoric can be traced to Coleridge's criticism, and for instance, to the reaction to the Enlightenment. Coleridge's brief treatise On Poesy or Art sets forth a theory of imitation which bears a remarkable resemblance to that of Sidney. The contemporary impact of Sidney's Apology is largely derivative of the humanistic precepts that inform the work, and its linkage of the rhetorical with the civic virtue of prudence. Prudence offers a middle ground between two extremes. Prudence, as a virtue, places a greater value on praxis than gnosis. Action is thus more important than abstract knowledge. It deals with the question of how to combine stability with innovation.

Sidney's influence on future critics and poets relates more closely to his view of the place of poets in society. Sidney describes poetry as creating a separate reality. The Romantic notion, as seen in Wordsworth, is that poetry privileges perception, imagination and modes of understanding. Wordsworth seeks to go back to nature for moments recollected in tranquility. Sidney, like Shelley and Wordsworth, sees the poet as being separate from society. To Sidney the poet is not tied to any subjection. He saw art as equivalent to "skill," a profession to be learned or developed, and nature as the objective, empirical world. The poet can invent, and thus in effect grows another nature.

Sidney writes that there "is no art delivered to mankind that hath not the works of nature for his principal object". The poet then does not depart from external nature. His works are "imitation" or "fiction," made of the materials of nature, and are shaped by the artist's vision. This vision is one that demands the reader's awareness of the art of imitation created through the "maker," the poet. Sidney's notion of "fore-conceit" means that a conception of the work must exist in the poet's mind before it is written. Free from the limitations of nature, and independent from nature, poetry is capable of "making things either better than Nature bringeth forth, or, quite anew, forms such as never were in Nature".

Sidney's doctrine presents the poet as creator. The poet's mediating role between two worlds – transcendent forms and historical actuality – corresponds to the Neoplatonic doctrine of emanation. A complement to this doctrine is the concept of return or catharsis, which finds a parallel in Sidney's contemplation of virtue, based on man's rational desire. Apology contains only elements of Neoplatonism without adhering to the full doctrine.

Thirdly, Sidney implies a theory of metaphoric language in his work. A recurring motif in Apology is painting or "portraiture". Apology applies language use in a way suggestive of what is known in modern literary theory as semiotics. His central premise is that poetry is an art of imitation, that is a "representing, counterfeiting, or figuring forth" not unlike a "speaking picture". Sidney pays his homage to Aristotle. Yet he develops his own idea of metaphoric language, one that it is based on an analogy through universal correspondences. Sidney's humanist poetics and his tendency to harmonize disparate extremes – to seek mediation – find expression in poetic works by John Donne. The life and writings of Sir Philip Sidney remain a legacy. In 1819, Thomas Campbell concludes that Sidney's life was "poetry in action," and then in 1858 William Stigant wrote that "Sidney's real poem was his life, and his teaching was his example". Sidney, the man, is apparent everywhere in his works: a study of Sidney's works is a study of the man.

Significance

An Apology for Poetry is the most important contribution to Renaissance literary theory. Sidney advocates a place for poetry within the framework of an aristocratic state, while showing concern for both literary and national identity. Sidney responds in Apology to an emerging antipathy to poetry as expressed in Stephen Gosson's The Schoole of Abuse (1579). Gosson offers what is in essence a puritan attack on imaginative literature. What is at stake in Sidney's argument is a defence of poetry's nobility. The significance of the nobility of poetry is its power to move readers to virtuous action. True poets must teach and delight – a view that dates back to Horace.

In an era of antipathy to poetry and puritanical belief in the corruption engendered by literature, Sidney's defence was a significant contribution to the genre of literary criticism. It was England's first philosophical defence in which he describes poetry's ancient and indispensable place in society, its mimetic nature, and its ethical function. Among Sidney's gifts to his contemporaries were his respect for tradition and willingness to experiment.

An example of the latter is his approach to Plato. He reconfigures Plato's argument against poets by saying poets are "the least liar". Poets never claim to know the truth, nor "make circles around your imagination," nor rely on authority (Letich 349). As an expression of a cultural attitude descending from Aristotle, Sidney, when stating that the poet "never affirmeth," makes the claim that all statements in literature are hypothetical or pseudo-statements. Sidney, as a traditionalist, however, gives attention to drama in contradistinction to poetry. Drama, writes Sidney, is "observing neither rules of honest civility nor of skillful poetry" and thus cannot do justice to this genre.

In Sidney's day anti-theatricality, an aesthetic and ideological concern, flourished among Sidney's circle at court. Theatre became a contentious issue in part because of the culmination of a growing contempt for the values of the emergent consumer culture. An expanding money economy encouraged social mobility.

Europe, at this time, had its first encounter with inflation. London's theatres at that time grew in popularity so much that by 1605, despite the introduction of charges, London commercial theatres could accommodate up to eight thousand men and women. Sidney had his own views on drama. In Apology, he shows opposition to the current of his day that pays little attention to unity of place in drama, but more specifically, his concern is with the "manner" that the "matter" is conveyed. He explains that tragedy is not bound to history or the narrative but to "laws of poesy," having "liberty, either to feign a quite new matter, or to frame the history to the most most tragical conveniency".

Sidney employs a number of strategies to assert the proper place of poetry. For instance, he argues against the way in which poetry was misaligned with youth, the effeminate and the timorous. He does so by introducing the idea that "poetry is the companion of camps" and by invoking the heroes of ages past. Sidney's reverence for the poet as soldier is significant because he himself was a soldier at one time. Poetry, in Apology, becomes an art that requires the noble stirring of courage. Sidney writes An Apology for Poetry in the form of a judicial oration for the defence, and thus it is like a trial in structure. Crucial to his defence is the descriptive discourse and the idea that poetry creates a separate reality. Sidney employs forensic rhetoric as a tool to make the argument that poetry not only conveys a separate reality, but that it has a long and venerable history, and it does not lie. It is defensible in its own right as a means to move readers to virtuous action.

Sidney's Method

Censorship is one issue Sidney had to overcome through his use of rhetorical devices in the Apology. Sidney was also versed in the phenomenon of courtiership. As part of his strategy against the threat of censorship, Sidney uses the structure of classical oration with its conventional divisions such as exordium and peroration. Sidney's use of classical oration stems from his humanist education. He uses this method to build his argument, by making use of the rhetorical methods in such guides as Thomas Wilson's Arte of Rhetorique (1553). Sidney also uses metaphor and allegory, to conceal and reveal his position.

For instance, his use of horsemanship as imagery and analogy substantiates his vision of the transformational power of poetry. Sidney, as author, enters his work undetected in that the etymology of his name "Philip" is "horse-lover". From the opening discourse on horsemanship, Sidney expands on the horse and saddle metaphor throughout his work by the "enlarging of a conceit". It is Sidney who then guards against a falling out with the "poet-whippers". Sidney also attends to the rhetorical concept of memory. Poetry, apart from its ability to delight, has an affinity with memory.

Method and style are thus key components of the Apology to overcome the problem of censorship. For this reason, Sidney consciously defends fiction, and he attacks the privilege that is accorded to "fact." He argues that the poet makes no literal claims of truth, is under no illusions, and thus creates statements that are in a sense "fictional" and as true as any others. What is at stake then is not only the value of poetry in the sense of its utility, but also its place in a world replete with strife, the contingent and the provisional.

Chapter 2

Biographical Note

Born into great expectations at the estate of Penshurst, Kent, on 30 November 1554, Philip Sidney was educated at Shrewsbury Grammar School in Shropshire, and entered Corpus Christi College, Oxford, in 1568. After three years, he departed for the traditional "Grand Tour" of continental Europe, arriving in Paris 1572, the year of the St. Bartholomew's Day Massacre, of which he was an eyewitness. He became friends with the noted humanist scholar Hubert Languet, and spent the winter with him at Frankfort.

In 1573 he passed through Hungary and Vienna on his way to Venice, and the following winter visited Padua, Florence, and Genoa. Sidney joined Edward Wotton for an embassy to the Imperial Court at Vienna, 1574-5, and returned to England, after a visit to Poland, in June 1575. In 1576, he became Queen Elizabeth's cupbearer and traveled to Ireland to take part in the campaign with Essex. For several years, the gallant, dashing, and well-traveled young Sidney, who was greatly admired on the Continent and at home, waited for an opportunity to serve his Queen in some capacity commensurate with his abilities, but no such opportunity came— perhaps because his volatile temperament could not safely be employed in the temporizing style of government she required to ensure stability.

It was probably in 1578 that Sidney's small pageant, The Lady of May, was presented before the Queen in vain hopes of persuading her to look with more favour on his uncle Leicester (and by extension, himself). At this time he also began work on the Old Arcadia, which he completed about 1581.

Finding employment at Court virtually denied him, Sidney at this time (1578-82) divided his time between visits with his friends (including Edmund Spenser, who published The Shepheardes Calendar in 1579) and his own writing, including The Defence of Poesie [1580-81], Certaine Sonets [1581], and Astrophel and Stella [1581-2]. He also began, but did not complete, a new version of the Arcadia.

Beginning about 1583, it seemed Sidney's fortunes might be about to turn. He was knighted in that year, so that he could stand in for his absent friend Prince Casimir of the Palatinate in installation as a Knight of the Garter. An important appointment came to him soon after, assisting the Earl of Warwick, Master of Ordinance, in preparing the defence of England against possible invasion by the Spanish. In the fall, he married Frances Walsingham.

It was Sidney's belief that the best way to slow the advance of the Spanish empire on the Continent was to attack the colonies of Spain in the New World. He arranged, in 1584, to sail with Sir Francis Drake on such an expedition but was recalled by the Queen at the last moment and made governor of Flushing, in the Netherlands. Sidney took up the cause of the overextended and unpaid garrison but discovered that his uncle, the Earl of Leicester, had diverted the allocated funds to his own use. Sidney nevertheless rallied the troops as best he could, and, going to the relief of the garrison at Zutphen, 22 September 1586, was wounded in the thigh by a musket ball. The wound festered, and he died, in great pain, at Arnheim, 17 October. All of Europe was stunned by the loss, and the body of Philip Sidney was laid to rest with a lavish state funeral at St. Paul's cathedral, London, 16 February 1587 (Kimbrough, unpaginated chronology, Sir Philip Sidney).

The Defence of Poesie

Sidney's famous essay is said to be a response to an attack on poetry and stage plays, which had been dedicated to him without his permission, by Stephen Gosson, a former playwright: The Schoole of Abuse, 1579. Another reply, inferior but interesting, had been published by Thomas Lodge in 1580.

Henry Olney produced a printing of An Apologie for

Poetrie in the spring of 1595; this edition proved to be unauthorized, as William Ponsonby had entered the work in the Stationer's register on November 29, 1594. Olney was directed to halt sale and turn over his remaining copies to Ponsonby, who replaced the title page with his own and sold the copies along with his own printing.

These combined copies, and those of Ponsonby's own edition printed by Thomas Creede, are rare, whereas Olney's exists in a number of copies. Four versions of the Defence are known: The Penshurst manuscript, De L'Isle MS. no. 1226; The Norwich manuscript found in 1966 in a commonplace book of Francis Blomefield's; An Apologie for Poetrie, Olney's printing of 1595, and Ponsonby's The Defence of Poesie of the same year. An examination of the paper used in the two manuscript versions, which was done at the request of Mary Mohl, the discoverer of the Norwich maunuscript, suggested that the latter, though in some respects inferior, is the older of the two (The Apology for Poetry xxiv). If this is the case, a stemma of these documents might appear as follows:

Fair Copy (no longer extant)
Copy seen by both Copy seen by both
Ponsonby's compositor Norwich scribe and
— — —Penshurst scribe Olney's compositor—
(no longer extant) (no longer extant)
Norwich, 1584-1595 (?)
Ponsonby, 1595 Olney, 1595
Penshurst (Robert Sidney's copy) ca. 1600

A definitive edition, collating all these, and recording all variants, with excellent endnotes, may be found in Miscellaneous Prose of Sir Philip Sidney [1973], edited by Katherine Duncan-Jones and Jan Van Dorsten. See also Katherine Duncan-Jones' excellent contribution to the Oxford Authors Series of Oxford University Press, Sir Philip Sidney [1989]. The notes are, as is usual in the series, outstanding, especially in tracing Sidney's reading in Scaliger and the classical authors.

Many scholars, some of whom have devoted a lifetime with skill and devotion to the task, have written on Sidney and on the Defence, so a definitive general introduction will not be attempted here. There is one aspect of the Defence, however, that has been often noted only in passing, and often dismissively, and as I feel it is Sidney's main point I will attempt to throw a little light on it. Sidney is conscious throughout his defence that it is fiction he is defending, and that his strength lies in attacking the privilege generally accorded to "fact." He says that "of all writers under the Sunne, the Poet is the least lyer"; that is, the practitioners of what we now call the academic disciplines are regularly betrayed by their literalism, while the poet, who is under no illusions, freely creates "fictional" statements as true as any other, and the truer for not being asserted as literal. Sidney's approach is characteristic of Renaissance humanism, and more closely akin to modern semiotic theory than is generally appreciated.

Renaissance education came to specialize in rhetoric at a time in which political and economic power came to be concentrated in the courts of princes. This can hardly be a coincidence. Every courtier was trained to the art of sprezzatura, of skill in seeming effortlessness in horsemanship, swordplay, singing, dancing, speaking, and writing, so as to catch the eye of those higher in the hierarchy, and especially that of the prince. Self-presentation has always been and remains the first move in the game of self-advancement, but for the Renaissance in general and Elizabethans especially, "fashioning a self," to echo Spenser, was an obsession. Peter Ramus and the humanist rhetoricians provided a timely operating environment for such pursuits, because their foregrounding of the provisional status of any assertion helped the courtiers to understand self-image as a work in progress rather than as a cynical device.

The Defence of Poesie reflects the humanist education which Shrewsbury and Oxford had given to Sidney, and reflects on the rhetorical aims of self-presentation with which an underemployed Elizabethan gentleman would undertake such a work. It follows the rules and outline of a standard argument: exordium, proposition, division, examination, refutation, digression, peroration; and does so with a spirit and style that must have done its author great credit in the eyes of his contemporaries.

The Defence serves almost as a copia of Renaissance theory, for Sidney brings every available gun to bear on his objective: Pliny, Musaeus, Homer, Hesiod, Orpheus, Linus, Amphion, Livius Andronicus, Ennius, Dante, Boccaccio, Petrarch, Gower, Chaucer, Thales, Empedocles, Parmenides, Pythagoras, Phocilydes, Herodotus, Virgil, Xenophon, Tremellius, Junius, Tyrtaeus, Lucretius, Manilius, Pontanus, Lucan, Cicero, Heliodorus, Plato, Aristotle, Cornelius Agrippa, Horace, Terence, More, Erasmus, "Dares Phrygius," Plautus, Euripides, Phocion, Sannazaro, Boethius, Persius, Plutarch, Pindar, Tasso, Ovid, Dio Cassius, Ariosto, Scaliger, Bembo, Bibbiena, Beze, Melancthon, Fracastorio, Muret, Buchanan, Hurault, Juvenal, Surrey, Spenser, Sackville, Norton, Apuleius, Demosthenes, Landino, and both Old and New Testaments are all cited in support of his position, which as every critic will tell you is that poetry is useful because it delights as it teaches, a view that dates back to Horace and beyond.

The venerable tradition of didacticism, and Sidney's heavy reliance upon it in the Defence, has sometimes led to a tendency to dismiss the Defence as derivative: "not a very original theorist," says Hazard Adams in Critical Theory Since Plato. Adams himself, however, notices something that "sounds modern" in Sidney's argument that the poet "nothing affirmeth, and therefore never lieth." He perceptively compares Sidney on this point to I.A. Richards, but concludes that the comparison will go nowhere because "Sidney does not have a modern theory of language". While it is obvious that Sidney had not the advantage, in his education, of having read Ferdinand de Saussure and his successors, I believe it is a mistake, on the basis of our own historical chauvinism, not to seek the implications of Sidney's argument, and to callously assume that Sidney did not himself see some of those implications. Nor was Sidney alone in so seeing; Renaissance humanists, of whom Sidney was one, understood not merely formal rhetoric but epistemology and even ontology in terms of appearances.

Throughout the period, diagrams appeared in books, such as Andrew Borde's The First Book of the Introduction to Knowledge [1542], or Robert Fludd's Utriusque Cosmi Historia [1616], relating the Ptolemaic cosmology to the idea of a "great chain of being" in which the cosmos is arranged as a hierarchy in which each successive level downward in the hierarchy contains entities which are analogies of entities in the preceding level; to begin to understand the world view of those who produced these diagrams, it may help to visualize ourselves not as "made in the image of God" in the sense that we are independent objects that resemble God, but are actual depictions of God, like paintings.

In this view, nature is not divided from God in the way in which we are accustomed, after Descartes, to think, but is something more like a thought or imagination in the mind of God. As imago dei, we reflect our Maker in all that we do, and most of all in doing what our Maker does: to make, especially by imagining. To attempt to improve one's image is then not the dishonest activity, which an Enlightenment materialist assumes it to be, but in imitatio dei, is to participate in the creative activity of the Cosmos. Such a world view will hold that all epistemological practice will be mimetic in procedure, and this is in fact what Sidney tells us early on:

There is no Art delivered unto mankind that hath not the works of nature for his principal object, without which they could not consist, and on which they so depend, as they become Actors & Plaiers, as it were of what nature will have set forth. So doth the Astronomer looke upon the starres, and by that he seeth set downe what order nature hath taken therein. So doth the Geometritian & Arithmetitian, in their divers sorts of quantities. So doth the Musitians intimes tel you, which by nature agree, which not.

The natural Philosopher thereon hath his name, and the morall Philosopher standeth uppon the naturall vertues, vices, or passions of man: and follow nature saith he therein, and thou shalt not erre. The Lawier saith, what men have determined. The Historian, what men have done. The Gramarian, speaketh onely of the rules of speech, and the

Rhetoritian and Logitian, considering what in nature wil soonest proove, and perswade thereon, give artificiall rules, which still are compassed within the circle of a question, according to the proposed matter.

The Phisitian wayeth the nature of mans bodie, & the nature of things helpfull, or hurtfull unto it. And the Metaphisicke though it be in the second & abstract Notions, and therefore be counted supernaturall, yet doth hee indeed build upon the depth of nature.

"By that he seeth set down what order nature hath taken therein." The sciences map the patterns of their objects of inquiry. The poet has the advantage over these, says Sidney, in that he creates a meta-map, or seeks to re-present the mind itself ("first nature") in which nature ("second nature") is but a thought. Poetic imagination brings forth a model on which readers or audiences can build their own characters for the better: it worketh, not onely to make a Cyrus, which had bene but a particular excellency as nature might have done, but to bestow a Cyrus upon the world to make many Cyrusses, if they will learne aright, why and how that maker made him.

It is this poetic mold from which so many Cyruses can be formed that Sidney refers to as architectonike, the science of sciences. The argument between the philosopher and the historian which Sidney vividly describes is a battle for the honour of being taken for the prescribing artist. The philosopher gives precepts but does not map them onto the world; the historian gives a picture of the world, but cannot by mere description point us to the precepts which would bring it into harmony with the divine mind; the poet then takes away the honour from them both by relating the precepts to the world, mapping "should" onto "is," as it were:

> Now doth the peerlesse Poet performe both [the work of the philosopher and the historian], for whatsoever the Philosopher saith should be done, he gives a perfect picture of it by some one, by whom he presupposeth it was done, so as he coupleth the generall notion with the particuler example.

The poet's "presupposition" makes no assertion of fact, though it is important to note that it does imply an assertion that the model presented is, if "rightly" done, exemplary. Every practitioner of an "art" or "science" proceeds by mimetic activity, in observing and then in proceeding through metaphor to represent to society what has been observed. Only the poet (here, creator of fiction, or literary practitioner) trades in metaphor itself rather than in its product.

This is not strictly true, even for Sidney, for he admits that the priest or preacher takes precedence in such trading. But he does not admit that theologians work in anything "better" than metaphor; instead, he refers to David and Jesus as poets, and suggests, albeit obliquely, that all didacticism is dependent upon a merely posited and purely metaphorical world view. A simpler way to put all this is that there is unfortunately no alternative to simply taking our belief in God, the cosmos, our earth as we perceive it, and our society as we experience it, on faith and not as anything known directly in and of itself. The lines drawn ("coupleth") in mental space between "notion" and "example" are the very stuff of which all knowledge, Sidney implies, is made. Sidney hammers this point home by his argument on "lies." Poets are accused of lying, since there is no necessary connection between their models and observed phenomena. His reply is that in all the other arts, the assumption is made that models re-present observations accurately; but this is never so.

Therefore he can assert that of all writers under the Sunne, the Poet is the least lyer: and though he wold, as a Poet can scarecely be a lyer. The Astronomer with his cousin the Geometrician, can hardly escape, when they take upon them to measure the height of the starres. How often thinke you do the Phisitians lie, when they averre things good for sicknesses, which afterwards send Charon a great number of soules drowned in a potion, before they come to his Ferrie? And no lesse of the rest, which take upon them to affirme. Now for the Poet, he nothing affirmeth, and therefore never lieth: for as I take it, to lie, is to affirme that to bee true, which is false. So as the other Artistes, and especially the Historian, affirming manie things, can in the clowdie knowledge of mankinde, hardly escape from manie lies.

The argument is at first glance specious. Of course fictions are false; that is what fiction means. Our common sense (empiricist) assumption, which has gained ground greatly since the age of Hobbes and Newton, is that while Sidney's point is well taken, in that our technicians have as yet gotten the facts wrong, but he must be joking, for the facts are nevertheless there, and they will get them right eventually. But I believe Sidney is serious here. He says, "in the clowdy knowledge of mankinde," with no qualifiers. That he does so provides us with the crux of his argument.

From Petrarch on, the assumption of scholars during the Renaissance was that the centuries from the fall of Rome until their own time were a "dark age," in which the great knowledge of the ancients fell into disuse; it was their mission to recover something of the glory of Greece and Rome by recovering and mastering their literature and "arts," or, interchangeably, "sciences." History, Philosophy, Mathematics, Astronomy, and Medicine were among these, as were painting and sculpture, music, and the production of literary works, especially epic, tragedy, comedy, satire, lyric, pastoral, and other forms, which some authorities gathered together under the heading of "poesie."

A student in England in the age of Ascham and Wilson could expect to be exposed to a wide range of "arts" and literary and historical works under the curriculum—an adaptation of the medieval trivium—by which means students had for centuries been taught grammar, rhetoric, and dialectic. Although this curriculum was often taught under the implicit assumption that it formed a seamless and perfect whole, it contained a contradiction that produced (and still produces today) considerable friction among thinkers and artists. Plato had regarded rhetoric as a highly suspect art, productive of immorality.

He argued for dialectic to be used in its place, which he defined as the science of understanding (architectonike) as oppposed to merely convincing; he desired that the conclusion of a syllogism be true of the world to which it refers (Theatetus, Sophist, Phaedrus, Republic). Aristotle had made a place for rhetoric within dialectic by claiming that dialectic is simply the use of complete syllogisms to understand truth while rhetoric is the use of partial syllogisms to attain specific ends, such as convincing a jury of one's innocence, regardless of one's actual guilt (Rhetoric).

But attacks against the primacy of dialectic had been made, notably by Peter Ramus, whose doctoral dissertation was on the topic "everything Aristotle said was wrong." Ramus chose to invert Aristotle's position and upheld that dialectic is but a part of rhetoric, thus re-privileging rhetoric as the architectonike, or science of sciences, as it had been formerly held by the Sophists to be. Ramus' insight was that an assumption generally made by dialecticians is that true premises can be found upon which to base the complete syllogisms that are intended to lead to true, that is, ontological, knowledge. Ramus's system of logic, unlike that of Aristotle, assumes that a premise is always only posited, and any conclusions based on it are likewise only posited.

The empiricist view is that the senses report a "real" or literal world that is like our conception of it. The empiricist view of language is that words refer to objects in a "real" world, and that metaphor is a distortion of reference, so that a word can be used out of its proper context in order to make a useful statement about another kind of object in another context. Thus, we can say of a wise prince: "behold Cyrus!" — transferring reference from the real Cyrus who was wise onto someone who is not Cyrus, but whose wisdom we wish to praise. Sidney calls our attention to the unsupportable assumption in the phrase "real Cyrus." What real Cyrus? Historians cannot show us one; they are only repeating what they have heard. Their Cyrus is posited only. This realization undermines the empiricist view of language and suggests that contrary to what we expect, all reference is metaphorical. It is our insistence on literality that is the distortion, for the literal is only metaphor that we have agreed among ourselves to regard as somehow non- metaphorical.

This idea is at the root both of the effectiveness of the art of rhetoric and of our uneasy but continued acceptance of it.

Plato sought an immaterial reality, Aristotle a material one; Sidney suspects that neither can be found by us, but at best a model of a posited model, or copy of a posited copy (Plato's nightmare) can be fashioned and tested.

This utilitarian view is the basis of rhetorical theory, and can be traced from the Sophists through Scaliger, Ramus, and the humanists, to Sidney, to Milton, to the reaction to the Enlightenment in Coleridge's criticism, and in our own time to suggestions made by C.S. Peirce, William James, Karl Popper, Owen Barfield, W.V. Quine, Benjamin Lee Whorf, Stanley Fish, and many others.

Why, then, do critics feel that Sidney "does not have a modern theory of language"? The answer is that he does not follow through on his own insight but applies the very principle he has just refuted, that of the common-sense privileging of literality, in his criticism of the current drama; of it he complains that:Now you shall have three Ladies walke to gather flowers, and then we must beleeve the stage to be a garden. By and by we heare newes of shipwrack in the same place, then we are too blame if we accept it not for a Rock. Upon the back of that, comes out a hidious monster with fire and smoke, and then the miserable beholders are bound to take it for a Cave: while in the mean time two Armies flie in, represented with foure swords & bucklers, and then what hard hart will not receive it for a pitched field.

The complaint here is of the English habit of paying little or no attention to "unity of place." Sidney believed, along with Lodovico Castelvetro and others, that Aristotle had proscribed dramatic action beyond one circuit of the sun. The name of Aristotle as the authority behind the notion of "unity of time" could hardly be ignored. Greeks in the time of Aristotle regarded physical presentation in drama (and dance) as a sacred activity, and it was as important not to do confusing things with time as it would be not to get the words of a spell out of sequence. Literality mattered; one cannot move twenty years in one's own body, so one's "stage" body ought not to do this either; it is an insult to the persona inhabited by the actor to be treated quite so cavalierly. Renaissance critics sensed that jumping the action from one location to another involved the same problem as jumping it from one time to another; if we cannot get from the garden to the battlefield in three minutes ourselves, we should not have our actors do so.

But in English drama, eighteen hundred years after the drama described by Aristotle, the tabu against representing a long story as nimbly with one's body as Homer was free to do with his words has largely disappeared. The actors engage our imaginations only, are visual as well as auditory metaphors, and the audience can provide narrative unity itself by the use of memory. Though Sidney does not see that his own destruction of literality points to the success, rather than failure, of the native theatrical tradition, he provides a glimpse of the solution even as he argues mistakenly for the literalism of observing the unities: you shall have Asia of the one side, and Affricke of the other, and so mannie other under Kingdomes, that the Player when he comes in, must ever begin

The charge that Sidney's theory of language is not modern is misdirected. He is accurate in his assessment of language, and goes astray only when adopting a poetics that runs counter to his own theory. In Twelfth Night, which our unfortunate Sir Philip did not live to witness, we have both the refutation of the literalist theory with which he was saddled, and the confirmation of the metaphorical theory he so brilliantly elucidated. In refutation, we easily conceive the three months of the action, and its movement from seacoast to palace, street, and garden; the work is unified by its being a kind of land voyage of discovery, or rather recovery, of the losses that were sustained on the high seas. In confirmation, the play is, as Sidney recommends, an invention that is eikastike, and not phantastike, in that it figures forth good things, showing its Viola as one who should be emulated and its Malvolio as one who, perhaps, should not, though he never lacks his humanity. And these are inventions all, the "lies" of the poet. Yet if anyone should call Viola a lie, would we not give them the lie-direct? She lives in our minds, and not necessarily in our minds alone: so far substantially is she worked, not only to make a Viola, which had been but a particular excellency, as nature might have done, but to bestow a Viola upon the world, to make many Violas, if we will learn aright why and how that maker made her!

We all use metaphors, says Sidney, for we cannot communicate our various knowledges without them, literal reference being a prerogative of a higher Nature than that we are born to. But to some of us it is given to not merely use metaphors, but to create them. If, says he, we are so blinded by our literality that we must condemn our metaphor-makers out of hand, then we bring upon ourselves the curse of oblivion, for our memorials are necessarily constructed entirely of metaphor: and when you die, your memorie die from the earth for want of an Epitaphe. The Defence of Poesie cannot be charged with lack of modernity until its linguistic premise can be shown to have been superseded. This has not yet occurred.

Risa Stephanie Bear, 1992

Chapter 3

Apologizing for Pleasure in Sidney's 'Apology for Poetry': the Nurse of Abuse Meets the Tudor Grammar School

As one of its major strategies for defending poetry, Sidney's Apology describes poetry's capacity simultaneously to teach and to delight, to instruct effectively by appealing to pleasure. According to the Apology, it is pleasure, which creates poetry as superior to history and philosophy, for poetry's ability to delight moves readers to virtue, rather than subjecting them to tedious discussions or ambiguous examples. Even in the initial stages of civilization, it was the "sweet delights" of poetry, which prepared early peoples to exercise their minds for the reception of knowledge. But on the other side of the Apology's claim that poetry's delight enlivens its teaching lies the inference that the experience of delight must be justified by instruction.

This inference becomes explicit in the Apology's limitation of its defence to a definition of poetry as "feigning notable images of virtues, vices, or what else, with... delightful teaching". When separated from its moral function, poetry's pleasure renders it a "nurse of abuse," dangerously capable of eliciting the wrong sort of pleasure to infect its readers with "pestilent desires". By exploring the "nurse of abuse" image, together with other highly gendered figures, this essay advances the following argument: to the explicit charges against which Sidney's Apology defends poetry—that it lies, it promotes immorality, it was banished from Plato's ideal republic, and that it serves no useful purpose—can be added an implicit charge, that the pleasures offered by poetry rendered it dangerously effeminizing.

A reading of Sidney's Apology as defending poetry against charges of effeminacy was perhaps first performed in a passing comment by Walter Ong, who suggested that the anxiety, common among Renaissance humanists, that "literature, and poetry in particular, was actually soft or effeminate" motivated Sidney's claim that the Amadis de Gaule moved men to courage. More recently, M. J. Doherty's gendered reading of the Apology has also linked Sidney's poet and femininity.

Interpreting the Apology's Lady Poesy in terms of the ancient figure of Sophia or Wisdom, Doherty's work represents Sidney's poet as appropriating a feminine self-knowledge which poses no threat, however, to his masculinity. Fran Dolan's essay on the dichotomies between art and nature, on the other hand, locates Sidney's Apology within a tradition representing poetry as an erotic threat precisely because of a long-standing association between poetry's "pleasure and desire with the feminine." Dolan claims that, like Puttenham and Montaigne, Sidney uses a "gendered and eroticized" construction of poetry to "convey the vulnerability and impairment of the masculine poet." While much remains to be done with the gendered metaphors and concepts in the Apology, these discussions of the inextricable entanglement of poetry in gender issues provide a radically new approach, which promises to recover ideological operations working deeply within the early modern culture and its texts.

Any full-scale rereading of the Apology in terms of gender must first, however, take into account recent work representing a crisis in early modern gender ideology. Since Laqueur uncovered the one-sex model of early modern gender, scholars have newly understood that in this period, in a more literal sense than in modern times, gender was a question of performance—of costume, of gesture, of status—rather than of ontological being. In her study of Gosson's Schoole of Abuse, a work dedicated to Sidney and convincingly claimed as a major impetus for his Apology, Laura Levine describes how this one-sex model created "an unmanageable anxiety that there is no such thing as a masculine self." Thus, for Gosson and others, the spectacle of boys on stage in women's clothing embodied the culture's worst fantasy concerning the reversability of male gender, as adopting the costume and gestures of femininity, the boy actor became in some sense the part he played.

Extending Levine's argument, Stephen Orgel discovers an early modern anxiety that heterosexual love can turn men not only into women, but "back into women," for "in the medical literature we all started as women, and the culture confirmed this by dressing all children in skirts until the age of seven or so." Laqueur's performative version of masculinity further explains Orgel's perception of the essential femininity of early modern boys: in his dependence upon women who dominated him, a boy was not yet able to enact his masculinity. But these essays do not account for the source of this threat of infantilization. What within the nature of heterosexual love was understood to propel boys (or men) helplessly back to this degraded, effeminate state?

Sidney's Apology provides an ideal vehicle through which to study this fear of regression in its representation of the wrong sort of poetry as a "nurse of abuse." Enacting a sort of demonic pieta reducing grown men to the passivity of sleeping infants, this nightmare figure recurs in various texts to embody a widespread anxiety that the pleasures of poetry somehow unleashed the most infantilizing effects of female domination on adult males.

In Spenser's Faerie Queene, she appears as Acrasia, cradling the limp Verdant who has left his "suspended instruments" hanging in a nearby tree to sink into a helpless (and seemingly permanent) post-coital lethargy; critics have noted that Acrasia's Bower of Bliss is described in the same terms used by contemporary defenders of poetry. On a lighter note, Shakespeare's comic artist-figure Bottom takes the place of the changeling child to be pleasured and dominated in the arms of the fairy queen in A Midsummer Night's Dream before he attempts to write a "ballad of this dream." In the Schoole of Abuse, Gosson's scorn for men who choose "wallowing in ladies lappes" over "wrastling at arms" includes a warning against "all suche delights as may winne us to pleasure." Gosson's description of how such delights may "rocke us in sleep" enacts this same merger of adult lust with regressive infantilism.

While Sidney may have been directly influenced by Gosson, the presence of this figure in the works of Shakespeare and Spenser shows that the fear of this regressive process, elicited by the pleasures of poetry, was widespread in the early modern culture. These anxieties, and their link to poetry, are expressed with special clarity in Sidney's "nurse of abuse" passage: " is the nurse of abuse, infecting us with many pestilent desires; with a siren's sweetness drawing the mind to the serpent's tail of sinful fancies... both in other nations and in ours, before poets did soften us, we were full of courage, given to martial exercises, the pillars of warlike liberty, and not lulled asleep in shady idleness with poet's pastimes.". This splitting of the male self between the warrior of the past and the infant-like reader, nursed and "lulled asleep" in the present controls much of the argument and the imagery of the Apology.

Like rabbits and ducks, warriors and infants perform a mental trompe d'oeil as they vie for the prominent position in the Apology which will render the loser invisible. Any victory is only temporary. They repeatedly exchange places because in the binary oppositions which construct them, the existence of each depends upon the absencepresence of the other. The effeminacy of the infantilized readers of poetry is necessary to define the highly phallic masculinity of the warrior: hard (not softened by poetry), strengthened by continual effort (not weakened by idle pleasure), oriented towards war (not towards sexual desire). But like most alien Others, this effeminate infant lies not outside but within the warrior. Following Theweleit's depiction of the soldier-male, the phallic depiction of men as pillars connotes the hard body surface—the armor—of the warrior male, which sharply differentiates him from others and from the desiring "female" (or the effeminate child) which remains within the self.

Pleasure plays a central role in this process. Theweleit describes the conversion of pleasure into anxiety in this splitting of the self between female (or childish) interior and male exterior: for the warrior male, pleasure evokes a fear that "dissolution may occur along the borders of the body", that the defined male self might become lost in the "desiring-production of the unconscious". The worst fears described in Theweleit's paradigm are realized abundantly in this passage. Dramatizing poetry's irresistible power, the merging of nurse's lullaby with siren's song enacts a destructive female engulfment of readers who are simultaneously infants and adult males. Readers once "full of courage" now have no more will to resist the pleasures of poetry than infants who cannot resist a lullaby or refuse disease-laden nurses' milk. Equating nurses with sirens recasts the narrative pleasures of lullabies, and the closeness with dominant women they enact, as a seductive desire which draws men to their death. Lured by an irresistible pleasure in poetry which dissolves the boundaries between adult love and infantile passivity, readers of love poetry helplessly regress to the time of female dominance when they were not yet male.

If the reader is infantilized, the poet is cross-dressed. It is one matter for poetry to be represented as a woman; it is another to represent even the wrong sort of poetry as nurses' milk and sirens' songs. The lullaby function of "poet's pastimes" which lulls readers' (moral) selves asleep not only blurs the distinctions between adult poetry and the songs and nursery rhymes of childhood; it also blurs the boundaries between the poet's voice and the voices of nurses. Feminizing the poet even more radically, the image of siren acts out the reversibility of gender inherent in the one sex gender system. The homonym of "tail" and "tale" in the description of the "siren's sweetness drawing the mind to the serpent's tail of sinful fancies" locates the wrong kind of poetry within the tails or genitalia of women. This homonym measures the extent to which textual pleasures, even the textual pleasures offered by poems written by adult males, were perceived as sexual pleasures, and both were encoded as female.

It might be argued that the Apology presents the "nurse of abuse" passage as one of various attacks against which Sidney defends poetry. But Sidney's counter-argument does not deny the role of poetry in this regressive process. In his impassioned claim "not that poetry abuses man's wit, but that man's wit abuses poetry", Sidney defends moral kinds of poetry by distinguishing them from love poetry. But, as Helgerson notes, against the wrong kind of poetry which "trains man's wit to wanton sinfulness and lustful love," the charges still stand. Moreover, the very terms of Sidney's counter-argument confirm the gender anxieties elicited by the "nurse of abuse" passage: "I yield that Poesy may not only be abused, but that being abused, by reason of his sweet charming force, it can do more hurt than any other army of words". Explicitly countering the effeminizing force of nurse-sirens in the imagery of poetry as an "army of words," the Apology personifies poetry as masculine for the first time in this text. But the stereotypically feminine adjectives "sweet charming" suggest that even as a military force, poetry's masculinity is vulnerable to the reverses imagined within a one sex gender system.

Anxieties elicited by this reversibility of gender identity similarly underlie the rigid polarities contrasting poetry and needlecraft in the counter-argument: "Truly a needle cannot do much hurt, and as truly (with leave of ladies be it spoken) it cannot do much good. With a sword thou mayest kill thy father, and with a sword thou mayest defend thy prince and country. So that, as in calling poets the fathers of lies they say nothing, so in this their agument of abuse they prove the commendation". The silent emendation of the original accusation leveled against poetry as the "mother of lies" to call poets the "father of lies" suggests the extent to which gender has become a sensitive issue in this passage. The phallocentric anxiety revealed by the contrast between the man's large sword to the woman's small needle has pushed the Apology's argument into a false position. Instead of defending poetry's morality, as this passage purports to do, it presents the ability to kill fathers as a necessary, if regrettable, aspect of poetry's virility.

This morally dubious assertion of the poet's masculinity is further undercut by the terms it employs. In size, the poet's pen resembles a woman's needle more than a warrior's sword; and like needles, poet's pens mark a flat surface within a private, domestic space. The inherent instability of this comparison of pens to swords calls into question an entire line of martial representations of poetry in the Apology. But to understand the wider cultural context which gives meaning to these representations, it is necessary to return to the "nurse of abuse," this time to consider the social formations by which middle- or upper-class males were installed into a prominent form of early modern masculinity.

Like most nightmare figures, Sidney's "nurse of abuse" embodies both a fear and a wish; it enacts both the desire and the threat of that desire to regress to female nurturance and domination. At this time, when according to Aries, "the effeminization of little boys" "had reached its height," a natural nostalgia for childhood posed a threat to gender identity. Yet while a desire for a release from masculinity was rendered unspeakable within this highly patriarchal culture, it was also an almost inevitable result of an abrupt childhood transition commonly experienced by privileged males. Sometime between seven and ten years of age, most upper class boys were suddenly separated from a relatively easy-going environment dominated by women to learn Latin from tutors or schoolmasters.

A significant force in shaping the elite male subject was not only this abrupt separation of seven-year-old boys from their extended families, but the meanings invested in this transition by the culture. One primary meaning was the conferral of a dominant early modern version of masculinity. William Kerrigan has eloquently represented the project of the early modern grammar school as the rebirth of the students' "linguistic ego" into a masculine world of Latin. For Walter Ong, the learning of Latin, and the severe methods through which it was taught, formed a "male puberty rite."

The learning of Latin functioned not only to mark gender, but to justify it as a means of transforming young boys into men worthy of assuming power. This process left little time for play. As T. W. Baldwin put it, Elizabethans "did not found schools to let boys play; in fact, invented all kinds of sinister devices to attempt to thwart that natural instinct.... They wanted taught to be men." The discipline required for a boy to spend most of his waking hours memorzing Latin grammar, translating from Latin and then back to English, and reciting lessons from rote, installed him within the prevailing grammar school ethic of "instinctual renunciation." This considerable mental discipline, reinforced at most schools with whippings and canings, was to be internalized to create a student population "'broken and bridled'" into strict control of the passions.

The theory advanced for this submission appealed to the elite nature of its population: training in obedience enabled children better to claim their proper positions of authority over others as adults. This rationalization is, in fact, explicitly stated in a letter to Philip Sidney from his father: "Be humble and obedient to your masters, for, unless your frame yourself to obey others—yea, and feel in yourself what obedience is, you shall never be able to teach others how to obey you." This obedience was to be internal as well as external, as stated in, for example, the common schooltext Erasmus's Adages: "Nemo bene imperat": "A man must fyrst rule his own lustes, and be himselfe obedient to ryght reason, ere he can well governe other."

Central to the grammar school project was the forceful assertion of the difference of boys both from women and from androgynous children they had been under their charge. Richard Halperin's general argument, that the Tudor education and culture were shaped by a troubling awareness of a vagrant class of the new poor which it could not quite "banish from its unconscious", is even more true for the determinative influence of the women and "effeminate" children of childhood. In the schoolroom culture where reason and self-control were constructed as masculine, the intensely desiring body had no legitimate space. For Vives, physical pleasures decrease virility and even threaten penetration: "Therefore our inner judgment must discover this inclination toward the love of our body, and the desire of things here in this life, which is customarily called our self-love. Such self-love enervates the strength and virility of our minds to such a degree that nothing can be so minute but that it is easily able to penetrate therein" (italics mine).

The simple, sensual pleasures of early childhood became something that, by and large, schoolboys were to give up. Not to give up the pleasures of the maternal environment meant not to enter the arena where male adulthood was achieved, according to a "learned man," a friend of Vives, who thanked God for the death of his mother, for "if she had lyved, I had never come to Paris to lerne: but had syt styll at home all my lyfe, among dicying, drabbes, delycates, and pleasures, as I begonne." The immense power given by Vives's friend to his mother, who had to die before he could attend school in Paris, resembles the power given to the mothers, nurses, and other women of childhood, who formed a silent binary term shaping (and threatening) the projects and even the curriculum of the early modern grammar school. One sign of their power appears in pedagogical writings which endow the vernacular fictions or nursery rhymes first heard in childhood with a dangerously effeminizing power. As Halperin has mentioned, one function of this educational system was to alienate boys from a popular and a specifically female culture whose influence was embodied in its stories.

Erasmus's advice reveals the extent to which these tales were contaminated by the gender of their female narrators: "A boy learn a pretty story from the ancient poets, or a memorable tale from history, just as readily as the stupid and vulgar ballad, or the old wives' fairy rubbish such as most children are steeped in nowadays by nurses and serving women."

As an enactment of an affectionate bond between children and women, the vernacular tales of childhood were rendered almost unspeakable. But scattered evidence—a childhood reminiscence, warnings in books on childrearing, histories of nursery rhymes—strongly suggests that these seldom-mentioned stories—of fairies, ghosts, and goblins—told by women to children remained widespread.

While the few remaining references to this oral tradition identify (and usually disparage) the narrators as women, sometimes narrators could, of course, be male. The Apology's allusion to a domestic scene of narration draws on this possibility in its argument that poetry teaches morality more effectively than philosophy. Enticing readers with delight rather than boring them with definitions, the poet begins "with a tale which holdeth children from play, and old men from the chimney corner". Conflating the pleasure offered by simple domestic narratives with that offered by all poetry, the Apology insists upon the childishness of literary response, a childishness which most adults never outgrow: "So it is in men (most of which are childish in the best things, till they be cradled in their graves): glad they will be to hear the tales of Hercules, Achilles, Cyrus, Aeneas".

The contrast between the childishness of this delight to direct instruction in morality which most readers resist, swearing "they be brought to school again," stresses its incompatibility with schoolroom experience. This contrast merges this childish delight, essential to the effectiveness of poetry, with the narrative pleasures later so infantilizing to readers of love poetry. The threat of this identification accounts for a troubling discrepancy in this passage. What is the significance of the fact that the heroes claimed for these tales—Hercules, Achilles, Cyrus, and Aeneas—were, in fact, the heroes of texts universally taught in schools? Were tales of Hercules prominent among the tales "which holdeth children from play," or were the more common "old wives' fairy rubbish" indefensible within the argument of the Apology?

The actual gender of Sidney's narrators of vernacular tales is less important than the ambiguous gendering of the boys who heard them; it was their childhood effeminacy, which created fictions as a threat to later masculinity. Still, the Apology's substitution of a male narrator of tales of Hercules for the more usual narrators of "old wives' tales" participates in a wider silence within the culture. The erasure of the influence of the women known in childhood could never be complete: abjected from the schoolroom, they returned as specters inhabiting the psyches of early modern males and the texts they produced.

Sidney's famous evocation of the poet's golden world is one such text haunted by the ghosts of childhood. As set apart from astronomers, mathematicians, musicians, and other intellectual professionals, poets alone attain true masculinity through the creativity of their minds:

Only the poet, disdaining to be tied to any such subjection, lifted up with the vigour of his own invention, doth grow in effect another nature, in making things either better than Nature bringeth forth, or, quite anew, forms such as were never in Nature, as the Heroes, Demigods, Cyclops, Chimeras, Furies, and such like: so as he goeth hand in hand with Nature, not enclosed within the narrow warrant of her gifts, but freely ranging only within the zodiac of his own wit... her world is brazen, the poets only deliver a golden.

In her exploration of early modern distinctions between nature and art, Dolan has aptly read this passage as the poet's attempt to create "a world that surpasses nature and bypasses the female role in reproduction," to ally his art with the "masculine and the divine". Dolan's interpretation of this passage can be pressed further, as an expression of the project of the early modern grammar school to provide the "rebirth" of the male subject into "another nature," where masculinity is constructed through the constant exercise of the intellect, with an ensuing disregard for the "natural" pleasures associated with the body and women.

Through the study of Latin, and the process through which that study was conducted, the male subject moved beyond the "old" nature now perceived as a confinement "within the narrow warrant" of Nature's "gifts." Through the sheer effort of intellectual endeavor, "lifted up with the vigour of his own invention, "the schoolboy learned to participate in a new subjectivity centered on the mind, taking precedence over the former subjectivity centered on the body.

Especially resonant of the early modern grammar school is the Apology's peopling of this new nature of the mind with figures encountered in a standard classical education. Besides revealing an educated familiarity with classical texts, the figures themselves embody in exaggerated from the privileges of class and gender forming the basis for the early modern grammar school. Through military deeds or the privilege of birth, male figures can be elevated to heroes or even (following Aeneas and Caesar) demigods. They can also be degraded to the stupidity of the despised Cyclops, the strong but clod-dish wooer of Galathea so easily outwitted by Ulysses. (Indeed Erasmus used the Cyclops figure to warn his students to study by comparing him to a person "who has great strength of body, but not of mind."

Within this new and misogynistic nature, women can only appear as monsters. Their depiction as furies embodies the anger projected upon women and the guilt they elicit, the "painful remorse and gnawing of conscience, horribly tormenting wicked mindes" in hell. Their representation as chimeras, or "unreal creatures of the imagination" (OED), points to their elision from the misogynistic discourses informing the grammar schools. Constructed within yet outside language, women are yet present in this wholly male environment as dangerous illusions. This chimera image may also refer to women's narratives. According to Puttenham, chimeras were bred only by "distempered imaginations" rather than the fantasies of "good poets."In its resemblance to the serpent's tail of the chimera, Sidney's image of poetry with a serpent's tail tale of "sinful fancies" enacts the denigration of women's fictions within the humanist culture of the schoolroom.

This rejection of the brazen world of sensual pleasures for a golden world of intellectual accomplishments created a problem within an institution designed to transform androgynous boys into virile leaders of men. Poetry remained essential to students as a repository of eloquence, but because of its pleasures, poetry became a site of conflict, or at least of suspicion, in the grammar school curriculum. Helgerson points out that among humanists, whose ideas were so formative for early modern schools, poetry was "soft and effeminate, weakening boys and leading them to lascivious pleasure rather than manly and courageous accomplishment".

The dangers posed by poetry to the establishment of the disciplined schcolboy were eloquently expressed in Gosson's passage describing their progress from the lower to the upper forms in the Schoole of Abuse: You are no soner entred but libertie looseth the reynes and geves you head, placing you with poetrie in the lowest forme, when his skill is showne too make his scholer as good as ever twangde: he preferres to pyping, from pyping to playing, from play to pleasure, from pleasure to slouth, from slouth to sleepe, from sleepe to sinne, from sinne to death, from death too the Divil, if you take your learning apace, and passe through every forme without revolting.

Richard Halperin has argued that this crisis posed by poetry to humanist teaching derived from its subject matter, which was "pleasure itself" without reference to "social utility or seriousness"; poetry offered the possibility of "detaching language's pleasing or persuasive force from its ideological anchor." But a startling contrast in gendered metaphors describing poetry's role in education reveals the extent to which the pleasure of poetry brought on a crisis of gender as well as of meaning. Simultaneously representing poetry as a nurse and a military agent, works such as Thomas Elyot's The Book Named the Governor signal radically unstable gender assignments for boys as (effeminate) infants and (masculine) warriors. The presence of both of these contradictory identities corresponds to the uneasy splitting of the self between the effeminate child of the nursery and the masculine youth of the schoolroom.

These radically opposed metaphors for poetry, and the unresolved gender identities for students they imply, enter the Tudor grammar school curriculum in its two contrasting strategies for dealing with the effeminizing potential of poetry. On the one hand, the emphasis on epic poetry, and especially the martial episodes of epic poems by Homer and Virgil, in the curriculum was to promote not only morality but martial courage. Ong's claim that the "masculine" appeal of epic was responsible for its privileging in grammar schools and in the culture generally is well substantiated by, for example, Thomas Elyot's recommendation of the reading of "noble poets," particularly Virgil and Homer, to teach boys the "marciall and discipline of armes" as well as to inflame their "courage". The second strategy presented the pleasures of poetry as especially appropriate for younger students, who needed to be "nursed" or enticed into learning Latin at this early stage of their education. Any effeminizing effects of the pleasure offered by poetry in the lower forms were then to be counteracted by dispensing a healthy antidote of history and moral philosophy in the upper forms.

The prominence of both of these strategies in Sidney's Apology creates the Tudor grammar school as an important cultural context through which to read Sidney's defence of poetry. By moving readers to martial rather than purely moral ends, military representations of poetry in the Apology attempt to recuperate poetry's pleasure as "courage."

The Amadis de Gaule, for example, has moved readers' hearts to the exercise of "courtesy, liberality, and especially courage". For the citizens of Hungary, songs of their "ancestor's valour" were the "chiefest kindlers of brave courage" in that "soldier-like nation". Sidney attests to the power of that "the old song of Percy and Douglas" to move his own heart "more than with a trumpet".

Alexander's admiration for the "pattern of Achilles" stirred up his courage on the battlefield. Edward Berry has analyzed these and other military allusions as Sidney's attempt to transform the "marginal figure of the poet's vocation into the leader of a militant aristocracy."Surely, both Sideney's metaphors and his military aspirations participate in a wider project: to assert the masculinity of poets (including himself) and their readers. More than the actual utility claimed for fictional works, the claim that "Orlando Furioso, or the honest King Arthur will never displease a solider" attests to the masculinity of the pleasure taken by soldier-readers in these texts. The Apology does not adopt this strategy for defending poetry uncritically; it also tests it to reveal its limitations and the limitations of the version of masculinity it constructs. As in the comparison of swords to needles, a disturbing gender instability lurks within the representation of poetry as the "companion of the camps": the phrase could as easily apply to the male and female prostitutes commonly following the troops. In the emphasis on poetry as a warrior-art, the Apology's argument shows more signs of strain.

As Katherine Duncan Jones has succinctly put it, Sidney's own poems were "hardly the stuff to give the troops. "With what "seriousness" was this military use for poetry advanced? Was it part of an intellectual experiment to see how strongly a position could be defended, according to oratorical practice in schoolrooms and law courts? As Peter Herman has recently noted, at the time he wrote the Apology, Sidney also directed a letter to Edward Denny to recommend books to further his knowledge of "soldiery"; all mention of poetry is conspicuously absent.

Within the Apology itself, the representation of the warrior-reader is most undercut by its portrait of John Pietro Pugliano in its opening frame. The admiration for soldiers expressed in the Apology is exaggerated to absurdity in Pugliano's overly enthusiastic defence of soldiers as the "noblest estate of mankind, and horsemen the noblest of soldiers". The "strong affections and weak arguments" of this soldier, whose very name means "fighter," cast into doubt the plausibility of the soldier reader who reads Homer before battle. Pugliano's unthinking fervor validates, by contrast, Sidney's delicate irony; Sidney's wit makes the martial form of masculinity look obtuse so that poets, even effeminate ones, seem attractive by contrast. But Pugliano presents too broad a target. Despite Sidney's own death from battlewounds, the feudal warrior was fast becoming an anachronism in this proto-capitalistic society; the majority of grammar school graduates finally entered the professions or the court's bureaucracy rather than the military. The primary function of the warrior-reader within the grammar school was not, then, so much to improve courage in battle, as to cast a mystique over a less glamorous masculinity better adapted to the hierarchical social structures of early modern England.

This masculinity of the disciplined subject revived a model dating from classical times by which (male) passion was to exert mastery over (female) passions within the self. Pleasure threatened these gender boundaries; for yielding to a pleasure, especially a sensual pleasure, strong enough to overturn reason's control transformed otherwise rational men to not-men: to women or, I would argue, to children, dominated by passions. This hierarchical model of masculinity enacted a defence not only against the desiring female within the self, but also against the androgynous child, whose traces it records.

The Apology contests the effeminizing threat posed by poetry by appropriating its power to inculcate a disciplined form of masculinity delineated especially well in its portraits of Cyrus and Aeneas. The Apology's treatment of these two denizens of the poet's golden world of intellect may well reflect the way the Cyropedia and Aeneid were read at Sidney's own grammar school; for both works figured prominently as required texts at Shrewsbury.

In praising Xenophon for his "effigiem justi imperii, 'the portraiture of a just empire'" under the name of Cyrus, the Apology alludes not so much to Cyrus' skill in battle as to his ability to create order both in his realm and within himself by exerting rigorous control over his passions and sensual desires. The ascetic Cyrus presents an especially good example of a disciplined subject; his contempt for physical pleasures may well have contributed a military panache to grammar school discipline, as he addresses his soldiers, for example: "yt becometh a ruler to exceed his subjects, not in easiness of life, but in the care of provision, and prest courage of travel." Thus, by bestowing the Idea of Cyrus "upon the world to make many Cyruses", the poet was imitating not only his heavenly Maker but also the project of the grammar school curriculum.

In its depiction of how Virgil's Aeneid "stirreth and instructeth the mind... with desire to be worthy, and informs with counsel how to be worthy", the Apology explicitly argues poetry's power to produce within its readers the ideal of the disciplined subject, who like Aeneas excels both in his "inward self" and his "outward government." These traits are revealed in Aeneas' reverence to patriarchal values shown in "preserving his old father, and carrying away his religious ceremonies." They are revealed in his obedience to duty, including "god's commandment" to leave Dido to fulfill his epic destiny.

Obedience to hard patriarchal duty, the suppression of soft emotions emerging from relationships with women, the choice of a future destiny over a present pleasure: each of these triumphs of (masculine) reason over the(effeminate) desiring body was as essential to the creation of the disciplined grammar school subject as to the founding of Rome. Suzuki's recent reading of the Dido episode as representing "Aeneas' passage from a dependence on a maternal figure to a position of leadership in a society of male comrades" suggests an apt analogy to the similarly difficult passage experienced by grammar school boys.

The protest expressed in Sidney's description of Aeneas's abandonment of Dido despite "all passionate kindness," against even "the human consideration of virtuous gratefulness", suggests a conflict in Sidney's own loyalties to patriarchal values. Like his subversion of the warrior-reader in his portrait of Pugliano, this empathy with Dido suggests that Sidney's interpellation as a disciplined subject was not complete. The instability in Sidney's loyalties is symptomatic of a larger instability within the early modern culture, which proceeds from the splitting of the male self between effeminate child and masculine adult.

This splitting is reflected in the widespread metaphor of poetry as nurse, which makes visible the effeminate child it was precisely the function of the warrior imagery to conceal. Within grammar school pedagogy, nurse imagery permitted the pleasure of poetry as appropriate to an early stage in what

Kerrigan has aptly termed a "rebirth" of the pedagogical subject into the masculine world of intellect. Thus, William Kempe's ideal schoolmaster acts as a "paineful nurse" to beginning students as, reducing Latin to its simplest elements, he "cheweth it all in small pieces, and thrusteth it into the childs mouth." Elyot recommends Virgil as a nurse to young students: "this noble Virgile like to a good norise giveth to a childe if he will take it every thing apte for his witte and capacities".

Robertello, an Italian scholar, revived Strabo's representation of poems as functioning as nurses to entire cultures, for their "fables gradually suckled and nurtured men until the time they would be more capable of understanding matters in philosophy which are most difficult." The representation of poetry and the schoolmasters who taught it as "nurses" in this early stage of the educational process appropriated the formative pleasures of the child's earlier experience with female nurses even as it attempted to erase the traces of their influence.

In its own use of nurse imagery, the Apology draws on the grammar school strategy of justifying the pleasures of poetry as part of a longer process. The Apology's description of "the poet as food for the tenderest stomachs" presents literature as uniquely qualified to teach because of the pleasure it offers to those who are very young in intellect.

Its specific reference to Aesop's tales as an example of pleasurable teaching draws upon current educational practice, for these fables (in Latin or Greek) were commonly recommended for beginning students precisely for the charm of their arguments in which "children moche do delite." The Apology extends the range of grammar school practice in its representation of poetry as a necessary preliminary for more difficult subjects, not only for students but for nations: even for the "noblest nations and languages," poetry acted as the "first nurse, whose milke by little and little enabled them to feed afterwards of tougher knowledges". The Apology represents poetry as operating for Indians the same way it was to operate for boys in grammar schools, to prepare their minds for more difficult studies ahead: "Until they find a pleasure in the exercises of the mind, great promises of much knowledge will little persuade them that know not the fruits of knowledge".

This strategy for justifying poetry as a stage in learning depended on the introduction of more serious subjects—especially history and moral philosophy—later in the curriculum. To some extent, this pattern prevailed in the grammar schools, although it was no means absolute, for it competed with the pressure to begin with the easier Latin texts before moving on to more difficult ones.

Thus, Philip Sidney would have read some moral philosophy in the relatively simple Latin of Vives and Cato in his early years at Shrewsbury before he advanced to the sophisticated Latin poetry of Ovid and Virgil. But Sidney's own general sense that history and moral philosophy were appropriate for older students emerges in his recommendations to Edmund Denny for a course of study.

If Denny were younger, Sideny would have directed him to study Latin, Greek, and logic. Since Denny is older, however, he recommends history and moral philosophy. Sidney's recommendations to Denny lend credence to Sidney's own deprecatory representations of the Arcadia as a "toy full book" and an "ink-wasting toy" as more than simple modesty. As Ong has noted, "literary studies in the Renaissance were for youngsters". This perception of poetry sheds insight on Joseph Loewenstein's findings, drawn from the many references in the Astrophel and Stella to the schoolroom and the nursery, that poetry was perceived as essentially childish.

What, then, can be made of the Apology's claim that pleasure creates poetry as a more efficient teacher of morality than history or philosophy? Not only does this argument run counter to Sidney's advice to Denny, but within the context of the grammar school curriculum, the Apology's advocacy of poetry's pleasure was no less than revolutionary.

The privileging of history and moral philosophy in grammar schools was more than a curricular choice; this hierarchy of studies was to replicate itself within the subjectivities of schoolboys. Read according to grammar school dieologies, the Apology's defence of poetry subverted not only the early modern curriculum but also the pedagogical subject it attempted to shape. The very desire for pleasure which history and philosophy were to "bridle" as schoolboys advanced in discipline became, in the Apology, the standard of judgment by which these later studies are found wanting. In the Apology, pleasure becomes equated with, rather than opposed to, morality; for without offering pleasure, texts can have no effect upon the minds and actions of their readers.

The seriousness of Sidney's argument hinges on whether the representations of philosophers and historians are read as portraits or as caricatures. Read as portraits, they further subvert the grammar school project by questioning the ability of philosophers and historians to inculcate virtues they obviously do not possess. Moral philosophers are unable even to follow their own teaching that "passion... must be mastered," for the passions dominating their own souls are only too apparent as they approach "with a sullen gravity," "angry with any man in whom they see the foul fault of anger". A very "tyrant in table talk," the historian is no better.

The very "great chafe" with which he denies that "any man for teaching of virtue, and virtuous actions is comparable to him" in fact reveals the falsity of his position. But these representations can also be read as caricatures, as vicious as they are hilarious. Read this way, the presence of these morally dubious pleasures undercuts the Apology's defence of pleasure as a moral force.

In this section of the Apology, any pretense of reasonable fairmindedness has begun to slip. In its passionate defence of its own highly self-interested argument, the Apology employs the unfair tactic of contrasting the worst traits of historians and philosophers to the best traits of poets: only the "peerless poet" appears as a model of rationality as he combines moral teachings and uplifting examples to "entice any man to enter" upon the path of a virtuous life. The exclusion of the amoral poets who offer pleasure without instruction—the writers of love poetry or (even worse) the lower class, female narrators of fairy tales—finally grants to them the considerable power of very bad dreams. Hovering in the moonlit spaces around and between the words of the text, these ghostly presences assume silent control of the central arguments of the Apology.

More than poetry, and even more than pleasure, is at stake in Sidney's Apology for Poetry. Sidney's text marks a transitional stage in the history of the bourgeois subject; it traces the process through which anxiety became installed in the very experience of pleasure.

The stringent civilizing process shaping the privileged male subject provides a context through which to read the Apology, which recapitulates its figures, its experiences, and its ideologies in its imagery and its argument. Like the Cartesian subject described by Francis Barker, the early modern privileged male had begun to harbor a "profound and corporeal guilt," to internalize a "self-disciplinary fixation predicated on the outlawing of the body and its passions." The stirrings of the Cartesian splitting of the self, with the location of subjectivity securely in the cogito, were already present in the early modern grammar school, where the desiring body was tainted with effeminacy. Unable to reject absolutely this emerging gender ideology, Sidney strains logic to clear a legitimate space for the pleasure offered by poetry. While Sidney records his own interpellation as an early modern masculine subject, he also contests it, casting a lingering look backward to the androgynous subjectivity of childhood.

Chapter 4

Text

Philip Sidney was born at Penshurst, in Kent, on the 29th of November, 1554. His father, Sir Henry Sidney, had married Mary, eldest daughter of John Dudley, Duke of Northumberland, and Philip was the eldest of their family of three sons and four daughters. Edmund Spenser and Walter Raleigh were of like age with Philip Sidney, differing only by about a year, and when Elizabeth became queen, on the 17th of November, 1558, they were children of four or five years old. In the year 1560 Sir Henry Sidney was made Lord President of Wales, representing the Queen in Wales and the four adjacent western counties, as a Lord Deputy represented her in Ireland.

The official residence of the Lord President was at Ludlow Castle, to which Philip Sidney went with his family when a child of six. In the same year his father was installed as a Knight of the Garter. When in his tenth year Philip Sidney was sent from Ludlow to Shrewsbury Grammar School, where he studied for three or four years, and had among his schoolfellows Fulke Greville, afterwards Lord Brooke, who remained until the end of Sidney's life one of his closest friends. When he himself was dying he directed that he should be described upon his tomb as "Fulke Greville, servant to Queen Elizabeth, counsellor to King James, and friend to Sir Philip Sidney." Even

Dr. Thomas Thornton, Canon of Christ Church, Oxford, under whom Sidney was placed when he was entered to Christ Church in his fourteenth year, at Midsummer, in 1568, had it afterwards recorded on his tomb that he was "the tutor of Sir Philip Sidney."

Sidney was in his eighteenth year in May, 1572, when he left the University to continue his training for the service of the state, by travel on the Continent. Licensed to travel with horses for himself and three servants, Philip Sidney left London in the train of the Earl of Lincoln, who was going out as ambassador to Charles IX., in Paris. He was in Paris on the 24th of August in that year, which was the day of the Massacre of St. Bartholomew.

He was sheltered from the dangers of that day in the house of the English Ambassador, Sir Francis Walsingham, whose daughter Fanny Sidney married twelve years afterwards. From Paris Sidney travelled on by way of Heidelberg to Frankfort, where he lodged at a printer's, and found a warm friend in Hubert Languet, whose letters to him have been published. Sidney was eighteen and Languet fifty-five, a French Huguenot, learned and zealous for the Protestant cause, who had been Professor of Civil Law in Padua, and who was acting as secret minister for the Elector of Saxony when he first knew Sidney, and saw in him a future statesman whose character and genius would give him weight in the counsels of England, and make him a main hope of the Protestant cause in Europe. Sidney travelled on with Hubert Languet from Frankfort to Vienna, visited Hungary, then passed to Italy, making for eight weeks Venice his head-quarters, and then giving six weeks to Padua. He returned through Germany to England, and was in attendance it the Court of Queen Elizabeth in July, 1575. Next month his father was sent to Ireland as Lord Deputy, and Sidney lived in London with his mother.

At this time the opposition of the Mayor and Corporation of the City of London to the acting of plays by servants of Sidney's uncle, the Earl of Leicester, who had obtained a patent for them, obliged the actors to cease from hiring rooms or inn yards in the City, and build themselves a house of their own a little way outside one of the City gates, and wholly outside the Lord Mayor's jurisdiction. Thus the first theatre came to be built in England in the year 1576. Shakespeare was then but twelve years old, and it was ten years later that he came to London.

In February, 1577, Philip Sidney, not yet twenty-three years old, was sent on a formal embassy of congratulation to Rudolph II. upon his becoming Emperor of Germany, but under the duties of the formal embassy was the charge of watching for opportunities of helping forward a Protestant League among the princes of Germany. On his way home through the Netherlands he was to convey Queen Elizabeth's congratulations to William of Orange on the birth of his first child, and what impression he made upon that leader of men is shown by a message William sent afterwards through Fulke Greville to Queen Elizabeth. He said "that if he could judge, her Majesty had one of the ripest and greatest counsellors of State in Philip Sidney that then lived in Europe; to the trial of which he was pleased to leave his own credit engaged until her Majesty was pleased to employ this gentleman, either amongst her friends or enemies."

Sidney returned from his embassy in June, 1577. At the time of his departure, in the preceding February, his sister Mary, then twenty years old, had become the third wife of Henry Herbert, Earl of Pembroke, and her new home as Countess of Pembroke was in the great house at Wilton, about three miles from Salisbury. She had a measure of her brother's genius, and was of like noble strain. Spenser described her as

"The gentlest shepherdess that lives this day,
And most resembling, both in shape and spright,
Her brother dear."

Ben Jonson, long after her brother had passed from earth, wrote upon her death the well-known epitaph:-

"Underneath this sable herse
Lies the subject of all verse,
Sidney's sister, Pembroke's mother.
Death, ere thou hast slain another,
Learn'd, and fair, and good as she,
Time shall throw a dart at thee."

Sidney's sister became Pembroke's mother in 1580, while her brother Philip was staying with her at Wilton. He had early in the year written a long argument to the Queen against the project of her marriage with the Duke of Anjou, which she then found it politic to seem to favour. She liked Sidney well, but resented, or appeared to resent, his intrusion of advice; he also was discontented with what seemed to be her policy, and he withdrew from Court for a time. That time of seclusion, after the end of March, 1580, he spent with his sister at Wilton.

They versified psalms together; and he began to write for her amusement when she had her baby first upon her hands, his romance of "Arcadia." It was never finished. Much was written at Wilton in the summer of 1580, the rest in 1581, written, as he said in a letter to her, "only for you, only to you... for severer eyes it is not, being but a trifle, triflingly handled. Your dear self can best witness the manner, being done in loose sheets of paper, most of it in your presence, the rest by sheets sent unto you as fast as they were done."

He never meant that it should be published; indeed, when dying he asked that it should be destroyed; but it belonged to a sister who prized the lightest word of his, and after his death it was published in 1590 as "The Countess of Pembroke's Arcadia."

The book reprinted in this volume was written in 1581, while sheets of the "Arcadia" were still being sent to Wilton. But it differs wholly in style from the "Arcadia." Sidney's "Arcadia" has literary interest as the first important example of the union of pastoral with heroic romance, out of which came presently, in France, a distinct school of fiction. But the genius of its author was at play, it followed designedly the fashions of the hour in verse and prose, which tended to extravagance of ingenuity. The "Defence of Poesy" has higher interest as the first important piece of literary criticism in our literature. Here Sidney was in earnest.

His style is wholly free from the euphuistic extravagance in which readers of his time delighted: it is clear, direct, and manly; not the less, but the more, thoughtful and refined for its unaffected simplicity. As criticism it is of the true sort; not captious or formal, still less engaged, as nearly all bad criticism is, more or less, with indirect suggestion of the critic himself as the one owl in a world of mice. Philip Sidney's care is towards the end of good literature. He looks for highest aims, and finds them in true work, and hears God's angel in the poet's song. The writing of this piece was probably suggested to him by the fact that an earnest young student, Stephen Gosson, who came from his university about the time when the first theatres were built, and wrote plays, was turned by the bias of his mind into agreement with the Puritan attacks made by the pulpit on the stage (arising chiefly from the fact that plays were then acted on Sundays), and in 1579 transferred his pen from service of the players to attack on them, in a piece which he called "The School of Abuse, containing a Pleasant Invective against Poets, Pipers, Players, Jesters, and such like Caterpillars of a Commonwealth; setting up the Flag of Defiance to their mischievous exercise, and overthrowing their Bulwarks, by Profane Writers, Natural Reason, and Common Experience: a Discourse as pleasant for Gentlemen that favour Learning as profitable for all that will follow Virtue." This Discourse Gosson dedicated "To the right noble Gentleman, Master Philip Sidney, Esquire."

Sidney himself wrote verse, he was companion with the poets, and counted Edmund Spenser among his friends. Gosson's pamphlet was only one expression of the narrow form of Puritan opinion that had been misled into attacks on poetry and music as feeders of idle appetite that withdrew men from the life of duty. To show the fallacy in such opinion, Philip Sidney wrote in 1581 this piece, which was first printed in 1595, nine years after his death, as a separate publication, entitled "An Apologie for Poetrie." Three years afterwards it was added, with other pieces, to the third edition of his "Arcadia," and then entitled "The Defence of Poesie." In sixteen subsequent editions it continued to appear as "The Defence of Poesie."

The same title was used in the separate editions of 1752 and 1810. Professor Edward Arber re-issued in 1869 the text of the first edition of 1595, and restored the original title, which probably was that given to the piece by its author. One name is as good as the other, but as the word "apology" has somewhat changed its sense in current English, it may be well to go on calling the work "The Defence of Poesie."

In 1583 Sidney was knighted, and soon afterwards in the same year he married Frances, daughter of Sir Francis Walsingham. Sonnets written by him according to old fashion, and addressed to a lady in accordance with a form of courtesy that in the same old fashion had always been held to exclude personal suit—personal suit was private, and not public—have led to grave misapprehension among some critics.

They supposed that he desired marriage with Penelope Devereux, who was forced by her family in 1580—then eighteen years old—into a hateful marriage with Lord Rich. It may be enough to say that if Philip Sidney had desired her for his wife, he had only to ask for her and have her. Her father, when dying, had desired— as any father might—that his daughter might become the wife of Philip Sidney. But this is not the place for a discussion of Astrophel and Stella sonnets. In 1585 Sidney was planning to join Drake it sea in attack on Spain in the West Indies.

He was stayed by the Queen. But when Elizabeth declared war on behalf of the Reformed Faith, and sent Leicester with an expedition to the Netherlands, Sir Philip Sidney went out, in November, 1585, as Governor of Flushing. His wife joined him there. He fretted at inaction, and made the value of his counsels so distinct that his uncle Leicester said after his death that he began by "despising his youth for a counsellor, not without bearing a hand over him as a forward young man. Notwithstanding, in a short time he saw the sun so risen above his horizon that both he and all his stars were glad to fetch light from him." In May, 1586, Sir Philip Sidney received news of the death of his father. In August his mother died. In September he joined in the investment of Zutphen.

On the 22nd of September his thigh-bone was shattered by a musket ball from the trenches. His horse took fright and galloped back, but the wounded man held to his seat. He was then carried to his uncle, asked for water, and when it was given, saw a dying soldier carried past, who eyed it greedily. At once he gave the water to the soldier, saying, "Thy necessity is yet greater than mine." Sidney lived on, patient in suffering, until the 17th of October. When he was speechless before death, one who stood by asked Philip Sidney for a sign of his continued trust in God. He folded his hands as in prayer over his breast, and so they were become fixed and chill, when the watchers placed them by his side; and in a few minutes the stainless representative of the young manhood of Elizabethan England passed away.

An Apologie for Poetrie

When the right virtuous Edward Wotton and I were at the Emperor's court together, we gave ourselves to learn horsemanship of Gio. Pietro Pugliano; one that, with great commendation, had the place of an esquire in his stable; and he, according to the fertileness of the Italian wit, did not only afford us the demonstration of his practice, but sought to enrich our minds with the contemplation therein, which he thought most precious. But with none, I remember, mine ears were at any time more laden, than when (either angered with slow payment, or moved with our learner-like admiration) he exercised his speech in the praise of his faculty.

He said, soldiers were the noblest estate of mankind, and horsemen the noblest of soldiers. He said, they were the masters of war and ornaments of peace, speedy goers, and strong abiders, triumphers both in camps and courts; nay, to so unbelieved a point he proceeded, as that no earthly thing bred such wonder to a prince, as to be a good horseman; skill of government was but a "pedanteria" in comparison.

Then would he add certain praises by telling what a peerless beast the horse was, the only serviceable courtier, without flattery, the beast of most beauty, faithfulness, courage, and such more, that if I had not been a piece of a logician before I came to him, I think he would have persuaded me to have wished myself a horse. But thus much, at least, with his no few words, he drove into me, that self love is better than any gilding, to make that seem gorgeous wherein ourselves be parties.

Wherein, if Pugliano's strong affection and weak arguments will not satisfy you, I will give you a nearer example of myself, who, I know not by what mischance, in these my not old years and idlest times, having slipped into the title of a poet, am provoked to say something unto you in the defence of that my unelected vocation; which if I handle with more good will than good reasons, bear with me, since the scholar is to be pardoned that followeth the steps of his master.

And yet I must say, that as I have more just cause to make a pitiful defence of poor poetry, which, from almost the highest estimation of learning, is fallen to be the laughing-stock of children; so have I need to bring some more available proofs, since the former is by no man barred of his deserved credit, whereas the silly latter hath had even the names of philosophers used to the defacing of it, with great danger of civil war among the Muses.

At first, truly, to all them that, professing learning, inveigh against poetry, may justly be objected, that they go very near to ungratefulness to seek to deface that which, in the noblest nations and languages that are known, hath been the first light-giver to ignorance, and first nurse, whose milk by little and little enabled them to feed afterwards of tougher knowledges. And will you play the hedgehog, that being received into the den, drove out his host? or rather the vipers, that with their birth kill their parents?

Let learned Greece, in any of her manifold sciences, be able to show me one book before Musaeus, Homer, and Hesiod, all three nothing else but poets. Nay, let any history he brought that can say any writers were there before them, if they were not men of the same skill, as Orpheus, Linus, and some others are named, who having been the first of that country that made pens deliverers of their knowledge to posterity, may justly challenge to be called their fathers in learning. For not only in time they had this priority (although in itself antiquity be venerable) but went before them as causes to draw with their charming sweetness the wild untamed wits to an admiration of knowledge. So as Amphion was said to move stones with his poetry to build Thebes, and Orpheus to be listened to by beasts, indeed, stony and beastly people, so among the Romans were Livius Andronicus, and Ennius; so in the Italian language, the first that made it to aspire to be a treasure-house of science, were the poets Dante, Boccace, and Petrarch; so in our English were Gower and Chaucer; after whom, encouraged and delighted with their excellent foregoing, others have followed to beautify our mother tongue, as well in the same kind as other arts.

This did so notably show itself that the philosophers of Greece durst not a long time appear to the world but under the mask of poets; so Thales, Empedocles, and Parmenides sang their natural philosophy in verses; so did Pythagoras and Phocylides their moral counsels; so did Tyrtaeus in war matters; and Solon in matters of policy; or rather they, being poets, did exercise their delightful vein in those points of highest knowledge, which before them lay hidden to the world; for that wise Solon was directly a poet it is manifest, having written in verse the notable fable of the Atlantic Island, which was continued by Plato. And, truly, even Plato, whosoever well considereth shall find that in the body of his work, though the inside and strength were philosophy, the skin, as it were, and beauty depended most of poetry.

For all stands upon dialogues; wherein he feigns many honest burgesses of Athens speaking of such matters that if they had been set on the rack they would never have confessed them; besides, his poetical describing the circumstances of their meetings, as the well-ordering of a banquet, the delicacy of a walk, with interlacing mere tiles, as Gyges's Ring, and others; which, who knows not to be flowers of poetry, did never walk into Apollo's garden.

And even historiographers, although their lips sound of things done, and verity be written in their foreheads, have been glad to borrow both fashion and, perchance, weight of the poets; so Herodotus entitled the books of his history by the names of the Nine Muses; and both he, and all the rest that followed him, either stole or usurped, of poetry, their passionate describing of passions, the many particularities of battles which no man could affirm; or, if that be denied me, long orations, put in the months of great kings and captains, which it is certain they never pronounced.

So that, truly, neither philosopher nor historiographer

could, at the first, have entered into the gates of popular judgments, if they had not taken a great disport of poetry; which in all nations, at this day, where learning flourisheth not, is plain to be seen; in all which they have some feeling of poetry. In Turkey, besides their lawgiving divines they have no other writers but poets. In our neighbour-country Ireland, where, too, learning goes very bare, yet are their poets held in a devout reverence. Even among the most barbarous and simple Indians, where no writing is, yet have they their poets who make and sing songs, which they call "Arentos," both of their ancestor's deeds and praises of their gods.

A sufficient probability, that if ever learning comes among them, it must be by having their hard dull wits softened and sharpened with the sweet delight of poetry; for until they find a pleasure in the exercise of the mind, great promises of much knowledge will little persuade them that know not the fruits of knowledge.

In Wales, the true remnant of the ancient Britons, as there are good authorities to show the long time they had poets, which they called bards, so through all the conquests of Romans, Saxons, Danes, and Normans, some of whom did seek to ruin all memory of learning from among them, yet do their poets, even to this day, last; so as it is not more notable in the soon beginning than in long-continuing.

But since the authors of most of our sciences were the Romans, and before them the Greeks, let us, a little, stand upon their authorities; but even so far, as to see what names they have given unto this now scorned skill. Among the Romans a poet was called "vates," which is as much as a diviner, foreseer, or prophet, as by his conjoined words "vaticinium," and "vaticinari," is manifest; so heavenly a title did that excellent people bestow upon this heart- ravishing knowledge! And so far were they carried into the admiration thereof, that they thought in the changeable hitting upon any such verses, great foretokens of their following fortunes were placed. Whereupon grew the word of sortes Virgilianae; when, by sudden opening Virgil's book, they lighted upon some verse, as it is reported by many, whereof the histories of the Emperors' lives are full.

As of Albinus, the governor of our island, who, in his childhood, met with this verse -

Arma amens capio, nec sat rationis in armis and in his age performed it. Although it were a very vain and godless superstition; as also it was, to think spirits were commanded by such verses; whereupon this word charms, derived of "carmina," cometh, so yet serveth it to show the great reverence those wits were held in; and altogether not without ground, since both the oracles of Delphi and the Sibyl's prophecies were wholly delivered in verses; for that same exquisite observing of number and measure in the words, and that high-flying liberty of conceit proper to the poet, did seem to have some divine force in it.

And may not I presume a little farther to show the reasonableness of this word "vates," and say, that the holy David's Psalms are a divine poem? If I do, I shall not do it without the testimony of great learned men, both ancient and modern. But even the name of Psalms will speak for me, which, being interpreted, is nothing but Songs; then, that is fully written in metre, as all learned Hebricians agree, although the rules be not yet fully found. Lastly, and principally, his handling his prophecy, which is merely poetical.

For what else is the awaking his musical instruments; the often and free changing of persons; his notable prosopopoeias, when he maketh you, as it were, see God coming in His majesty; his telling of the beasts' joyfulness, and hills leaping; but a heavenly poesy, wherein, almost, he sheweth himself a passionate lover of that unspeakable and everlasting beauty, to be seen by the eyes of the mind, only cleared by faith? But truly, now, having named him, I fear I seem to profane that holy name, applying it to poetry, which is, among us, thrown down to so ridiculous an estimation. But they that, with quiet judgments, will look a little deeper into it, shall find the end and working of it such, as, being rightly applied, deserveth not to be scourged out of the church of God.

But now let us see how the Greeks have named it, and how they deemed of it. The Greeks named him [Greek text], which name hath, as the most excellent, gone through other languages; it cometh of this word [Greek text], which is TO MAKE; wherein, I know not whether by luck or wisdom, we Englishmen have met with the Greeks in calling him "a maker," which name, how high and incomparable a title it is, I had rather were known by marking the scope of other sciences, than by any partial allegation.

There is no art delivered unto mankind that hath not the works of nature for his principal object, without which they could not consist, and on which they so depend as they become actors and players, as it were, of what nature will have set forth. So doth the astronomer look upon the stars, and by that he seeth set down what order nature hath taken therein. So doth the geometrician and arithmetician, in their diverse sorts of quantities. So doth the musician, in times, tell you which by nature agree, which not.

The natural philosopher thereon hath his name; and the moral philosopher standeth upon the natural virtues, vices, or passions of man; and follow nature, saith he, therein, and thou shalt not err. The lawyer saith what men have determined. The historian, what men have done. The grammarian speaketh only of the rules of speech; and the rhetorician and logician, considering what in nature will soonest prove and persuade, thereon give artificial rules, which still are compassed within the circle of a question, according to the proposed matter.

The physician weigheth the nature of man's body, and the nature of things helpful and hurtful unto it. And the metaphysic, though it be in the second and abstract notions, and therefore be counted supernatural, yet doth he, indeed, build upon the depth of nature. Only the poet, disdaining to be tied to any such subjection, lifted up with the vigour of his own invention, doth grow, in effect, into another nature; in making things either better than nature bringeth forth, or quite anew; forms such as never were in nature, as the heroes, demi-gods, Cyclops, chimeras, furies, and such like; so as he goeth hand in hand with Nature, not enclosed within the narrow warrant of her gifts, but freely ranging within the zodiac of his own wit. Nature never set forth the earth in so rich tapestry as divers poets have done; neither with so pleasant rivers, fruitful trees, sweet-smelling flowers, nor whatsoever else may make the too- much-loved earth more lovely; her world is brazen, the poets only deliver a golden.

But let those things alone, and go to man; for whom as the other things are, so it seemeth in him her uttermost cunning is employed; and know, whether she have brought forth so true a lover as Theagenes; so constant a friend as Pylades; so valiant a man as Orlando; so right a prince as Xenophon's Cyrus; and so excellent a man every way as Virgil's AEneas? Neither let this be jestingly conceived, because the works of the one be essential, the other in imitation or fiction; for every understanding knoweth the skill of each artificer standeth in that idea, or fore-conceit of the work, and not in the work itself.

And that the poet hath that idea is manifest by delivering them forth in such excellency as he had imagined them; which delivering forth, also, is not wholly imaginative, as we are wont to say by them that build castles in the air; but so far substantially it worketh not only to make a Cyrus, which had been but a particular excellency, as nature might have done; but to bestow a Cyrus upon the world to make many Cyruses; if they will learn aright, why, and how, that maker made him. Neither let it be deemed too saucy a comparison to balance the highest point of man's wit with the efficacy of nature; but rather give right honour to the heavenly Maker of that maker, who having made man to His own likeness, set him beyond and over all the works of that second nature; which in nothing he showeth so much as in poetry; when, with the force of a divine breath, he bringeth things forth surpassing her doings, with no small arguments to the incredulous of that first accursed fall of Adam; since our erected wit maketh us know what perfection is, and yet our infected will keepeth us from reaching unto it. But these arguments will by few be understood, and by fewer granted; thus much I hope will be given me, that the Greeks, with some probability of reason, gave him the name above all names of learning.

Now let us go to a more ordinary opening of him, that the truth may be the more palpable; and so, I hope, though we get not so unmatched a praise as the etymology of his names will grant, yet his very description, which no man will deny, shall not justly be barred from a principal commendation. Poesy, therefore, is an art of imitation; for so Aristotle termeth it in the word [Greek text]; that is to say, a representing, counterfeiting, or figuring forth: to speak metaphorically, a speaking picture, with this end, to teach and delight.

Of this have been three general kinds: the CHIEF, both in antiquity and excellency, which they that did imitate the inconceivable excellencies of God; such were David in the Psalms; Solomon in the Song of Songs, in his Ecclesiastes, and Proverbs; Moses and Deborah in their hymns; and the writer of Job; which, beside others, the learned Emanuel Tremellius and Fr. Junius do entitle the poetical part of the scripture; against these none will speak that hath the Holy Ghost in due holy reverence. In this kind, though in a wrong divinity, were Orpheus, Amphion, Homer in his hymns, and many others, both Greeks and Romans. And this poesy must be used by whosoever will follow St. Paul's counsel, in singing psalms when they are merry; and I know is used with the fruit of comfort by some, when, in sorrowful pangs of their death-bringing sins, they find the consolation of the never-leaving goodness.

The SECOND kind is of them that deal with matter philosophical; either moral, as Tyrtaeus, Phocylides, Cato, or, natural, as Lucretius, Virgil's Georgics; or astronomical, as Manilius and Pontanus; or historical, as Lucan; which who mislike, the fault is in their judgment, quite out of taste, and not in the sweet food of sweetly uttered knowledge.

But because this second sort is wrapped within the fold of the proposed subject, and takes not the free course of his own invention; whether they properly be poets or no, let grammarians dispute, and go to the THIRD, indeed right poets, of whom chiefly this question ariseth; betwixt whom and these second is such a kind of difference, as betwixt the meaner sort of painters, who counterfeit only such faces as are set before them; and the more excellent, who having no law but wit, bestow that in colours upon you which is fittest for the eye to see; as the constant, though lamenting look of Lucretia, when she punished in herself another's fault; wherein he painteth not Lucretia, whom he never saw, but painteth the outward beauty of such a virtue. For these three be they which most properly do imitate to teach and delight; and to imitate, borrow nothing of what is, hath been, or shall be; but range only, reined with learned discretion, into the divine consideration of what may be, and should be.

These be they, that, as the first and most noble sort, may justly be termed "vates;" so these are waited on in the excellentest languages and best understandings, with the fore-described name of poets. For these, indeed, do merely make to imitate, and imitate both to delight and teach, and delight to move men to take that goodness in hand, which, without delight they would fly as from a stranger; and teach to make them know that goodness whereunto they are moved; which being the noblest scope to which ever any learning was directed, yet want there not idle tongues to bark at them.

These be subdivided into sundry more special denominations; the most notable be the heroic, lyric, tragic, comic, satyric, iambic, elegiac, pastoral, and certain others; some of these being termed according to the matter they deal with; some by the sort of verse they like best to write in; for, indeed, the greatest part of poets have apparelled their poetical inventions in that numerous kind of writing which is called verse. Indeed, but apparelied verse, being but an ornament, and no cause to poetry, since there have been many most excellent poets that never versified, and now swarm many versifiers that need never answer to the name of poets. For Xenophon, who did imitate so excellently as to give us effigiem justi imperii, the portraiture of a just of Cyrus, as Cicero saith of him, made therein an absolute heroical poem. So did Heliodorus, in his sugared invention of Theagenes and Chariclea; and yet both these wrote in prose; which I speak to show, that it is not rhyming and versing that maketh a poet (no more than a long gown maketh an advocate, who, though he pleaded in armour should be an advocate and no soldier); but it is that feigning notable images of virtues, vices, or what else, with that delightful teaching, which must be the right describing note to know a poet by.

Although,indeed, the senate of poets have chosen verse as their fittest raiment; meaning, as in matter they passed all in all, so in manner to go beyond them; not speaking table-talk fashion, or like men in a dream, words as they changeably fall from the mouth, but piecing each syllable of each word by just proportion, according to the dignity of the subject.

Now, therefore, it shall not be amiss, first, to weight this latter sort of poetry by his WORKS, and then by his PARTS; and if in neither of these anatomies he be commendable, I hope we shall receive a more favourable sentence. This purifying of wit, this enriching of memory, enabling of judgment, and enlarging of conceit, which commonly we call learning under what name so ever it come forth, or to what immediate end so ever it be directed; the final end is, to lead and draw us to as high a perfection as our degenerate souls, made worse by, their clay lodgings, can be capable of.

This, according to the inclination of man, bred many formed impressions; for some that thought this felicity principally to be gotten by knowledge, and no knowledge to be so high or heavenly as to be acquainted with the stars, gave themselves to astronomy; others, persuading themselves to be demigods, if they knew the causes of things, became natural and supernatural philosophers.

Some an admirable delight drew to music, and some the certainty of demonstrations to the mathematics; but all, one and other, having this scope to know, and by knowledge to lift up the mind from the dungeon of the body to the enjoying his own divine essence. But when, by the balance of experience, it was found that the astronomer, looking to the stars, might fall in a ditch; that the enquiring philosopher might be blind in himself; and the mathematician might draw forth a straight line with a crooked heart; then lo! did proof, the over-ruler of opinions, make manifest that all these are but serving sciences, which, as they have a private end in themselves, so yet are they all directed to the highest end of the mistress knowledge, by the Greeks called [Greek text], which stands, as I think, in the knowledge of a man's self; in the ethic and politic consideration, with the end of well doing, and not of well knowing only; even as the saddler's next end is to make a good saddle, but his farther end to serve a nobler faculty, which is horsemanship; so the horseman's to soldiery; and the soldier not only to have the skill, but to perform the practice of a soldier.

So that the ending end of all earthly learning being virtuous action, those skills that most serve to bring forth that have a most just title to be princes over all the rest; wherein, if we can show it rightly, the poet is worthy to have it before any other competitors. Among whom principally to challenge it, step forth the moral philosophers; whom, methinks, I see coming toward me with a sullen gravity (as though they could not abide vice by daylight), rudely clothed, for to witness outwardly their contempt of outward things, with books in their hands against glory, whereto they set their names; sophistically speaking against subtlety, and angry with any man in whom they see the foul fault of anger.

These men, casting largesses as they go, of definitions, divisions, and distinctions, with a scornful interrogative do soberly ask: Whether it be possible to find any path so ready to lead a man to virtue, as that which teacheth what virtue is; and teacheth it not only by delivering forth his very being, his causes and effects; but also by making known his enemy, vice, which must be destroyed; and his cumbersome servant, passion, which must be mastered, by showing the generalities that contain it, and the specialities that are derived from it; lastly, by plain setting down how it extends itself out of the limits of a man's own little world, to the government of families, and maintaining of public societies?

The historian scarcely gives leisure to the moralist to say so much, but that he (laden with old mouse-eaten records, authorizing himself, for the most part, upon other histories, whose greatest authorities are built upon the notable foundation of hearsay, having much ado to accord differing writers, and to pick truth out of partiality; better acquainted with a thousand years ago than with the present age, and yet better knowing how this world goes than how his own wit runs; curious for antiquities, and inquisitive of novelties, a wonder to young folks, and a tyrant in table-talk) denieth, in a great chafe, that any man for teaching of virtue and virtuous actions, is comparable to him.

I am "Testis temporum, lux veritatis, vita memoriae, magistra vitae, nuncia vetustatis". The philosopher, saith he, teacheth a disputative virtue, but I do an active; his virtue is excellent in the dangerless academy of Plato, but mine showeth forth her honourable face in the battles of Marathon, Pharsalia, Poictiers, and Agincourt: he teacheth virtue by certain abstract considerations; but I only bid you follow the footing of them that have gone before you: old-aged experience goeth beyond the fine-witted philosopher; but I give the experience of many ages. Lastly, if he make the song book, I put the learner's hand to the lute; and if he be the guide, I am the light.

Then would he allege you innumerable examples, confirming story by stories, how much the wisest senators and princes have been directed by the credit of history, as Brutus, Alphonsus of Aragon (and who not? if need be). At length, the long line of their disputation makes a point in this, that the one giveth the precept, and the other the example. Now whom shall we find, since the question standeth for the highest form in the school of learning, to be moderator? Truly, as me seemeth, the poet; and if not a moderator, even the man that ought to carry the title from them both, and much more from all other serving sciences.

Therefore compare we the poet with the historian, and with the moral philosopher; and if he go beyond them both, no other human skill can match him; for as for the Divine, with all reverence, he is ever to be excepted, not only for having his scope as far beyond any of these, as eternity exceedeth a moment, but even for passing each of these in themselves; and for the lawyer, though "Jus" be the daughter of Justice, the chief of virtues, yet because he seeks to make men good rather "formidine poenae" than "virtutis amore," or, to say righter, doth not endeavour to make men good, but that their evil hurt not others, having no care, so he be a good citizen, how bad a man he be: therefore, as our wickedness maketh him necessary, and necessity maketh him honourable, so is he not in the deepest truth to stand in rank with these, who all endeavour to take naughtiness away, and plant goodness even in the secretest cabinet of our souls.

And these four are all that any way deal in the consideration of men's manners, which being the supreme knowledge, they that best breed it deserve the best commendation. The philosopher, therefore, and the historian are they which would win the goal, the one by precept, the other by example; but both, not having both, do both halt. For the philosopher, setting down with thorny arguments the bare rule, is so hard of utterance, and so misty to be conceived, that one that hath no other guide but him shall wade in him until he be old, before he shall find sufficient cause to be honest.

For his knowledge standeth so upon the abstract and general, that happy is that man who may understand him, and more happy that can apply what he doth understand. On the other side the historian, wanting the precept, is so tied, not to what should be, but to what is; to the particular truth of things, and not to the general reason of things; that his example draweth no necessary consequence, and therefore a less fruitful doctrine.Now doth the peerless poet perform both; for whatsoever the philosopher saith should be done, he giveth a perfect picture of it, by some one by whom he pre-supposeth it was done, so as he coupleth the general notion with the particular example.

A perfect picture, I say; for he yieldeth to the powers of the mind an image of that whereof the philosopher bestoweth but a wordish description, which doth neither strike, pierce, nor possess the sight of the soul, so much as that other doth. For as, in outward things, to a man that had never seen an elephant, or a rhinoceros, who should tell him most exquisitely all their shape, colour, bigness, and particular marks? or of a gorgeous palace, an architect, who, declaring the full beauties, might well make the hearer able to repeat, as it were, by rote, all he had heard, yet should never satisfy his inward conceit, with being witness to itself of a true living knowledge; but the same man, as soon as he might see those beasts well painted, or that house well in model, should straightway grow, without need of any description, to a judicial comprehending of them; so, no doubt, the philosopher, with his learned definitions, be it of virtue or vices, matters of public policy or private government, replenisheth the memory with many infallible grounds of wisdom, which, notwithstanding, lie dark before the imaginative and judging power, if they be not illuminated or figured forth by the speaking picture of poesy.

Tully taketh much pains, and many times not without poetical help, to make us know the force love of our country hath in us. Let us but hear old Anchises, speaking in the midst of Troy's flames, or see Ulysses, in the fulness of all Calypso's delights, bewail his absence from barren and beggarly Ithaca. Anger, the Stoics said, was a short madness; let but Sophocles bring you Ajax on a stage, killing or whipping sheep and oxen, thinking them the army of Greeks, with their chieftains Agamemnon and Menelaus; and tell me, if you have not a more familiar insight into anger, than finding in the schoolmen hA perfect pictureA perfect pictureA perfect picture is genus and difference?

See whether wisdom and temperance in Ulysses and Diomedes, valour in Achilles, friendship in Nisus and Euryalus, even to an ignorant man, carry not an apparent shining; and, contrarily, the remorse of conscience in OEdipus; the soon-repenting pride in Agamemnon; the self-devouring cruelty in his father Atreus; the violence of ambition in the two Theban brothers; the sour sweetness of revenge in Medea; and, to fall lower, the Terentian Gnatho, and our Chaucer's Pandar, so expressed, that we now use their names to signify their trades; and finally, all virtues, vices, and passions so in their own natural states laid to the view, that we seem not to hear of them, but clearly to see through them?

But even in the most excellent determination of goodness, what philosopher's counsel can so readily direct a prince as the feigned Cyrus in Xenophon? Or a virtuous man in all fortunes, as AEneas in Virgil? Or a whole commonwealth, as the way of Sir Thomas More's Utopia? I say the way, because where Sir Thomas More erred, it was the fault of the man, and not of the poet; for·that way of patterning a commonwealth was most absolute, though he, perchance, hath not so absolutely performed it.

For the question is, whether the feigned image of poetry, or the regular instruction of philosophy, hath the more force in teaching. Wherein, if the philosophers have more rightly showed themselves philosophers, than the poets have attained to the high top of their profession, (as in truth, "Mediocribus esse poetis Non Di, non homines, non concessere columnae," it is, I say again, not the fault of the art, but that by few men that art can be accomplished.

Certainly, even our Saviour Christ could as well have given the moral common-places of uncharitableness and humbleness, as the divine narration of Dives and Lazarus; or of disobedience and mercy, as the heavenly discourse of the lost child and the gracious father; but that his thorough searching wisdom knew the estate of Dives burning in hell, and of Lazarus in Abraham's bosom, would more constantly, as it were, inhabit both the memory and judgment.

Truly, for myself (me seems), I see before mine eyes the lost child's disdainful prodigality turned to envy a swine's dinner; which, by the learned divines, are thought not historical acts, but instructing parables. For conclusion, I say the philosopher teacheth, but he teacheth obscurely, so as the learned only can understand him; that is to say, he teacheth them that are already taught.

But the poet is the food for the tenderest stomachs; the poet is, indeed, the right popular philosopher. Whereof AEsop's tales give good proof; whose pretty allegories, stealing under the formal tales of beasts, make many, more beastly than beasts, begin to hear the sound of virtue from those dumb speakers. But now may it be alleged, that if this managing of matters be so fit for the imagination, then must the historian needs surpass, who brings you images of true matters, such as, indeed, were done, and not such as fantastically or falsely may be suggested to have been done.

Truly, Aristotle himself, in his Discourse of Poesy, plainly determineth this question, saying, that poetry is [Greek text], that is to say, it is more philosophical and more ingenious than history.

His reason is, because poesy dealeth with [Greek text], that is to say, with the universal consideration, and the history [Greek text], the particular. "Now," saith he, "the universal weighs what is fit to be said or done, either in likelihood or necessity; which the poesy considereth in his imposed names; and the particular only marks, whether Alcibiades did, or suffered, this or that:" thus far Aristotle. Which reason of his, as all his, is most full of reason. For, indeed, if the question were, whether it were better to have a particular act truly or falsely set down? There is no doubt which is to be chosen, no more than whether you had rather have Vespasian's picture right as he was, or, at the painter's pleasure, nothing resembling?

But if the question be, for your own use and learning, whether it be better to have it set down as it should be, or as it was? then, certainly, is more doctrinable the feigned Cyrus in Xenophon, than the true Cyrus in Justin; and the feigned AEneas in Virgil, than the right AEneas in Dares Phrygius; as to a lady that desired to fashion her countenance to the best grace, a painter should more benefit her, to portrait a most sweet face, writing Canidia upon it, than to paint Canidia as she was, who, Horace sweareth, was full ill-favoured. If the poet do his part aright, he will show you in Tantalus, Atreus, and such like, nothing that is not to be shunned; in Cyrus, AEneas, Ulysses, each thing to be followed; where the historian, bound to tell things as things were, cannot be liberal, without he will be poetical, of a perfect pattern; but, as in Alexander, or Scipio himself, show doings, some to be liked, some to be misliked; and then how will you discern what to follow, but by your own discretion, which you had, without reading Q. Curtius? And whereas, a man may say, though in universal consideration of doctrine, the poet prevaileth, yet that the history, in his saying such a thing was done, doth warrant a man more in that he shall follow; the answer is manifest: that if he stand upon that WAS, as if he should argue, because it rained yesterday therefore it should rain to-day; then, indeed, hath it some advantage to a gross conceit.

But if he know an example only enforms a conjectured likelihood, and so go by reason, the poet doth so far exceed him, as he is to frame his example to that which is most reasonable, be it in warlike, politic, or private matters; where the historian in his bare WAS hath many times that which we call fortune to overrule the best wisdom. Many times he must tell events whereof he can yield no cause; or if he do, it must be poetically.

For, that a feigned example bath as much force to teach as a true example (for as for to move, it is clear, since the feigned may be tuned to the highest key of passion), let us take one example wherein an historian and a poet did concur. Herodotus and Justin do both testify, that Zopyrus, King Darius's faithful servant, seeing his master long resisted by the rebellious Babylonians, feigned himself in extreme disgrace of his King; for verifying of which he caused his own nose and ears to be cut off, and so flying to the Babylonians, was received; and, for his known valour, so far credited, that he did find means to deliver them over to Darius. Much-like matters doth Livy record of Tarquinius and his son.

Xenophon excellently feigned such another stratagem, performed by Abradatus in Cyrus's behalf. Now would I fain know, if occasion be presented unto you to serve your prince by such an honest dissimulation, why do you not as well learn it of Xenophon's fiction as of the other's verity? and, truly, so much the better, as you shall save your nose by the bargain; for Abradatus did not counterfeit so far.

So, then, the best of the historians is subject to the poet; for, whatsoever action or faction, whatsoever counsel, policy, or war stratagem the historian is bound to recite, that may the poet, if he list, with his imitation, make his own, beautifying it both for farther teaching, and more delighting, as it please him: having all, from Dante's heaven to his hell, under the authority of his pen. Which if I be asked, What poets have done so? as I might well name some, so yet, say I, and say again, I speak of the art, and not of the artificer. Now, to that which commonly is attributed to the praise of history, in respect of the notable learning which is got by marking the success, as though therein a man should see virtue exalted, and vice punished: truly, that commendation is peculiar to poetry, and far off from history; for, indeed, poetry ever sets virtue so out in her best colours, making fortune her well-waiting handmaid, that one must needs be enamoured of her. Well may you see Ulysses in a storm, and in other hard plights; but they are but exercises of patience and magnanimity, to make them shine the more in the near following prosperity. And, on the contrary part, if evil men come to the stage, they ever go out (as the tragedy writer answered to one that misliked the show of such persons) so manacled, as they little animate folks to follow them. But history being captive to the truth of a foolish world, in many times a terror from well- doing, and an encouragement to unbridled wickedness.

For see we not valiant Miltiades rot in his fetters? the just Phocion and the accomplished Socrates put to death like traitors? the cruel Severus live prosperously? the excellent Severus miserably murdered? Sylla and Marius dying in their beds? Pompey and Cicero slain then when they would have thought exile a happiness? See we not virtuous Cato driven to kill himself, and rebel Caesar so advanced, that his name yet, after sixteen hundred years, lasteth in the highest honour? And mark but even Caesar's own words of the forenamed Sylla, (who in that only did honestly, to put down his dishonest tyranny), "literas nescivit:" as if want of learning caused him to do well.

He meant it not by poetry, which, not content with earthly plagues, deviseth new punishment in hell for tyrants: nor yet by philosophy, which teacheth "occidentes esse:" but, no doubt, by skill in history; for that, indeed, can afford you Cypselus, Periander, Phalaris, Dionysius, and I know not how many more of the same kennel, that speed well enough in their abominable injustice of usurpation. I conclude, therefore, that he excelleth history, not only in furnishing the mind with knowledge, but in setting it forward to that which deserves to be called and accounted good: which setting forward, and moving to well-doing, indeed, setteth the laurel crowns upon the poets as victorious; not only of the historian, but over the philosopher, howsoever, in teaching, it may be questionable.

For suppose it be granted, that which I suppose, with great reason, may be denied, that the philosopher, in respect of his methodical proceeding, teach more perfectly than the poet, yet do I think, that no man is so much [Greek text], as to compare the philosopher in moving with the poet. And that moving is of a higher degree than teaching, it may by this appear, that it is well nigh both the cause and effect of teaching; for who will be taught, if he be not moved with desire to be taught? And what so much good doth that teaching bring forth (I speak still of moral doctrine) as that it moveth one to do that which it doth teach.

For, as Aristotle saith, it is not Greek text but Greek text must be the fruit: and how [Greek text] can be, without being moved to practise, it is no hard matter to consider. The philosopher showeth you the way, he informeth you of the particularities, as well of the tediousness of the way and of the pleasant lodging you shall have when your journey is ended, as of the many by-turnings that may divert you from your way; but this is to no man, but to him that will read him, and read him with attentive, studious painfulness; which constant desire whosoever hath in him, hath already passed half the hardness of the way, and therefore is beholden to the philosopher but for the other half.

Nay, truly, learned men have learnedly thought, that where once reason hath so much over-mastered passion, as that the mind hath a free desire to do well, the inward light each mind hath in itself is as good as a philosopher's book: since in nature we know it is well to do well, and what is well and what is evil, although not in the words of art which philosophers bestow upon us; for out of natural conceit the philosophers drew it; but to be moved to do that which we know, or to be moved with desire to know, "hoc opus, hic labor est." Now, therein, of all sciences (I speak still of human and according to the human conceit), is our poet the monarch. For he doth not only show the way, but giveth so sweet a prospect into the way, as will entice any man to enter into it; nay, he doth, as if your journey should lie through a fair vineyard, at the very first give you a cluster of grapes, that full of that taste you may long to pass farther.

He beginneth not with obscure definitions, which must blur the margin with interpretations, and load the memory with doubtfulness, but he cometh to you with words set in delightful proportion, either accompanied with, or prepared for, the well- enchanting skill of music; and with a tale, forsooth, he cometh unto you with a tale which holdeth children from play, and old men from the chimney-corner; and, pretending no more, doth intend the winning of the mind from wickedness to virtue; even as the child is often brought to take most wholesome things, by hiding them in such other as have a pleasant taste; which, if one should begin to tell them the nature of the aloes or rhubarbarum they should receive, would sooner take their physic at their ears than at their mouth; so it is in men (most of them are childish in the best things, till they be cradled in their graves); glad they will be to hear the tales of Hercules, Achilles, Cyrus, AEneas; and hearing them, must needs hear the right description of wisdom, valour, and justice; which, if they had been barely (that is to say, philosophically) set out, they would swear they be brought to school again.

That imitation whereof poetry is, hath the most conveniency to nature of all other; insomuch that, as Aristotle saith, those things which in themselves are horrible, as cruel battles, unnatural monsters, are made, in poetical imitation, delightful. Truly, I have known men, that even with reading Amadis de Gaule, which, God knoweth, wanteth much of a perfect poesy, have found their hearts moved to the exercise of courtesy, liberality, and especially courage.

Who readeth AEneas carrying old Anchises on his back, that wisheth not it were his fortune to perform so excellent an act? Whom doth not those words of Turnus move (the tale of Turnus having planted his image in the imagination) "— fugientem haec terra videbit? Usque adeone mori miserum est?" Where the philosophers (as they think) scorn to delight, so much they be content little to move, saving wrangling whether "virtus" be the chief or the only good; whether the contemplative or the active life do excel; which Plato and Boetius well knew; and therefore made mistress Philosophy very often borrow the masking raiment of poesy.

For even those hard-hearted evil men, who think virtue a school- name, and know no other good but "indulgere genio," and therefore despise the austere admonitions of the philosopher, and feel not the inward reason they stand upon; yet will be content to be delighted, which is all the good-fellow poet seems to promise; and so steal to see the form of goodness, which seen, they cannot but love, ere themselves be aware, as if they took a medicine of cherries. Infinite proofs of the strange effects of this poetical invention might be alleged; only two shall serve, which are so often remembered, as, I think, all men know them.

The one of Menenius Agrippa, who, when the whole people of Rome had resolutely divided themselves from the senate, with apparent show of utter ruin, though he were, for that time, an excellent orator, came not among them upon trust, either of figurative speeches, or cunning insinuations, and much less with far-fetched maxims of philosophy, which, especially if they were Platonic, they must have learned geometry before they could have conceived; but, forsooth, he behaveth himself like a homely and familiar poet.

He telleth them a tale, that there was a time when all the parts of the body made a mutinous conspiracy against the belly, which they thought devoured the fruits of each other's labour; they concluded they would let so unprofitable a spender starve. In the end, to be short (for the tale is notorious, and as notorious that it was a tale), with punishing the belly they plagued themselves. This, applied by him, wrought such effect in the people as I never read that only words brought forth; but then so sudden, and so good an alteration, for upon reasonable conditions a perfect reconcilement ensued.

The other is of Nathan the prophet, who, when the holy David had so far forsaken God, as to confirm adultery with murder, when he was to do the tenderest office of a friend, in laying his own shame before his eyes, being sent by God to call again so chosen a servant, how doth he it? but by telling of a man whose beloved lamb was ungratefully taken from his bosom. The application most divinely true, but the discourse itself feigned; which made David (I speak of the second and instrumental cause) as in a glass see his own filthiness, as that heavenly psalm of mercy well testifieth.

By these, therefore, examples and reasons, I think it may be manifest that the poet, with that same hand of delight, doth draw the mind more effectually than any other art doth. And so a conclusion not unfitly ensues; that as virtue is the most excellent resting-place for all worldly learning to make his end of, so poetry, being the most familiar to teach it, and most princely to move towards it, in the most excellent work is the most excellent workman.

But I am content not only to decipher him by his works (although works in commendation and dispraise must ever hold a high authority), but more narrowly will examine his parts; so that (as in a man) though all together may carry a presence full of majesty and beauty perchance in some one defectious piece we may find blemish.

Now, in his parts, kinds, or species, as you list to term them, it is to be noted that some poesies have coupled together two or three kinds; as the tragical and comical, whereupon is risen the tragi-comical; some, in the manner, have mingled prose and verse, as Sannazaro and Boetius; some have mingled matters heroical and pastoral; but that cometh all to one in this question; for, if severed they be good, the conjunction cannot be hurtful.

Therefore, perchance, forgetting some, and leaving some as needless to be remembered, it shall not be amiss, in a word, to cite the special kinds, to see what faults may be found in the right use of them. Is it, then, the pastoral poem which is misliked? For, perchance, where the hedge is lowest, they will soonest leap over. Is the poor pipe disdained, which sometimes, out of Melibaeus's mouth, can show the misery of people under hard lords and ravening soldiers? And again, by Tityrus, what blessedness is derived to them that lie lowest from the goodness of them that sit highest? Sometimes under the pretty tales of wolves and sheep, can include the whole considerations of wrong doing and patience; sometimes show, that contentions for trifles can get but a trifling victory; where, perchance, a man may see that even Alexander and Darius, when they strove who should be cock of this world's dunghill, the benefit they got was, that the after-livers may say, "Haec memini, et victum frustra contendere Thyrsim.

Ex illo Corydon, Corydon est tempore nobis." Or is it the lamenting elegiac,which in a kind heart, would move rather pity than blame; who bewaileth, with the great philosopher Heraclitus, the weakness of mankind, and the wretchedness of the world; who, surely, is to be praised, either for compassionately accompanying just causes of lamentations, or for rightly pointing out how weak be the passions of woefulness? Is it the bitter, but wholesome iambic, who rubs the galled mind, making shame the trumpet of villany, with bold and open crying out against naughtiness? Or the satiric? who, "Omne vafer vitium ridenti tangit amico;" who sportingly never leaveth, until he make a man laugh at folly, and, at length, ashamed to laugh at himself, which he cannot avoid without avoiding the folly; who, while "circum praecordia ludit," giveth us to feel how many headaches a passionate life bringeth us to; who when all is done, "Est Ulubris, animus si nos non deficit aequus." No, perchance, it is the comic; whom naughty play-makers and stage-keepers have justly made odious.

To the arguments of abuse I will after answer; only thus much now is to be said, that the comedy is an imitation of the common errors of our life, which he representeth in the most ridiculous and scornful sort that may be; so as it is impossible that any beholder can be content to be such a one. Now, as in geometry, the oblique must be known as well as the right, and in arithmetic, the odd as well as the even; so in the actions of our life, who seeth not the filthiness of evil, wanteth a great foil to perceive the beauty of virtue.

This doth the comedy handle so, in our private and domestical matters, as, with hearing it, we get, as it were, an experience of what is to be looked for, of a niggardly Demea, of a crafty Davus, of a flattering Gnatho, of a vain-glorious Thraso; and not only to know what effects are to be expected, but to know who be such, by the signifying badge given them by the comedian. And little reason hath any man to say, that men learn the evil by seeing it so set out; since, as I said before, there is no man living, but by the force truth hath in nature, no sooner seeth these men play their parts, but wisheth them in "pistrinum;" although, perchance, the sack of his own faults lie so behind his back, that he seeth not himself to dance in the same measure, whereto yet nothing can more open his eyes than to see his own actions contemptibly set forth; so that the right use of comedy will, I think, by nobody be blamed.

And much less of the high and excellent tragedy, that openeth the greatest wounds, and showeth forth the ulcers that are covered with tissue; that maketh kings fear to be tyrants, and tyrants to manifest their tyrannical humours; that with stirring the effects of admiration and commiseration, teacheth the uncertainty of this world, and upon how weak foundations gilded roofs are builded; that maketh us know, "qui sceptra saevos duro imperio regit, timet timentes, metus in authorem redit." But how much it can move, Plutarch yielded a notable testimony of the abominable tyrant Alexander Pheraeus; from whose eyes a tragedy, well made and represented, drew abundance of tears, who without all pity had murdered infinite numbers, and some of his own blood; so as he that was not ashamed to make matters for tragedies, yet could not resist the sweet violence of a tragedy.

And if it wrought no farther good in him, it was that he, in despite of himself, withdrew himself from hearkening to that which might mollify his hardened heart. But it is not the tragedy they do dislike, for it were too absurd to cast out so excellent a representation of whatsoever is most worthy to be learned. Is it the lyric that most displeaseth, who with his tuned lyre and well-accorded voice, giveth praise, the reward of virtue, to virtuous acts? who giveth moral precepts and natural problems? who sometimes raiseth up his voice to the height of the heavens, in singing the lauds of the immortal God?

Certainly, I must confess mine own barbarousness; I never heard the old song of Percy and Douglas, that I found not my heart moved more than with a trumpet; and yet it is sung but by some blind crowder, with no rougher voice than rude style; which being so evil apparelled in the dust and cobweb of that uncivil age, what would it work, trimmed in the gorgeous eloquence of Pindar? In Hungary I have seen it the manner at all feasts, and all other such-like meetings, to have songs of their ancestors' valour, which that right soldier-like nation think one of the chiefest kindlers of brave courage.

The incomparable Lacedaemonians did not only carry that kind of music ever with them to the field, but even at home, as such songs were made, so were they all content to be singers of them; when the lusty men were to tell what they did, the old men what they had done, and the young what they would do.

And where a man may say that Pindar many times praiseth highly victories of small moment, rather matters of sport than virtue; as it may be answered, it was the fault of the poet, and not of the poetry, so, indeed, the chief fault was in the time and custom of the Greeks, who set those toys at so high a price, that Philip of Macedon reckoned a horse-race won at Olympus among three fearful felicities. But as the inimitable Pindar often did, so is that kind most capable, and most fit, to awake the thoughts from the sleep of idleness, to embrace honourable enterprises.

There rests the heroical, whose very name, I think, should daunt all backbiters. For by what conceit can a tongue be directed to speak evil of that which draweth with him no less champions than Achilles, Cyrus, AEneas, Turus, Tydeus, Rinaldo? who doth not only teach and move to truth, but teacheth and moveth to the most high and excellent truth: who maketh magnanimity and justice shine through all misty fearfulness and foggy desires? who, if the saying of Plato and Tully be true, that who could see virtue, would be wonderfully ravished with the love of her beauty; this man setteth her out to make her more lovely, in her holiday apparel, to the eye of any that will deign not to disdain until they understand.

But if any thing be already said in the defence of sweet

poetry, all concurreth to the maintaining the heroical, which is not only a kind, but the best and most accomplished kind, of poetry. For, as the image of each action stirreth and instructeth the mind, so the lofty image of such worthies most inflameth the mind with desire to be worthy, and informs with counsel how to be worthy.

Only let AEneas be worn in the tablet of your memory, how he governeth himself in the ruin of his country; in the preserving his old father, and carrying away his religious ceremonies; in obeying God's commandments, to leave Dido, though not only passionate kindness, but even the human consideration of virtuous gratefulness, would have craved other of him; how in storms, how in sports, how in war, how in peace, how a fugitive, how victorious, how besieged, how besieging, how to strangers, how to allies, how to enemies; how to his own, lastly, how in his inward self, and how in his outward government; and I think, in a mind most prejudiced with a prejudicating humour, he will be found in excellency fruitful. Yea, as Horace saith, "Melius Chrysippo et Crantore:" but, truly, I imagine it falleth out with these poet-whippers as with some good women who often are sick, but in faith they cannot tell where. So the name of poetry is odious to them, but neither his cause nor effects, neither the sum that contains him, nor the particularities descending from him, give any fast handle to their carping dispraise.

Since, then, poetry is of all human learnings the most ancient, and of most fatherly antiquity, as from whence other learnings have taken their beginnings; since it is so universal that no learned nation doth despise it, nor barbarous nation is without it; since both Roman and Greek gave such divine names unto it, the one of prophesying, the other of making, and that indeed that name of making is fit for him, considering, that where all other arts retain themselves within their subject, and receive, as it were, their being from it, the poet only, only bringeth his own stuff, and doth not learn a conceit out of a matter, but maketh matter for a conceit; since neither his description nor end containeth any evil, the thing described cannot be evil; since his effects be so good as to teach goodness, and delight the learners of it; since therein (namely, in moral doctrine, the chief of all knowledges) he doth not only far pass the historian, but, for instructing, is well nigh comparable to the philosopher; for moving, leaveth him behind him; since the Holy Scripture (wherein there is no uncleanness) hath whole parts in it poetical, and that even our Saviour Christ vouchsafed to use the flowers of it; since all his kinds are not only in their united forms, but in their severed dissections fully commendable; I think, and think I think rightly, the laurel crown appointed for triumphant captains, doth worthily, of all other learnings, honour the poet's triumph. But because we have ears as well as tongues, and that the lightest reasons that may be, will seem to weigh greatly, if nothing be put in the counterbalance, let us hear, and, as well as we can, ponder what objections be made against this art, which may be worthy either of yielding or answering.

First, truly, I note, not only in these, poet-haters, but in all that kind of people who seek a praise by dispraising others, that they do prodigally spend a great many wandering words in quips and scoffs, carping and taunting at each thing, which, by stirring the spleen, may stay the brain from a thorough beholding, the worthiness of the subject.

Those kind of objections, as they are full of a very idle uneasiness (since there is nothing of so sacred a majesty, but that an itching tongue may rub itself upon it), so deserve they no other answer, but, instead of laughing at the jest, to laugh at the jester. We know a playing wit can praise the discretion of an ass, the comfortableness of being in debt, and the jolly commodities of being sick of the plague; so, of the contrary side, if we will turn Ovid's verse, "Ut lateat virtus proximitate mali." "That good lies hid in nearness of the evil," Agrippa will be as merry in the showing the Vanity of Science, as Erasmus was in the commending of Folly; neither shall any man or matter escape some touch of these smiling railers. But for Erasmus and Agrippa, they had another foundation than the superficial part would promise.

Marry, these other pleasant fault-finders, who will correct the verb before they understand the noun, and confute others' knowledge before they confirm their own; I would have them only remember, that scoffing cometh not of wisdom; so as the best title in true English they get with their merriments, is to be called good fools; for so have our grave forefathers ever termed that humorous kind of jesters. But that which giveth greatest scope to their scorning humour, is rhyming and versing. It is already said, and, as I think, truly said, it is not rhyming and versing that maketh poesy; one may be a poet without versing, and a versifier without poetry. But yet, presuppose it were inseparable, as indeed, it seemeth Scaliger judgeth truly, it were an inseparable commendation; for if "oratio" next to "ratio," speech next to reason, be the greatest gift bestowed upon mortality, that cannot be praiseless which doth most polish that blessing of speech; which considereth each word, not only as a man may say by his forcible quality, but by his best measured quantity; carrying even in themselves a harmony; without, perchance, number, measure, order, proportion be in our time grown odious. But lay aside the just praise it hath, by being the only fit speech for music—music, I say, the most divine striker of the senses; thus much is undoubtedly true, that if reading be foolish without remembering, memory being the only treasure of knowledge, those words which are fittest for memory, are likewise most convenient for knowledge.

Now, that verse far exceedeth prose in the knitting up of the memory, the reason is manifest: the words, besides their delight, which hath a great affinity to memory, being so set as one cannot be lost, but the whole work fails: which accusing itself, calleth the remembrance back to itself, and so most strongly confirmeth it. Besides, one word so, as it were, begetting another, as, be it in rhyme or measured verse, by the former a man shall have a near guess to the follower.

Lastly, even they that have taught the art of memory, have showed nothing so apt for it as a certain room divided into many places, well and thoroughly known; now that hath the verse in effect perfectly, every word having his natural seat, which seat must needs make the word remembered. But what needs more in a thing so known to all men? Who is it that ever was a scholar that doth not carry away some verses of Virgil, Horace, or Cato, which in his youth he learned, and even to his old age serve him for hourly lessons? as, "Percontatorem fugito: nam garrulus idem est. Dum sibi quisque placet credula turba sumus."

But the fitness it hath for memory is notably proved by all delivery of arts, wherein, for the most part, from grammar to logic, mathematics, physic, and the rest, the rules chiefly necessary to be borne away are compiled in verses. So that verse being in itself sweet and orderly, and being best for memory, the only handle of knowledge, it must be in jest that any man can speak against it. Now then go we to the most important imputations laid to the poor poets; for aught I can yet learn, they are these.

First, that there being many other more fruitful knowledges, a man might better spend his time in them than in this. Secondly, that it is the mother of lies. Thirdly, that it is the nurse of abuse, infecting us with many pestilent desires, with a syren sweetness, drawing the mind to the serpent's tail of sinful fancies; and herein, especially, comedies give the largest field to ear, as Chaucer saith; how, both in other nations and ours, before poets did soften us, we were full of courage, given to martial exercises, the pillars of manlike liberty, and not lulled asleep in shady idleness with poets' pastimes.

And lastly and chiefly, they cry out with open mouth, as if they had overshot Robin Hood, that Plato banished them out of his commonwealth. Truly this is much, if there be much truth in it. First, to the first, that a man might better spend his time, is a reason indeed; but it doth, as they say, but "petere principium." For if it be, as I affirm, that no learning is so good as that which teacheth and moveth to virtue, and that none can both teach and move thereto so much as poesy, then is the conclusion manifest, that ink and paper cannot be to a more profitable purpose employed.

And certainly, though a man should grant their first assumption, it should follow, methinks, very unwillingly, that good is not good because better is better. But I still and utterly deny that there is sprung out of earth a more fruitful knowledge. To the second, therefore, that they should be the principal liars, I answer paradoxically, but truly, I think truly, that of all writers under the sun, the poet is the least liar; and though he would, as a poet, can scarcely be a liar.

The astronomer, with his cousin the geometrician, can hardly escape when they take upon them to measure the height of the stars. How often, think you, do the physicians lie, when they aver things good for sicknesses, which afterwards send Charon a great number of souls drowned in a potion before they come to his ferry. And no less of the rest which take upon them to affirm. Now for the poet, he nothing affirmeth, and therefore never lieth; for, as I take it, to lie is to affirm that to be true which is false: so as the other artists, and especially the historian, affirmeth many things, can, in the cloudy knowledge of mankind, hardly escape from many lies: but the poet, as I said before, never affirmeth; the poet never maketh any circles about your imagination, to conjure you to believe for true what he writeth: he citeth not authorities of other histories, but even for his entry calleth the sweet Muses to inspire into him a good invention; in troth, not labouring to tell you what is or is not, but what should or should not be.

And, therefore, though he recount things not true, yet because he telleth them not for true he lieth not; without we will say that Nathan lied in his speech, before alleged, to David; which, as a wicked man durst scarce say, so think I none so simple would say, that AEsop lied in the tales of his beasts; for who thinketh that AEsop wrote it for actually true, were well worthy to have his name chronicled among the beasts he writeth of. What child is there that cometh to a play, and seeing Thebes written in great letters upon an old door, doth believe that it is Thebes? If then a man can arrive to the child's age, to know that the poet's persons and doings are but pictures what should be, and not stories what have been, they will never give the lie to things not affirmatively, but allegorically and figuratively written; and therefore, as in history, looking for truth, they may go away full fraught with falsehood, so in poesy, looking but for fiction, they shall use the narration but as an imaginative ground-plot of a profitable invention. But hereto is replied, that the poets give names to men they write of, which argueth a conceit of an actual truth, and so, not being true, proveth a falsehood.

And doth the lawyer lie then, when, under the names of John of the Stile, and John of the Nokes, he putteth his case? But that is easily answered, their naming of men is but to make their picture the more lively, and not to build any history. Painting men, they cannot leave men nameless; we see we cannot play at chess but that we must give names to our chess-men: and yet, methinks, he were a very partial champion of truth that would say we lied for giving a piece of wood the reverend title of a bishop. The poet nameth Cyrus and AEneas no other way than to show what men of their fames, fortunes, and estates should do.

Their third is, how much it abuseth men's wit, training it to a wanton sinfulness and lustful love. For, indeed, that is the principal if not only abuse I can hear alleged. They say the comedies rather teach, than reprehend, amorous conceits; they say the lyric is larded with passionate sonnets; the elegiac weeps the want of his mistress; and that even to the heroical Cupid hath ambitiously climbed.

Alas! Love, I would thou couldst as well defend thyself, as thou canst offend others! I would those on whom thou dost attend, could either put thee away or yield good reason why they keep thee! But grant love of beauty to be a beastly fault, although it be very hard, since only man, and no beast, hath that gift to discern beauty; grant that lovely name of love to deserve all hateful reproaches, although even some of my masters the philosophers spent a good deal of their lamp-oil in setting forth the excellency of it; grant, I say, what they will have granted, that not only love, but lust, but vanity, but, if they list, scurrility, possess many leaves of the poets' books; yet, think I, when this is granted, they will find their sentence may, with good manners, put the last words foremost; and not say that poetry abuseth man's wit, but that man's wit abuseth poetry.

For I will not deny but that man's wit may make poesy, which should be [Greek text], which some learned have defined, figuring forth good things, to be [Greek text], which doth contrariwise infect the fancy with unworthy objects; as the painter, who should give to the eye either some excellent perspective, or some fine picture fit for building or fortification, or containing in it some notable example, as Abraham sacrificing his son Isaac, Judith killing Holofernes, David fighting with Goliath, may leave those, and please an ill-pleased eye with wanton shows of better-hidden matters.

But, what! shall the abuse of a thing make the right use odious? Nay, truly, though I yield that poesy may not only be abused, but that being abused, by the reason of his sweet charming force, it can do more hurt than any other army of words, yet shall it be so far from concluding, that the abuse shall give reproach to the abused, that, contrariwise, it is a good reason, that whatsoever being abused, doth most harm, being rightly used (and upon the right use each thing receives his title) doth most good.

Do we not see skill of physic, the best rampire to our often-assaulted bodies, being abused, teach poison, the most violent destroyer? Doth not knowledge of law, whose end is to even and right all things, being abused, grow the crooked fosterer of horrible injuries? Doth not (to go in the highest) God's word abused breed heresy, and His name abused become blasphemy? Truly, a needle cannot do much hurt, and as truly (with leave of ladies be it spoken) it cannot do much good. With a sword thou mayest kill thy father, and with a sword thou mayest defend thy prince and country; so that, as in their calling poets fathers of lies, they said nothing, so in this their argument of abuse, they prove the commendation.

They allege herewith, that before poets began to be in price, our nation had set their heart's delight upon action, and not imagination; rather doing things worthy to be written, than writing things fit to be done. What that before time was, I think scarcely Sphynx can tell; since no memory is so ancient that gives not the precedence to poetry.

And certain it is, that, in our plainest homeliness, yet never was the Albion nation without poetry. Marry, this argument, though it be levelled against poetry, yet it is indeed a chainshot against all learning or bookishness, as they commonly term it. Of such mind were certain Goths, of whom it is written, that having in the spoil of a famous city taken a fair library, one hangman, belike fit to execute the fruits of their wits, who had murdered a great number of bodies, would have set fire in it. "No," said another, very gravely, "take heed what you do, for while they are busy about those toys, we shall with more leisure conquer their countries."

This, indeed, is the ordinary doctrine of ignorance, and many words sometimes I have heard spent in it; but because this reason is generally against all learning as well as poetry, or rather all learning but poetry; because it were too large a digression to handle it, or at least too superfluous, since it is manifest that all government of action is to be gotten by knowledge, and knowledge best by gathering many knowledges, which is reading,; I only say with Horace, to him that is of that opinion, "Jubeo stultum esse libenter—" for as for poetry itself, it is the freest from this, objection, for poetry is the companion of camps. I dare undertake, Orlando Furioso, or honest King Arthur, will never displease a soldier: but the quiddity of "ens" and "prima materia" will hardly agree with a corslet. And, therefore, as I said in the beginning, even Turks and Tartars are delighted with poets.

Homer, a Greek, flourished before Greece flourished; and if to a slight conjecture a conjecture may be opposed, truly it may seem, that as by him their learned men took almost their first light of knowledge, so their active men receive their first notions of courage. Only Alexander's example may serve, who by Plutarch is accounted of such virtue that fortune was not his guide but his footstool; whose acts speak for him, though Plutarch did not; indeed, the phoenix of warlike princes. This Alexander left his schoolmaster, living Aristotle, behind him, but took dead Homer with him.

He put the philosopher Callisthenes to death, for his seeming philosophical, indeed mutinous, stubbornness; but the chief thing he was ever heard to wish for was that Homer had been alive. He well found he received more bravery of mind by the pattern of Achilles, than by hearing the definition of fortitude. And, therefore, if Cato misliked Fulvius for carrying Ennius with him to the field, it may be answered that if Cato misliked it the noble Fulvius liked it, or else he had not done it; for it was not the excellent Cato Uticensis whose authority I would much more have reverenced, but it was the former, in truth a bitter punisher of faults, but else a man that had never sacrificed to the Graces.

He misliked, and cried out against, all Greek learning, and yet, being fourscore years old, began to learn it, belike fearing that Pluto understood not Latin. Indeed, the Roman laws allowed no person to be carried to the wars but he that was in the soldiers' roll. And, therefore, though Cato misliked his unmustered person, he misliked not his work. And if he had, Scipio Nasica (judged by common consent the best Roman) loved him: both the other Scipio brothers, who had by their virtues no less surnames than of Asia and Afric, so loved him that they caused his body to be buried in their sepulture.

So, as Cato's authority being but against his person, and that answered with so far greater than himself, is herein of no validity. But now, indeed, my burthen is great, that Plato's name is laid upon me, whom, I must confess, of all philosophers I have ever esteemed most worthy of reverence; and with good reason, since of all philosophers he is the most poetical; yet if he will defile the fountain out of which his flowing streams have proceeded, let us boldly examine with what reason he did it.

First, truly, a man might maliciously object that Plato, being a philosopher, was a natural enemy of poets. For, indeed, after the philosophers had picked out of the sweet mysteries of poetry the right discerning of true points of knowledge, they forthwith, putting it in method, and making a school of art of that which the poets did only teach by a divine delightfulness, beginning to spurn at their guides, like ungrateful apprentices, were not content to set up shop for themselves, but sought by all means to discredit their masters; which, by the force of delight being barred them, the less they could overthrow them, the more they hated them.

For, indeed, they found for Homer seven cities strove who

should have him for their citizen, where many cities banished philosophers as not fit members to live among them. For only repeating certain of Euripides' verses many Athenians had their lives saved of the Syracusans, where the Athenians themselves thought many of the philosophers unworthy to live. Certain poets, as Simonides and Pindar, had so prevailed with Hiero the First, that of a tyrant they made him a just king; where Plato could do so little with Dionysius that he himself, of a philosopher, was made a slave.

But who should do thus, I confess, should requite the objections raised against poets with like cavillations against philosophers; as likewise one should do that should bid one read Phaedrus or Symposium in Plato, or the discourse of Love in Plutarch, and see whether any poet do authorise abominable filthiness as they do. Again, a man might ask, out of what Commonwealth Plato doth banish them? In sooth, thence where he himself alloweth community of women.

So, as belike this banishment grew not for effeminate wantonness, since little should poetical sonnets be hurtful, when a man might have what woman he listed. But I honour philosophical instructions, and bless the wits which bred them, so as they be not abused, which is likewise stretched to poetry. Saint Paul himself sets a watchword upon philosophy, indeed upon the abuse.

So doth Plato upon the abuse, not upon poetry. Plato found fault that the poets of his time filled the world with wrong opinions of the gods, making light tales of that unspotted essence, and therefore would not have the youth depraved with such opinions.

Herein may much be said; let this suffice: the poets did not induce such opinions, but did imitate those opinions already induced. For all the Greek stories can well testify that the very religion of that time stood upon many and many-fashioned gods; not taught so by poets, but followed according to their nature of imitation.

Who list may read in Plutarch the discourses of Isis and Osiris, of the cause why oracles ceased, of the Divine providence, and see whether the theology of that nation stood not upon such dreams, which the poets indeed superstitiously observed; and truly, since they had not the light of Christ, did much better in it than the philosophers, who, shaking off superstition, brought in atheism.

Plato, therefore, whose authority I had much rather justly construe than unjustly resist, meant not in general of poets, in those words of which Julius Scaliger saith, "qua authoritate, barbari quidam atque insipidi, abuti velint ad poetas e republica exigendos:" but only meant to drive out those wrong opinions of the Deity, whereof now, without farther law, Christianity hath taken away all the hurtful belief, perchance as he thought nourished by then esteemed poets. And a man need go no farther than to Plato himself to know his meaning; who, in his dialogue called "Ion," giveth high, and rightly, divine commendation unto poetry.

So as Plato, banishing the abuse, not the thing, not banishing it, but giving due honour to it, shall be our patron, and not our adversary. For, indeed, I had much rather, since truly I may do it, show their mistaking of Plato, under whose lion's skin they would make an ass- like braying against poesy, than go about to overthrow his authority; whom, the wiser a man is, the more just cause he shall find to have in admiration; especially since he attributeth unto poesy more than myself do, namely, to be a very inspiring of a divine force, far above man's wit, as in the fore-named dialogue is apparent.

Of the other side, who would show the honours have been by the best sort of judgments granted them, a whole sea of examples would present themselves; Alexanders, Caesars, Scipios, all favourers of poets; Laelius, called the Roman Socrates, himself a poet; so as part of Heautontimeroumenos, in Terence, was supposed to be made by him. And even the Greek Socrates, whom Apollo confirmed to be the only wise man, is said to have spent part of his old time in putting AEsop's Fables into verse; and, therefore, full evil should it become his scholar Plato to put such words in his master's mouth against poets.

But what needs more? Aristotle writes the "Art of Poesy;" and why, if it should not be written? Plutarch teacheth the use to be gathered of them; and how, if they should not be read? And who reads Plutarch's either history or philosophy, shall find he trimmeth both their garments with guards of poesy. But I list not to defend poesy with the help of his underling historiographer.

Let it suffice to have showed it is a fit soil for praise to dwell upon; and what dispraise may be set upon it is either easily overcome, or transformed into just commendation. So that since the excellences of it may be so easily and so justly confirmed, and the low creeping objections so soon trodden down; it not being an art of lies, but of true doctrine; not of effeminateness, but of notable stirring of courage; not of abusing man's wit, but of strengthening man's wit; not banished, but honoured by Plato; let us rather plant more laurels for to ingarland the poets' heads (which honour of being laureate, as besides them only triumphant captains were, is a sufficient authority to show the price they ought to be held in) than suffer the ill-favoured breath of such wrong speakers once to blow upon the clear springs of poesy. But since I have run so long a career in this matter, methinks, before I give my pen a full stop, it shall be but a little more lost time to inquire, why England, the mother of excellent minds, should be grown so hard a step-mother to poets, who certainly in wit ought to pass all others, since all only proceeds from their wit, being, indeed, makers of themselves, not takers of others.

How can I but exclaim, "Musa, mihi causas memora, quo numine laeso?" Sweet poesy! that hath anciently had kings, emperors, senators, great captains, such as, besides a thousand others, David, Adrian, Sophocles, Germanicus, not only to favour poets, but to be poets; and of our nearer times can present for her patrons, a Robert, King of Sicily; the great King Francis of France; King James of Scotland; such cardinals as Bembus and Bibiena; such famous preachers and teachers as Beza and Melancthon; so learned philosophers as Fracastorius and Scaliger; so great orators as Pontanus and Muretus; so piercing wits as George Buchanan; so grave councillors as, besides many, but before all, that Hospital of France, than whom, I think, that realm never brought forth a more accomplished judgment more firmly builded upon virtue; I say these, with numbers of others, not only to read others' poesies, but to poetise for others' reading: that poesy, thus embraced in all other places, should only find in our time a hard welcome in England, I think the very earth laments it, and therefore decks our soil with fewer laurels than it was accustomed.

For heretofore poets have in England also flourished; and, which is to be noted, even in those times when the trumpet of Mars did sound loudest. And now that an over-faint quietness should seem to strew the house for poets, they are almost in as good reputation as the mountebanks at Venice. Truly, even that, as of the one side it giveth great praise to poesy, which, like Venus (but to better purpose), had rather be troubled in the net with Mars, than enjoy the homely quiet of Vulcan; so serveth it for a piece of a reason why they are less grateful to idle England, which now can scarce endure the pain of a pen. Upon this necessarily followeth that base men with servile wits undertake it, who think it enough if they can be rewarded of the printer; and so as Epaminondas is said, with the honour of his virtue, to have made an office by his exercising it, which before was contemptible, to become highly respected; so these men, no more but setting their names to it, by their own disgracefulness, disgrace the most graceful poesy.

For now, as if all the Muses were got with child, to bring forth bastard poets, without any commission, they do post over the banks of Helicon, until they make their readers more weary than post-horses; while, in the meantime, they, "Queis meliore luto finxit praecordia Titan," are better content to suppress the outflowings of their wit, than by publishing them to be accounted knights of the same order. But I that, before ever I durst aspire unto the dignity, am admitted into the company of the paper-blurrers, do find the very true cause of our wanting estimation is want of desert, taking upon us to be poets in despite of Pallas.

Now, wherein we want desert, were a thankworthy labour to express. But if I knew, I should have mended myself; but as I never desired the title so have I neglected the means to come by it; only, overmastered by some thoughts, I yielded an inky tribute unto them. Marry, they that delight in poesy itself, should seek to know what they do, and how they do, especially look themselves in an unflattering glass of reason, if they be inclinable unto it. For poesy must not be drawn by the ears, it must be gently led, or rather it must lead; which was partly the cause that made the ancient learned affirm it was a divine, and no human skill, since all other knowledges lie ready for any that have strength of wit; a poet no industry can make, if his own genius be not carried into it. And therefore is an old proverb, "Orator fit, poeta nascitur." Yet confess I always, that as the fertilest ground must be manured, so must the highest flying wit have a Daedalus to guide him.

That Daedalus, they say, both in this and in other, hath three wings to bear itself up into the air of due commendation; that is art, imitation, and exercise. But these, neither artificial rules, nor imitative patterns, we much cumber ourselves withal. Exercise, indeed, we do, but that very forebackwardly; for where we should exercise to know, we exercise as having known; and so is our brain delivered of much matter which never was begotten by knowledge.

For there being two principal parts, matter to be expressed by words, and words to express the matter, in neither we use art or imitation rightly. Our matter is "quodlibet," indeed, although wrongly, performing Ovid's verse, "Quicquid conabor dicere, versus erit;" never marshalling it into any assured rank, that almost the readers cannot tell where to find themselves. Chaucer, undoubtedly, did excellently in his Troilus and Cressida; of whom, truly, I know not whether to marvel more, either that he in that misty time could see so clearly, or that we in this clear age go so stumblingly after him. Yet had he great wants, fit to be forgiven in so reverend antiquity. I account the Mirror of Magistrates meetly furnished of beautiful parts.

And in the Earl of Surrey's Lyrics, many things tasting of a noble birth, and worthy of a noble mind. The "Shepherds' Kalendar" hath much poesy in his eclogues, indeed, worthy the reading, if I be not deceived. That same framing of his style to an old rustic language, I dare not allow; since neither Theocritus in Greek, Virgil in Latin, nor Sannazaro in Italian, did affect it. Besides these, I do not remember to have seen but few (to speak boldly) printed that have poetical sinews in them. For proof whereof, let but most of the verses be put in prose, and then ask the meaning, and it will be found that one verse did but beget another, without ordering at the first what should be at the last; which becomes a confused mass of words, with a tinkling sound of rhyme, barely accompanied with reason. Our tragedies and comedies, not without cause, are cried out against, observing rules neither of honest civility nor skilful poetry. Excepting Gorboduc (again I say of those that I have seen), which notwithstanding, as it is full of stately speeches, and well- sounding phrases, climbing to the height of Seneca his style, and as full of notable morality, which it does most delightfully teach, and so obtain the very end of poesy; yet, in truth, it is very defectuous in the circumstances, which grieves me, because it might not remain as an exact model of all tragedies.

For it is faulty both in place and time, the two necessary companions of all corporal actions. For where the stage should always represent but one place; and the uttermost time presupposed in it should be, both by Aristotle's precept, and common reason, but one day; there is both many days and many places inartificially imagined.

But if it be so in Gorboduc, how much more in all the rest? where you shall have Asia of the one side, and Afric of the other, and so many other under kingdoms, that the player, when he comes in, must ever begin with telling where he is, or else the tale will not be conceived. Now shall you have three ladies walk to gather flowers, and then we must believe the stage to be a garden. By and by, we hear news of shipwreck in the same place, then we are to blame if we accept it not for a rock.

Upon the back of that comes out a hideous monster with fire and smoke, and then the miserable beholders are bound to take it for a cave; while, in the meantime, two armies fly in, represented with four swords and bucklers, and then, what hard heart will not receive it for a pitched field? Now of time they are much more liberal; for ordinary it is, that two young princes fall in love; after many traverses she is got with child; delivered of a fair boy; he is lost, groweth a man, falleth in love, and is ready to get another child; and all this in two hours' space; which, how absurd it is in sense, even sense may imagine; and art hath taught and all ancient examples justified, and at this day the ordinary players in Italy will not err in.

Yet will some bring in an example of the Eunuch in Terence, that containeth matter of two days, yet far short of twenty years. True it is, and so was it to be played in two days, and so fitted to the time it set forth. And though Plautus have in one place done amiss, let us hit it with him, and not miss with him. But they will say, How then shall we set forth a story which contains both many places and many times? And do they not know, that a tragedy is tied to the laws of poesy, and not of history; not bound to follow the story, but having liberty either to feign a quite new matter, or to frame the history to the most tragical convenience? Again, many things may be told, which cannot be showed: if they know the difference betwixt reporting and representing.

As for example, I may speak, though I am here, of Peru, and in speech digress from that to the description of Calicut; but in action I cannot represent it without Pacolet's horse. And so was the manner the ancients took by some "Nuntius," to recount things done in former time, or other place. Lastly, if they will represent an history, they must not, as Horace saith, begin "ab ovo," but they must come to the principal point of that one action which they will represent.

By example this will be best expressed; I have a story of young Polydorus, delivered, for safety's sake, with great riches, by his father Priamus to Polymnestor, King of Thrace, in the Trojan war time. He, after some years, hearing of the overthrow of Priamus, for to make the treasure his own, murdereth the child; the body of the child is taken up; Hecuba, she, the same day, findeth a sleight to be revenged most cruelly of the tyrant.

Where, now, would one of our tragedy-writers begin, but

with the delivery of the child? Then should he sail over into Thrace, and so spend I know not how many years, and travel numbers of places. But where doth Euripides? Even with the finding of the body; leaving the rest to be told by the spirit of Polydorus.

This needs no farther to be enlarged; the dullest wit may conceive it. But, besides these gross absurdities, how all their plays be neither right tragedies nor right comedies, mingling kings and clowns, not because the matter so carrieth it, but thrust in the clown by head and shoulders to play a part in majestical matters, with neither decency nor discretion; so as neither the admiration and commiseration, nor the right sportfulness, is by their mongrel tragi-comedy obtained. I know Apuleius did somewhat so, but that is a thing recounted with space of time, not represented in one moment: and I know the ancients have one or two examples of tragi-comedies as Plautus hath Amphytrio.

But, if we mark them well, we shall find, that they never, or very daintily, match horn-pipes and funerals. So falleth it out, that having indeed no right comedy in that comical part of our tragedy, we have nothing but scurrility, unworthy of any chaste ears; or some extreme show of doltishness, indeed fit to lift up a loud laughter, and nothing else; where the whole tract of a comedy should be full of delight; as the tragedy should be still maintained in a well-raised admiration. But our comedians think there is no delight without laughter, which is very wrong; for though laughter may come with delight, yet cometh it not of delight, as though delight should be the cause of laughter; but well may one thing breed both together.

Nay, in themselves, they have, as it were, a kind of contrariety. For delight we scarcely do, but in things that have a conveniency to ourselves, or to the general nature. Laughter almost ever cometh of things most disproportioned to ourselves and nature: delight hath a joy in it either permanent or present; laughter hath only a scornful tickling. For example: we are ravished with delight to see a fair woman, and yet are far from being moved to laughter; we laugh at deformed creatures, wherein certainly we cannot delight; we delight in good chances; we laugh at mischances; we delight to hear the happiness of our friends and country, at which he were worthy to be laughed at that would laugh: we shall, contrarily, sometimes laugh to find a matter quite mistaken, and go down the hill against the bias, in the mouth of some such men, as for the respect of them, one shall be heartily sorrow he cannot choose but laugh, and so is rather pained than delighted with laughter. Yet deny I not, but that they may go well together; for, as in Alexander's picture well set out, we delight without laughter, and in twenty mad antics we laugh without delight: so in Hercules, painted with his great beard and furious countenance, in a woman's attire, spinning at Omphale's commandment, it breeds both delight and laughter; for the representing of so strange a power in love procures delight, and the scornfulness of the action stirreth laughter.

But I speak to this purpose, that all the end of the comical part be not upon such scornful matters as stir laughter only, but mix with it that delightful teaching which is the end of poesy. And the great fault, even in that point of laughter, and forbidden plainly by Aristotle, is, that they stir laughter in sinful things, which are rather execrable than ridiculous; or in miserable, which are rather to be pitied than scorned. For what is it to make folks gape at a wretched beggar, and a beggarly clown; or against the law of hospitality, to jest at strangers, because they speak not English so well as we do? what do we learn, since it is certain, "Nil habet infelix pauperatas durius in se, Quam qnod ridiculos, homines facit." But rather a busy loving courtier, and a heartless threatening Thraso; a self-wise seeming school-master; a wry-transformed traveller: these, if we saw walk in stage names, which we play naturally, therein were delightful laughter, and teaching delightfulness: as in the other, the tragedies of Buchanan do justly bring forth a divine admiration.

But I have lavished out too many words of this play matter; I do it, because, as they are excelling parts of poesy, so is there none so much used in England, and none can be more pitifully abused; which, like an unmannerly daughter, showing a bad education, causeth her mother Poesy's honesty to be called in question. Other sorts of poetry, almost, have we none, but that lyrical kind of songs and sonnets, which, if the Lord gave us so good minds, how well it might be employed, and with how heavenly fruits, both private and public, in singing the praises of the immortal beauty, the immortal goodness of that God, who giveth us hands to write, and wits to conceive; of which we might well want words, but never matter; of which we could turn our eyes to nothing, but we should ever have new budding occasions.

But, truly, many of such writings as come under the banner of unresistible love, if I were a mistress, would never persuade me they were in love; so coldly they apply fiery speeches, as men that had rather read lover's writings, and so caught up certain swelling phrases, which hang together like a man that once told me, "the wind was at north-west and by south," because he would be sure to name winds enough; than that, in truth, they feel those passions, which easily, as I think, may be bewrayed by the same forcibleness, or "energia" (as the Greeks call it), of the writer. But let this be a sufficient, though short note, that we miss the right use of the material point of poesy.

Now for the outside of it, which is words, or (as I may term it) diction, it is even well worse; so is that honey-flowing matron eloquence, apparelled, or rather disguised, in a courtesan-like painted affectation. One time with so far-fetched words, that many seem monsters, but most seem strangers to any poor Englishman: another time with coursing of a letter, as if they were bound to follow the method of a dictionary: another time with figures and flowers, extremely winter-starved. But I would this fault were only peculiar to versifiers, and had not as large possession among prose printers: and, which is to be marvelled, among many scholars, and, which is to be pitied, among some preachers.

Truly, I could wish (if at least I might be so bold to wish, in a thing beyond the reach of my capacity) the diligent imitators of Tully and Demosthenes, most worthy to be imitated, did not so much keep Nizolian paper-books of their figures and phrases, as by attentive translation, as it were, devour them whole, and make them wholly theirs. For now they cast sugar and spice upon every dish that is served at the table: like those Indians, not content to wear ear-rings at the fit and natural place of the ears, but they will thrust jewels through their nose and lips, because they will be sure to be fine.

Tully, when he was to drive out Catiline, as it were with a thunderbolt of eloquence, often useth the figure of repetition, as "vivit et vincit, imo in senatum venit, imo in senatum venit,". Indeed, inflamed with a well-grounded rage, he would have his words, as it were, double out of his mouth; and so do that artificially which we see men in choler do naturally. And we, having noted the grace of those words, hale them in sometimes to a familiar epistle, when it were too much choler to be choleric.

How well, store of "similiter cadences" doth sound with the gravity of the pulpit, I would but invoke Demosthenes' soul to tell, who with a rare daintiness useth them. Truly, they have made me think of the sophister, that with too much subtlety would prove two eggs three, and though he may be counted a sophister, had none for his labour. So these men bringing in such a kind of eloquence, well may they obtain an opinion of a seeming fineness, but persuade few, which should be the end of their fineness.

Now for similitudes in certain printed discourses, I think all herbalists, all stories of beasts, fowls, and fishes are rifled up, that they may come in multitudes to wait upon any of our conceits, which certainly is as absurd a surfeit to the ears as is possible. For the force of a similitude not being to prove anything to a contrary disputer, but only to explain to a willing hearer: when that is done, the rest is a most tedious prattling, rather overswaying the memory from the purpose whereto they were applied, than any whit informing the judgment, already either satisfied, or by similitudes not to be satisfied.

For my part, I do not doubt, when Antonius and Crassus, the great forefathers of Cicero in eloquence; the one (as Cicero testifieth of them) pretended not to know art, the other not to set by it, because with a plain sensibleness they might win credit of popular ears, which credit is the nearest step to persuasion (which persuasion is the chief mark of oratory); I do not doubt, I say, but that they used these knacks very sparingly; which who doth generally use, any man may see, doth dance to his own music; and so to he noted by the audience, more careful to speak curiously than truly. Undoubtedly (at least to my opinion undoubtedly) I have found in divers small- learned courtiers a more sound style than in some professors of learning; of which I can guess no other cause, but that the courtier following that which by practice he findeth fittest to nature, therein (though he know it not) doth according to art, though not by art: where the other, using art to show art, and not hide art (as in these cases he should do), flieth from nature, and indeed abuseth art.

But what! methinks I deserve to be pounded for straying from poetry to oratory: but both have such an affinity in the wordish considerations, that I think this digression will make my meaning receive the fuller understanding: which is not to take upon me to teach poets how they should do, but only finding myself sick among the rest, to allow sonic one or two spots of the common infection grown among the most part of writers; that, acknowledging ourselves somewhat awry, we may bend to the right use both of matter and manner: whereto our language giveth us great occasion, being, indeed, capable of any excellent exercising of it.

I know some will say, it is a mingled language: and why not so much the better, taking the best of both the other? Another will say, it wanteth grammar. Nay, truly, it hath that praise, that it wants not grammar; for grammar it might have, but needs it not; being so easy in itself, and so void of those cumbersome differences of cases, genders, moods, and tenses; which, I think, was a piece of the tower of Babylon's curse, that a man should be put to school to learn his mother tongue. But for the uttering sweetly and properly the conceit of the mind, which is the end of speech, that hath it equally with any other tongue in the world, and is particularly happy in compositions of two or three words together, near the Greek, far beyond the Latin; which is one of the greatest beauties can be in a language.

Now, of versifying there are two sorts, the one ancient, the other modern; the ancient marked the quantity of each syllable, and according to that framed his verse; the modern, observing only number, with some regard of the accent, the chief life of it standeth in that like sounding of the words, which we call rhyme. Whether of these be the more excellent, would bear many speeches; the ancient, no doubt more fit for music, both words and time observing quantity; and more fit lively to express divers passions, by the low or lofty sound of the well-weighed syllable.

The latter, likewise, with his rhyme striketh a certain music to the ear; and, in fine, since it doth delight, though by another way, it obtaineth the same purpose; there being in either, sweetness, and wanting in neither, majesty.

Truly the English, before any vulgar language I know, is fit for both sorts; for, for the ancient, the Italian is so full of vowels, that it must ever be cumbered with elisions. The Dutch so, of the other side, with consonants, that they cannot yield the sweet sliding fit for a verse.

The French, in his whole language, hath not one word that hath his accent in the last syllable, saving two, called antepenultima; and little more, hath the Spanish, and therefore very gracelessly may they use dactiles. The English is subject to none of these defects. Now for rhyme, though we do not observe quantity, we observe the accent very precisely, which other languages either cannot do, or will not do so absolutely.

That "caesura," or breathing-place, in the midst of the verse, neither Italian nor Spanish have, the French and we never almost fail of. Lastly, even the very rhyme itself the Italian cannot put in the last syllable, by the French named the masculine rhyme, but still in the next to the last, which the French call the female; or the next before that, which the Italian calls "sdrucciola:" the example of the former is, "buono," "suono;" of the sdrucciola is, "femina," "semina." The French, of the other side, hath both the male, as "bon," "son," and the female, as "plaise," "taise;" but the "sdrucciola" he hath not; where the English hath all three, as "due," "true," "father," "rather," "motion," "potion;" with much more which might be said, but that already I find the trifling of this discourse is much too much enlarged.

So that since the ever praiseworthy poesy is full of virtue, breeding delightfulness, and void of no gift that ought to be in the noble name of learning; since the blames laid against it are either false or feeble; since the cause why it is not esteemed in England is the fault of poet-apes, not poets; since, lastly, our tongue is most fit to honour poesy, and to be honoured by poesy; I conjure you all that have had the evil luck to read this ink-wasting toy of mine, even in the name of the Nine Muses, no more to scorn the sacred mysteries of poesy; no more to laugh at the name of poets, as though they were next inheritors to fools; no more to jest at the reverend title of "a rhymer;" but to believe, with Aristotle, that they were the ancient treasurers of the Grecian's divinity; to believe, with Bembus, that they were the first bringers in of all civility; to believe, with Scaliger, that no philosopher's precepts can sooner make you an honest man, than the reading of Virgil; to believe, with Clauserus, the translator of Cornutus, that it pleased the heavenly deity by Hesiod and Homer, under the veil of fables, to give us all knowledge, logic, rhetoric, philosophy natural and moral, and "quid non?" to believe, with me, that there are many mysteries contained in poetry, which of purpose were written darkly, lest by profane wits it should be abused; to believe, with Landin, that they are so beloved of the gods that whatsoever they write proceeds of a divine fury. Lastly, to believe themselves, when they tell you they will make you immortal by their verses.

Thus doing, your names shall flourish in the printers' shops: thus doing, you shall be of kin to many a poetical preface: thus doing, you shall be most fair, most rich, most wise, most all: you shall dwell upon superlatives: thus doing, though you be "Libertino patre natus," you shall suddenly grow "Herculea proles," "Si quid mea Carmina possunt:" thus doing, your soul shall be placed with Dante's Beatrix, or Virgil's Anchisis.

But if (fie of such a but!) you be born so near the dull-making cataract of Nilus, that you cannot hear the planet-like music of poetry; if you have so earth-creeping a mind, that it cannot lift itself up to look to the sky of poetry, or rather, by a certain rustical disdain, will become such a Mome, as to be a Momus of poetry; then, though I will not wish unto you the ass's ears of Midas, nor to be driven by a poet's verses, as Bubonax was, to hang himself; nor to be rhymed to death, as is said to be done in Ireland; yet thus much curse I must send you in the behalf of all poets; that while you live, you live in love, and never get favour, for lacking skill of a sonnet; and when you die, your memory die from the earth for want of an epitaph.

Chapter 5

Reading Questions

"An Apology for Poetry" (1580-81, 1595).

- How does the poet's art differ from that of the astronomer, geometrician, moral philosopher, rhetorician, and others? What do poets "disdain," and how do they "grow in effect another nature"? Also, what is the distinction between the "brazen" world and the "golden" one?
- In what are we to recognize the "skill of the artificer"? In the work itself? Or in something else? Explain.
- In what special way does a poet show human beings to have been made in the image of God? How does poetry provide "no small argument" for the truth of the doctrine of original sin?
- What, according to Sidney, is the relationship between pleasure and learning? To what extent, ultimately, does he agree with Horace about the aim or "end" of poetry?
- Does "rhyming and versing" make a poet, according to Sidney? Why must the poet be skilled in "feigning notable images of virtues, vices, or what else"? That is, how does Sidney explain this requirement in moral terms?
- What, according to Sidney, did the Greeks mean by the philosophical term architectonike? (333) How does Sidney demonstrate that poetry — not philosophy or history — best furthers the "ending of all earthly learning"?

- How does Sidney summarize the case so far presented for giving the "laurel crown appointed to triumphing captains" to the poet?
- What are the four "most important imputations" that, according to Sidney, have been "laid to the door of poets"? How does he respond to the first one?
- How does Sidney reply to the second charge that poetry is the "mother of lies" or that poets are "the principal liars"? How is his response a defence against overzealous supporters of verisimilitude?
- Sidney argues that the third and most important of the charges against poetry — that it "abuseth men's wit"—can be "transformed into just commendation." How so?
- How does Sidney reply to the argument against poetry based on Plato's authority? What does Plato, according to Sidney, attribute "unto poetry more than myself do"? Is his reading of Plato accurate?
- What argument does Sidney make concerning the u nity of place—i.e. the idea that "the stage should always represent but one place"? Do his comments seem fitting? Why or why not?
- What two-part curse does Sidney send to one who has "so earth-creeping a mind that it cannot lift itself up to look to the sky of poetry"? On the whole, how would you characterize Sidney's argument in "An Apology for Poetry"—is his rhetoric mainly objective or mainly emotional? Do you find it convincing? Explain. Extra Discussion Questions
- Is Sidney's idea of mimesis Platonic or Aristotelian?
- Sidney argues that the "skill of the artificer standeth in that idea or foreconceit of the work, and not in the work itself." Is this distinction helpful or even meaningful? How can we judge the skill of the artist except by looking at his work where presumably the idea is embodied or revealed or expressed? But if the work is badly executed, how can we tell whether the idea behind it is nevertheless good? How might

it be argued that the image of the artist implied in this observation is Platonic rather than Aristotelian? Or Aristotelian rather than Platonic?

- Has Sidney, in your opinion, misread Plato's Ion?
- What assumptions seem to underlie Sidney's apparent belief in the ennobling efficacy of the "form of goodness" imaged forth by poetry?
- How might Socrates object to Sidney's notion that poetry can lead men toward virtuous action by "feigning noble images" of virtues and vices? Does Sidney seem to make psychological assumptions quite different from Socrates' assumptions in The Republic?
- Poets cannot be said to lie, according to Sidney, because they affirm nothing. So Aesop, for example, doesn't expect his reader literally to believe in the existence of speaking frogs or philosophical cranes. They are intended as nothing but allegories of certain moral truths. But can't it be supposed that the moral "truth" thus presented and therefore affirmed might itself be untrue, indeed be a pernicious falsehood? Thus, the poet can be accused of figuratively telling lies. Discuss this argument against Sidney's reply to the charge that poetry is the "mother of lies."

Chapter 6

The Truths of a Slippery World: Poetry and Tyranny in Sidney's Defence

Tyranny and Civil War Among The Muses

While prosecuting what the Defence of Poesy calls a "civil war among the muses," Philip Sidney marshals an especially crucial argument against Clio, the muse of history. Clio is the voice not of truth and moral persuasion, but of political turpitude. Just consider the kinds of stories that fill the history books, Sidney asks: Cypselus, Periander, Phalaris, and Dionysius Dionysius, king of Portugal: see Diniz. were all real-world tyrants who enjoyed quiet ends, unpunished for their crimes. Clio's reputed moral power emerges consequently as considerably less than exemplary, not merely because of the existence of such stories, but also more importantly because of the character of historical narrative itself.

Tied to the truths of a slippery world, history is condemned to narrating over and again the triumphs of tyranny. With an audacity as sly as it is comically hyperbolic, the Defence disposes in a single paragraph of centuries of humanistically inspired commentary on history's exemplary moral power. It is hardly the historian's fault that he is compelled to tell the truth, Sidney might have admitted if pressed, but therein lies the critical point: historical truth is simply inadequate, given the slipperiness of the world, to the demands of historical life.

It is useful to begin with renewed attention to how Sidney configures the relationship between poetry and history in his Defence, since that relationship is crucial for understanding his preoccupation with tyranny in the text and for reevaluating the connection between his poetics and his politics.

Tyranny has attracted a great deal of attention in studies of The New Arcadia, but little has been written about the tyrants who populate the Defence in such numbers. It is not only when taking the historian to task for his disciplinary shortfalls that Sidney interests us in tyranny. He muses too upon the failures of the philosopher.

Plato's real-life enslavement at the hands of Dionysius, the Sicilian tyrant whose education in virtue he failed to procure, becomes shorthand for the failure of philosophy generally in its confrontation with tyranny. In turn, the metamorphosis of Hiero I from tyrant to just king is credited to Simonides and Pindar, as another tribute to the superior powers of the poet. When Sidney wants to exemplify the "eikastic" powers of poetry — its capacity to "'figure forth good things"' — he does so, centrally, by alluding to a portrait of "Judith killing Holofernes," one of the great biblical prototypes of tyrannicide.

When he seeks to illustrate the power of the stage to create "divine admiration," he highlights the accomplishments of George Buchanan, that Scottish humanist whose specialty was tyrannicidal tragedy. The success of poets in confounding tyrants takes centre stage in Sidney's defence of tragedy as a genre. What the Defence terms the high and excellent Tragedy... maketh kings fear to be tyrants, and tyrants manifest their tyrannical humours".

Moreover, tyranny supplies the critical context for Sidney's most prominent and most telling exposition of poetic imitation, his illustration of the "speaking picture" of poetic mimesis by reference to the rape of Lucretia. The conjunction of historical event and poetic making is deeply purposeful. As the rape of Lucretia was the originary moment of Rome s freedom from tyranny — since it was the historical occasion motivating Brutus to extinguish Tarquin's line — that rape becomes in Sidney's text the foundation for a detailed account of how the "right poet" writes. Set free from history (unlike those historical and philosophical poets confined within the fold of the proposed subject"), the right poet ranges "with no law but his own wit... into the divine consideration of what may be and should be," depicting a Lucretia equally free from historical constraint.

She is painted not as she appeared in life, but as the "outward beauty of' her chastity. Her chastity is the "Idea" out of which the speaking picture is made, a universal whose reality is guaranteed by the access of the erected wit to truths that transcend the always corrupt and mutable world of history. In Sidney's version of the story, Lucretia is liberated twice, both times by the agency of her own virtue: once from the tyranny of Tarquin ("when she punished in herself another's fault") and a second time, from the tyranny of historical verisimilitude by the painter's speaking picture.

When history itself emerges as a form of tyranny — both history conceived as the brazen world of events, and history conceived as a science captive to the folly of the world of events — then the conjunction of poetics and politics is startlingly complete. Real freedom from tyranny becomes not just a possible subject of poetry, but also its necessary and important work. So often when Sidney writes about poetic action in idealizing terms, he does so with metaphors of the chaste body: in the portrait of Lucretia, in the repetition of Agrippa Agrippa (Ygr-p'Y), in Palestinian history: see Herod.'s tale about the divided body politic, and in the complementary stories of David's lust for Bathsheba's body and Nathan's healing fiction. The cleansing of the body — its government, its discipline, and its purgation — goes hand in hand with Sidney's desire to liberate history from tyranny.

To argue that Sidney understood history itself as a kind of tyranny and "right poetry" as a vehicle of liberation is to move against the mainstream of critical interpretation about the politics of Sidney's poetics — at least as that mainstream is measured by the critical literature of the 1990s. The argument presented here is a departure, centrally, from the most detailed and most influential of the cultural materialist readings of the Defence, Alan Sinfield's once startling depiction of Sidney's "puritan humanist" project as the originary text of a Soviet-style literary criticism haunting the tradition of English studies. As the product of what Sinfield terms "aesthetic absolutism," because of its pretensions to represent universals, the Defence is really propaganda (he claims) on behalf of "sectional interests" — Sidney's personal commitments as the member of a "puritan faction" that pursued an "earnest protestantism".

A prisoner of irremediable tensions between humanism and protestantism, Sidney 's aesthetic emerges in Sinfield's reading as an ideologically driven vehicle "correlated broadly with the absolutist aspirations of the Elizabethan state" and focused narrowly on driving that state "in a particular direction in order to reinforce a sectional stance". A decade after its publication, Sinfield's reading is now only "once" startling. The proliferation of new historicist and cultural materialist readings of Renaissance texts has made the historical move between Sidney and the Soviets a common rhetorical maneuver, a familiar leap on the historical trampoline achieved for persuasive effect, and no doubt intended for critical enlightenment. A decade later, however, such startling shifts between widely divergent times, places, and cultures have increasingly been called to account for endangering the very historical understanding that they sought to promote.

A genuinely historical appreciation of the politics of the Defence demands renewed scholarly attention to the history shaping Sidney's intellectual life. Sinfield is clearly right about both Sidney's commitment to a universalizing epistemology and the importance of his association with a specific community, informed by specific political and pious values. But Sinfield's essay, apart from some broad generalizing paragraphs about earnest puritans, never attempts to locate Sidney inside a historically specific community of that sort. By constructing a too-ready association between the Defense's universalizing epistemology and the oppressive absolutism of Soviet-style propaganda, he disregards those very historical conditions that lent Sidney's epistemology its political significance. This essay attempts a different approach by drawing attention to a particular historical community still largely neglected in current critical studies. More specifically, it argues that the epistemology of the Defence needs to be recontextualized as a governing body of assumptions about the nature of knowledge that Sidney derived from the revival of natural law theory among an intellectual elite closely associated with the late Philip Melanchthon (1497-1560) — the so-called Philippists — and the early proponents of tyrannomachist political philosophy. One specific source for the transmission of those assumptions to Sidney was his longtime mentor and friend, Hubert Languet (1518-81).

In this regard, the argument advanced here seeks to complement and extend the critically valuable labors of Beatrice Nicollier-de Weck, who in a recent biography of Languet has taken a familiar figure inside Sidney studies and made him unfamiliar again in ways that have major implications for preconceiving Sidney's piety; politics, and poetics. Until Nicollier-de Weck's biography, Languet's education in Wittenberg under Melanchthon and its influence on his own intellectual, political, and spiritual life have remained almost entirely unexamined, as well as its antecedent shaping power over the education in the Protestant cause that Languet labored to pass along to Philip Sidney. When the universalizing imperative of the Defence is seen in light of the historical conditions that supplied it with its meaning and its lived sense of urgency, Sidney's text emerges, surprisingly and with a genuinely historical power to startle, as the politically significant vehicle of a poetics of liberation.

Tyranny was a topic of enduring concern for Sidney. It shadowed everywhere that remarkable correspondence he pursued with Languet during the 1570s. As mentor and student exchanged information, analysis, even prayer about the machinations of papal and Spanish power, it was tyranny and the resistance to tyranny (not national interest or state power) that constituted their primary vocabulary for analyzing European politics.

That vocabulary speaks volumes about how they conceived of their own historical moment. Contemporary history was apocalyptically burdened, a battleground between the forces of light and darkness — the liberating power of the true church, on the one hand, imperilled by the tyranny of post-Tridentine Catholicism, on the other. In turn, that concept had practical consequences for Sidney's own actions. Real tyrants abroad and the perceived threat of tyranny at home influenced his decision to write against Queen Elizabeth's proposed marriage to Francis, Duke of Anjou Anjou (äNzh'), region and former province, W France, coextensive roughly with Maine-et-Loire and parts of Indre-et-Loire, Mayenne, and Sarthe depts. Angers, the historic capital, and Saumur are the chief towns.. Spanish tyranny helped to mo tivate Sidney's fascination with the Americas and his interest in Huguenot schemes for colonizing the new world, and that same fear of Spanish tyranny drew him at last, also, to the defence of Dutch freedom and to his death.

Not surprisingly, Sidney's lifelong preoccupation with tyranny found expression especially in his most important work: the elaboration of his New Arcadia, populated by notable numbers of tyrannical villains and by his twin tyrannomachist heroes, Pyrocles and Musidorus. Tyranny, then, was a familiar issue for Sidney, but Phalaris' inclusion in The Defencis rhetorically extended catalogue of history's bad exemplars is an especially pointed reminder about the personal character of those political concerns at stake for him in addressing contemporary tyrants.

Sidney had a history with Phalaris that is worth recounting. Phalaris, was a sixth-century BC tyrant of Acragas in Sicily, who became legendary for roasting his victims alive in a brazen bull. In July 1574, in a letter addressed to Languer, Sidney bitterly attacked a French humanist and politique, Guy du Faur, Sire de Pibrac (1529-84), for publishing a justification of the St. Bartholomew's Day Massacre — that current event supplying the most notorious evidence of Catholic tyranny at work. Languet responded in a remarkable letter (24 July 1574), which is at once a defence of Pibrac and a moral education for

Sidney. In that letter, Languet represents himself as unwilling to hold either Pibrac's Catholicism or his apology for the Massacre against him. Instead and surprisingly for Sidney to be sure, he praises Pibrac as "a man of such genius, learning, and eloquence, that I do not believe his equal is to be found in France." With the usual pointed ness of the teacher, Languet proceeds to extrapolate from the particular instance of Pibrac's fault — writing a letter that fear for his own death provoked — to a general lesson to be learned from his behaviour.

He was compelled to save his life by that letter, for which you find fault with him so grievously. I by no means admire his conduct, for, as the poet says. Phalaris licet imperet ut sis falsus et admoto dictet periuria tauro, summum crede nefas animam praeferre pudori, et propter vitam vivendi perdere causas. (though Phalaris himself should command you to tell lies and bring up his bull and dictate to you a perjury, believe it the greatest sin to prefer life to honour, and to lose for the sake of life, the cause of living.)

Good letters supply good lessons. At the moment that Languet urges Sidney's tolerance for Pibrac's all-too-human weakness, he supplies by way of Juvenal's Satires a corrective example to follow. Tyranny must be resisted, even as one must recognize the inevitable weakness of people who are oppressed by its power. Phalaris came to Sidney as a moral example in Languet's letters, and he figured prominently at a crucial moment in the political philosophy of another intimate friend, Philippe Du Plessis Mornay (1549-1623).

Languet mentored the two Philips, Mornay and Sidney, as twin students of the Protestant cause, and it is no accident that they employ the same historical vocabulary, even in response to the same historical events. Mornay's Vindiciae, contra tyrannos (1576) was the most carefully argued and the most notorious of all those resistance tracts produced in the aftermath of the Sr. Bartholomew's Day Massacre, and Phalaris makes an appearance in that tract precisely at one of those few moments in which the memory of the Massacre is specifically invoked. Moreover, the reference to Phalaris occurs in exactly the same literary context recalled by Languet's letter, Juvenal's Satire VIII.

In an argument in which Mornay imagines the response of the people to "a prince [who] commands that any innocent be killed, or that he be despoiled," he conjures into memory the example of "some Papinian [who]... will reproach Caracalla Caracalla (kãrYkãl`Y), 188–217, Roman emperor; son of Septimius Severus. His real name was Marcus Aurelius Antoninus, and he received his nickname from the caracalla, a Gallic tunic he regularly wore. to his face and will choose death rather than obedience: 'Even if Phalaris himself orders him to be false, and to dictate perjuries under threat of roasting alive." Drawing from the Scriptores historiae Augustae, Mornay inserts his allusion to the beastly Phalaris within the context of Roman imperial history — the story of the Emperor Caracalla's murder of his brother Geta, and the refusal of the praetorian prefect, Aemilius Papinianus, to compose a speech to the senate in justification of that murder.

The Român imperial allusion secures an obvious parallel to contemporary Huguenot interpretations of the Massacre (one more fratricidal tragedy in peril of a whitewash), while expressing simultaneously pointed optimism about the inevitability of resistance to tyranny: Papinian-style heroes always appear to undo tyrants, Mornay's text clearly implies — an echo of that long tradition of anti-tyrannical literature extending back to Cicero, then Christianized by John of Salisbury and Thomas Aquinas, in which tyrants providentially get their due. Read in light of Languet's correspondence with Sidney, Papinian's action becomes in Mornay's idealizing political philosophy the story of a Pibrac who operates as a Pibrac should — as a corrective example from the realm of history that shows how "one in whom... conscience remains will effectively counter tyranny. Its optimism is, in no small measure, intended as persuasion. For Sidney, Morna's appeal to Papinian — conjoined with the allusion to Juvenal — must also have carried a sharp reminder of the real-life Pibrac, a less sanguine reminder of how ineffectively tyranny found resistance on St. Bartholomew's Day, August 24th, 1572.

Sidney's allusion in The Defence to Phalaris comes

complete with a history, then, one that is important, first, because it draws attention to his own lived experience with tyranny. Phalaris was a figure whom Sidney knew both from the pages of Juvenal and from the streets of Paris. (Sidney was himself present at the St. Bartholomew's Day Massacre and may even have seen the mutilated corpse of Admiral Gaspard de Coligny.) The allusion matters also since Phalaris' name came loaded in Sidney's circle with certain specific, controversial political assumptions. In the same sentence from the Defence that he writes about Phalaris, Sidney mentions, as if in passing, that just as the poets have devised "new punishments in hell for tyrants," so philosophy teaches "occidendos esse" — that tyrants ought to be killed.

The "as if' quality of his phrasing is significant. He can write about tyrannicide as if it were a settled doctrine of political philosophy precisely because, for himself and for those friends wit h whom he was most closely connected, the doctrine needed neither argument nor proof. In fact, the whole of Sidney's discussion of tyrants in this passage, beginning with the allusion to Brutus' slaying of Caesar and proceeding to Dante's supposed invention of new torments for tyrants, echoes a tradition of republican literature descending from fifteenth-century Italy. The Defence does not argue the case for tyrannicide. It assumes tyrannicide as a good. The question posed by Phalaris' appearance in this passage and by Sidney's Defence as a whole — considered from the vantage of its public political purpose — is how best to counter tyranny, and it is from this perspective that the allusion to Phalaris matters most.

Phalaris was a name usefully invoked whenever the question arose in Sidney's own circle about how effectively to counter tyranny in practice — whether the issue concerned the private application of a moral philosophical principle (as in Languet's letter) or the public articulation of a political philosophy (as in Mornay's treatise).

Juvenal's Satire VIII was a shared point of reference among Languet, Mornay and Sidney. In its original form, Juvenal's poem is a fierce assault against the vices of the contemporary Roman nobility and a negative example —

exploitable to good pedagogical ends by the mentor Languet—that "nobilitas sola est atque unica virtus" (virtue is the one and only true nobility. More important, Juvenal's poem became inside this circle of friends a common point of reference for considering how to move from ought to is: for moving, that is, from the proposition that tyrants should be resisted to real resistance. What would have amazed, amused, and perhaps even dismayed his friends is Sidney's argument that poetry best supplies that vehicle for resisting tyranny rather than history or philosophy.

For in that argument was implied the relative inferiority of his friends' favored intellectual pursuits — the passion of Languet for history, of Mornay for moral and political philosophy. Juvenal matters, Sidney seems to say, for reasons better than his friends would have acknowledged.

Sidney's point really is one about Juvenal, or one about poetry, that is—and that fact lends a characteristically complicated tone to the whole of the Defence extended consideration of history's impotence before the onslaught of tyranny. It is characteristically complicated since it is a tone achieved with similar complexity as Sidney's argument repeatedly performs what can only be called a systematic downsizing of the historical within the realm of the poetic. Consider what happens rhetorically to the great world of history in the text. History's bloody civil wars become or at least threaten to become a civil war among the Muses"; Phalaris and Tarquin matter in the world of events, but the tyranny that matters most to Sidney's internal argument descends from "that tyrant in table talk," the historian; the senate that counts here consists not of patricians or politicians, but "of poets"; princes are transformed from authorities in sovereign states to "sovereign disciplines"; "monarch s" and "sacred majesty" are titles usurped by the makers of fictions; and the cause one fights for is no longer "the just cause" perpetually intoned in the correspondence with Languet, but instead the "just cause" of poetry.

In the course of these verbal exchanges, poetry appears at once ironically minimized (after all, these are only wars among the muses) and rhetorically enhanced (disciplinary disputes gain the grandeur of warfare), just as poetic action is made to seem both clearly distinct from the realm of events — wars among the muses produce no corpses — and urgently engaged with that world, since its presence is so constantly evoked by the very verbal moves in question. Sidney's attack on the historian's impotence before tyranny produces a tone so complicated because of the paradoxical logic at the heart of the argument. Poetry better remedies history's ills because it escapes confinement to the historical — hence its seeming triviality and its real potential for grandeur.

Sidney's point is one about poetry, then. But how he bolsters his position on behalf of poetry's power to undo the worst effects of tyranny with arguments that simultaneously draw upon and contest key intellectual assumptions of his friends, Languet and Mornay, forms an important and untold story about his Defence of Poesy. That story begins again with the interest of Sidney and his friends in Phalaris, a figure excoriated in the language of the Defence for his "abominable injustice" and reviled as a kind of dog unleashed from history's "kennel". As Sidney's vocabulary suggests, what made Phalaris' tyranny so striking was its very beastliness. Roasting his victims alive within a bronze bull that turned their screams into savage bellowing, all for the pleasure of his own entertainment, made Phalaris a memorable figure inside a circle of friends who defined tyranny as a violation of nature's law. Languet, Mornay, and Sidney all have recourse to that increasingly popular and potent political vocabulary com ing into renewed prominence inside sixteenth-century Europe, the vocabulary of natural law.

Natural Law and the Politics of Intellectualism

Scholars from Robert Hoopes to R. K. White have written extensively about the pervasive influence of natural law arguments in English Renaissance literature, and there is no need to rehearse their conclusions here. More to the point, Quentin Skinner has written about the significance of such arguments to the development of Renaissance political discourse, and most especially to their key role in the history of resistance theory.

In particular, Skinner argues persuasively about the struggle among the Huguenots after the St. Bartholomew's Day Massacre, as an embattled minority seeking religious freedom, to devise a logic and language for defending rebellion against tyranny that would have a broad national appeal transcending confessional boundaries. As Skinner makes clear, natural law arguments, with their appeal to unwritten universal laws inherent within the individual conscience, were crucial in bolstering the persuasiveness of the new resistance theory and, once more, he identifies Mornay's Vindiciae as tha t historically significant resistance text inside which natural law arguments enter first.

Skinner is clearly right about the importance of natural law to Mornay's argument, just as he is right about the intended cross-confessional character of its appeal. But where Skinner is demonstrably wrong—and this is a point that matters profoundly for understanding Sidney's role in this history—is in arguing for the novelty of these arguments in Mornay and in attributing, as cultural historians continue to do, the source of his new language and logic to Thomas Aquinas.

It may be an attractive historical irony to imagine the Protestant Mornay turning Catholic scholastic philosophy back against the post-Tridenrine Church, raiding Aquinas for the philosophical weaponry to topple the pope's minions from the throne of France. However, there is a more plausible explanation for the renewed popularity of natural law arguments in Mornay's Vindiciae, and for the popularity of those arguments in other resistance texts inside Britain: John Ponet's lucidly argued A shorte treatise of politike power (1556) and Geo rge Buchanan's influential Dejure regni apud Scotos (1579). Sidney's political writings and poetics display, too, a thorough-going dependence on natural law theory.

When Languet urged Sidney to moderate his criticisms of Pibrac, he did so as a mentor "by nature and by principle averse to judgments of this sort," explaining that "many people criticize me for this [moderation] and say that I derive it from my teacher, Melanchthon. Thus far I regret neither my teacher nor my principles, and shall not be led away from either by the criticisms of those who are naturally more captious or severe than I am. By identifying himself with Philip Melanchthon, Languet reminded Sidney about his distinctive political affiliation — the source of his own commitment to the Protestant cause — and, just as meaningfully, about the source of that political commitment in a distinctive brand of Protestant piety. Philip Melanchthon, it is useful to recall, was Luther's most tenacious and most brilliant ally, and among the Reformation's most influential and (for scholars of the English Renaissance) most forgotten architects.

A figure of polymathic productivity and universal learning, he pro duced the Reformation's first systematic theology, the Loci communes; he crafted its most comprehensive, most widely acclaimed statement of faith, the Augsburg Confession; and, in an age of great educators, this praeceptor germaniae was, as Johann Sturm put it, "the father of most educated men. " He was both influential and controversial — and controversy gave to his vision a distinctive focus. Especially in his later years, as the embattled guardian of what had been Luther's church, threatened by hostile imperial armies, Roman Catholic enemies, and fierce opposition from rival Protestants, Melanchthon became arguably sixteenth-century Europe's most temperate and most persistent champion of Christian liberty.

Melanchthon's appeal was cosmopolitan, and his followers disparagingly called "Philippists." Numbered among them were the two Camerarius, Joachim the Elder (1500-74) and Joachim the Younger (1534-98), both distinguished German philologists; Johannes Crato (1515-85), the Silesian physician whose great life labor was the liberation of the Bohemian church; Charles de l'Ecluse (1526-1609), the internationally esteemed French botanist; Joannes Sambucus (1531-84), the renowned Hungarian emblematist; and Daniel Rogers (1538?-91), the Anglo-Dutch poet and diplomat, a well-known figure in Elizabethan court circles, and a close friend of Sidney. Languet himself was a Burgundian by birth. As a group, the so-called Philippists were at once elite humanists — educated enthusiasts for the alliance of good letters and the good state — and politically sober Protestants, longing for the reunification of the true church from the ruins of its confessional divisions.

As a group, too, the Philippists echoed Melanchthon's frequent calls for freedom from theological disputation — including freedom from dark pronouncements about predestination and election, matters too terrifying to the souls of unlearned Christians. When forced into theological discussions, they were inclined to espouse a moderate position on free will, and an openness to compromise with rival Reformed and Catholic interpretations of the mass and the eucharist. As a body, moreover, they shared Melanchthon's political goal of achieving freedom from tyranny: his pragmatic regard for compromise, his irenic aversion from war, and his conservative ideal of the well-ordered aristocratic state, governed by the godly prince serving the godly church. Simultaneously, even paradoxically, they shared Melanchthon's providential reading of international politics and his fiercely anti-papal convictions representing Europe as a battleground between Christ's church on the one hand and Tridentine Catholicism on the other.

That battleground was no mere metaphor. Especially in the decades of the 1570s and 80s, Philip II's campaigns for military domination in the north seemed to make the dark tyranny of the Antichrist visible, and thereby marked the Netherlands for forward. Protestants generally and for Philippists particularly as the central battleground in a cause whose scope was international.

According to Paul Oskar Kristeller, "Melanchthon, the defender of rhetoric against philosophy,... had more influence on many aspects of Lutheran Germany than Luther himself and... was responsible for the humanistic tradition of the German Protestant schools down to the nineteenth century." That influence is measurable across an extensive disciplinary domain from dialectics to natural philosophy, and it is an influence demonstrable, too, in Melanchthon's pervasive employment of natural law arguments derived from Aristotle and his scholastic commentators in reshaping moral, political, and even theological learning for the Protestant north. That employment was central, not adventitious

- Accidental or acquired; not natural or hereditary.
- Found out of the normal or usual place.
- Adventitial.

adventitious (d, to his intellectual career, as his most recent scholars have demonstrated in considerable detail. Most important, however, for this argument is Melanchrhon's introduction of the language and logic of natural law into resistance theory during the War of the League of Schmalkaldan in the late 1540s. Under attack by imperial powers, the Protestant princes of Germany needed some means to justify armed defence against sovereign authority and consequently some radically different philosophical arguments from the ones Luther had employed against the peasant rebellions of earlier decades. The church's very survival demanded it.

Melanchthon's justification of resistance, originally published in German in 1547 as the Von der Notwehr Unterricht (Instruction Concerning Self-Defence), was subsequently retranslated into Latin as De defensione concessa humano generi jure naturae (About the Defence Permitted to Humankind by the Law of Nature). Its original publication in German speaks to its pointedly political purpose in swaying popular opinion, but it is its Latin title that articulates most clearly the logic of its central argument: self-defence derives its foundational authority from universal laws of nature inscribed in human kind — laws inscribed in the conscience by God, as this aggressively Protestant document constantly insists. By self-defence, what Melanchthon had in mind was more than passive disobedience or a refusal, Papinian-style, to follow the emperor's commands.

He justified as well an active military response, even tyrannicide. In answer to his central organizing question about whether active defence is permitted, M elanchthon wrote:

"Certum est omnes homines bona conscientia sequi & amplecti, quod statuit ius Naturae, quod vere ius divinum est. Est autem omnibus hominibus haec Lex, quasi lumen quoddam, divinitus impressa, quod in atroci & notoria iniuria, cum destituimur a Magistratu, liceat nobis uti defensione, adversus pares, & adversus superiores." (It is certain that all men should follow and be filled with good conscience, which is a law of nature, and which truly is a divine law.

Moreover this Law is a light to all men, having been divinely impressed on them, showing in cases of atrocious and notorious injuries, when we are oppressed by a Magistrate, that it is permissible for us to act in our defence against equals and against superiors.) Moreover, Melanchthon proceeded to argue that there are many cases in which natural law not only permitted self-defence, but also actually commanded ("sed etiam mandata") husbands to shield wives, fathers children, and magistrates their subjects. The Brutus who stabbe d Caesar and the wife of Alexander Pheraeus who murdered her tyrannical husband both acted according to natural law by punishing tyrants who had themselves defied those appropriate (those "natural" boundaries) inside which the power appropriate to the prince's calling should operate. They acted, in short, out of a natural duty to protect society and in defence of good order.

Tyrannicide is both the right and the obligation of a free people, an argument that Reformers eager to safeguard the liberty of the church from tyranny eagerly transplanted to England and Scotland. In 1556, John Ponet (1514?-56) dedicated his Short Treatise of politike power to "all true natural Englishe men," and mobilized against orthodox Tudor support of Queen Mary's sovereignty the newly potent language and logic of natural law (title page). A call to arms masquerading as a philosophical justification for tyrannicide, Ponet's treatise appeals for authority at every stage of its methodically organized argument to natural law theory. Natural law accounts for the origins of society, it endorses the exercise of right reason in government, it explains the predations of tyranny from the primitive to the contemporary church, and it enables the Treatise's climactic celebration of the wisdom of the ancients in acknowledging that "it is naturall to cutte awaie an incurable membre, which (being suffered) wolde destro ie the hole body".

Ponet's point about England's political body is plain: Mary Tudor must be excised. A decade later and a kingdom to the north, George Buchanan naturalized substantially the same arguments in his anatomy of tyranny and Scottish politics, the controversial Dejure regni apud Scotos (1579). Like Ponet, Buchanan grounds his argument on behalf of tyrannicide in natural law theory; Defending the right of a free people to resist tyranny or misgovernment requires, logically, an exposition of good government, "the original and cause of creating kings, and what the duties of kings are towards their people, and of people towards their kings".

That exposition, eriological in kind, generates an image of the state as a body whose natural condition is harmony, with king safeguarding people, and people safeguarded by law — an image that reason has power to expose, in turn, because of that natural "LIGHT infused by GOD into our Minds". While the "scope" of the king, as physician to the state, is to promote "the health of the body," the tyrant operates, as unnatural monster, to corrupt that body for his own lusts. Buchanan's point is made as plainly as Ponet's: "occidendos esse," tyrants must be killed. Natural law demands it.

Mornay was not the first, then, to espouse a right to resistance on the foundations of natural law theory. Ponet and Buchanan developed similar arguments by the same means. As a result, unless we assume with Skinner an unlikely rekindling of scholastic enthusiasm among these devoted Protestants, some alternative explanation for their shared language and logic is required. That alternative presents itself plausibly enough as the product of shared historical connections — the allegiance among these writers to the same republic of letters. John Ponet was a Marian exile who by his own report discovered in Melanchthon one of his principal "comforters." George Buchanan was a long-time friend and companion of Hubert Languet, that Burgundian who gave up friends, family, and homeland to devote his entire adult life to Melanchrhon's service. In the early 1560s, while a professor in Paris, Buchanan belonged to a circle of irenic humanists that included, in addition to Languet, Charles de l'Ecluse, Francois Baudoui n (1520-73), and Joannes Sambucus — all distinguished intellectuals and Philippists, students or devotees of Philip Melanchthon.

In the late 1570s. after his return to Scotland, Buchanan's closest friend in England was Daniel Rogers, himself an intimate of Languet's circle and the son of the Marian martyr and Philippist, John Rogers (1500?-55). Within this international republic of letters, constituted by Protestant humanists devoted to preserving the "true" church from its international enemies, Mornay's reliance on natural law theory could not have been interpreted as an act of ironic scholastic inversion. It would have been received instead as traditional argumentation derived from a long-standing political discourse with its roots in Melanchthon and its branches in Ponet and Buchanan. Since mid-century, natural law theory had itself been naturalized in the Protestant north as a response to what these humanists viewed as the threatening tempests of the Catholic League's tyranny.

It was one thing to contemplate taking arms against a sea of troubles. It was quite another, for humanists writing in this republic of letters, to counter tyranny with the pen. As Skinner has demonstrated so well, the appeal of natural law arguments to such writers was their confidence in the power of universal standards of reason to secure freedom from partisan wrangling. Such confidence existed everywhere inside this circle. It was found, for instance, in the last service Languet performed for the cause, his authorship in 1581 of An Apologie for William of Orange (1533-84), perceived as the great champion of liberty in Europe s most important political theater, the Netherlands. Consistently advancing arguments from natural law, Languet's Apologie employs the "strength and soundness of reason" to demonstrate how that Spanish Phalaris, Philip II, had sacrificed his natural claims upon sovereignty.

Mornay, too, evidences a similar desire to avoid partisanship, expressing confidence in his most impor tant controversial works in the near-geometric precision of reason. Whether addressing the problem of atheism in the De verite (1581) a plea for universal Christian truth in an age of irrational confessionalism, or Machiavellianism in the Contra tyrannos (an assault against the contamination of political culture by bad books), natural law arguments appeal inclusively to readers of "whichever party or nation or condition they belong" on the optimistic assumption that reason will naturally create agreement.

Beyond Skinner's point, then, at the foundations of such humanist textual labors are the assumptions of what can only be termed a deeply held intellectualism: a belief that real political change derives first and foremost from changes in how people think — especially in how they think about primary issues of moral and political philosophy. That intellectualism is reflected in the content of their shared agreements about the nature of tyranny — as a perversion (literally), an unnatural inversion of the nature of good government originating in the perversion of the individual mind or soul.

Tyranny is a form of self-love — or rather, a manifestation of self-love in the public arena. Ponet's fundamental political distinction is between the true king who maintains "justice, to the wealthe and benefite of the hole multitude" and the tyrant "that seketh his owne gayne". Buchanan defines justice, in good classical terms, as that principle that "allows every man his own," and then deepens classical prece pt with Christian charity, distinguishing between the true king who "beareth rule for the subjects welfare" and the tyrant who rules "for himself."

Mornay in the Vindiciae elaborates a similar paternalism, when he cites Augustine to demonstrate that "to command is nothing other than to show concern for the people," a selfless exercise of power mirrored in Seneca's accounts of kingship in the golden age, and contrasted — in these brazen years — by the predations of the unnatural tyrant "who serves only his own welfare and desires, who neglects and perverts all laws". Ponet, Buchanan, and Mornay represent tyranny in essentially similar ways, as one more point of agreement inside a community of humanists whose shared understandings are so often illuminated by commonplaces in Melanchthon's thought. Toward the conclusion of the Loci communes of 1555, when contemplating worldly authority, Melanchthon argues that God "gave men light, namely, understanding of natural law through which we know that we should make and keep order in governments, and are obliged to obey natural law as God's will"; once more, as he writes in application of this argument, such laws distinguish true kings from tyrants – the latter consistently distinguished from the former as rulers who pursue "their own general happiness" and "seek their own tyranny, welfare. pomp, sensual pleasure, and suppression of the truth".

Such commonplaces are illuminating because they underscore the logic of that shared intellectualism of the resistance theorists. A consistent correspondence is maintained between the public and the private spheres, political and moral life, because always for the Protestant humanist the reality that counts is the one that situates the individual in relation to God. Tyranny in the state proceeds from the tyranny of sin over the soul, as a repetition of Melanchthon's distinctive reading of Adam's fall as a sin of self-love. From the earliest version of the Loci communes (1521), the emphasis remains the same: "Thus it happens the soul being without celestial light and life is in darkness. As a result, it most ardently loves itself, seeks its own desires and wishes nothing but carnal things.... It cannot but be that a creature whom the love of God has not absorbed, loves itself in the highest degree". The rape of Lucretia is a speaking picture of tyrannical self-love at work in the state and the soul, and chastity; rightly interpreted, the agent of tyrannicide.

Recovering a history of Protestant resistance theory matters to the present argument, since it points to the Defence as a text in dialogue with a community of texts from this same republic of letters. Like Ponet, Buchanan, Mornay, and

Languet, Sidney too employs the language and logic of natural law theory. It highlights in advance the enormous promise of natural law arguments for a writer like Sidney, himself haunted by the nightmare of tyranny. It is necessary to write about the "promise" of this argumentative rhetoric — its serviceability in securing agreement across confessional boundaries, its employment history in support of the cause — rather than its appeal or power.

In the aftermath of St. Bartholomew's Day 1572 and the capitulations of well-educated humanists like Pibrac, Sidney acknowledged what his friends, Mornay and Languet, wished to ignore altogether: the helplessness of even the best historical examples and philosophical rules to undo the Phalaris of the world. Within his republic of letter s, Sidney was one among many writers employing the pen against tyranny, but he was unique for defending the poet's pen as an especially fit instrument for that labor. This does not mean that his Defence is a call to arms against tyranny. Nothing about the history of the text's circulation as a coterie work passing among family and friends suggests such a purpose. Sidney's purpose, of course, was to defend poetry, and tyrants populate the text in such large numbers because poetry's value in the public sphere, among such a community of like-minded readers (readers who shared similar political goals), can be measured only by reference to its value in subduing them.

Sidney's "Cosmopology" and the Poetics of Liberation

The tyranny of self-love looms large throughout the Defence of Poesy as a theme that binds private to public considerations, the pious to the political. Geography helps to illustrate the point. Sidney opens his Defence in the Vienna of Maximilian II, his chief place of residence during his three-year continental tour, where he spent several months reading and studying in the company of Languet and a variety of other irenicists and Philippists.

In the 1570s, Vienna was a cosmopolitan city, a magnet for an international cast of intellectuals. Distinguished for its coincidence of religious moderation and flourishing arts, the city was home to the physician and natural philosopher, Tomas Jordan (1539-85) a Hungarian resident of Vienna, as well as to Charles de l'Ecluse, Johannes Crato, and Joannes Sambucus — all devotees of Melanchthon. Similar to those other Philippists dispersed throughout Northern Europe, these humanists, while preaching the paradox of anti-confessionalism in an age of confessional confl icts, sought to put pious ideals into this-worldly practice as artists, doctors, natural philosophers and political activists.

By example of their labors, such a community highlighted one key message of Melanchthon's career, the value of humane studies for pious purposes. When Sidney opens his argument in the Defence, he evokes the memory of the irenic Vienna of Maximilian II (1564-76), that Holy Roman Emperor internationally famous for calling himself not a Catholic but a Christian. In part, Sidney's gesture is meaningful as an act of nostalgia, a brief act of mourning for the world lost there. For Maximilian's Vienna stood in conspicuous contrast to what Sidney considered that espaniolated, counter-Reformation Prague of the new Emperor Rudolf II (1576-1612), whose Tridentine tyranny threatened to undo civil life, civil arts, civil everything.

Sidney's main purpose in remembering Maximilian's Vienna, of course, is to summon into mind Signor Pugliano, that horseman whose comically splendid devotion to his art nearly makes Philip wish himself a horse — a monitory fable about "self-love" as "better than any gilding to make that seem gorgeous wherein ourselves are parties". Sidney distances himself from the mentor, and not for the last time. But as Pugliano's self-love is located in the vanished world of Maximilian's court, as sin threatening the unnatural metamorphosis of man to beast, the very location of the fable shadows a larger public world in which the tyranny of self-loving sovereigns operates unnaturally to darker ends.

Sidney returns to the theme of tyrannical self-love frequently in the Defence, and often with a similar lightness of touch. As one chief rival to the poets, he presents the arrogant philosophers, "casting largesse as they go of definitions, divisions, and distinctions, with a scornful interrogative... soberly asking whether it be possible to find any path so ready to lead a man to virtue". As the poet's other chief rival, Sidney ushers into view the similarly narcissistic historian: "a wonder to young folks and a tyrant in table talk, denying, in a great chafe, that any man for teaching of virtue is comparable to him".

The parodic philosopher and historian of the Defence are portraits in pomposity, speaking pictures of self-love tyrannizing over substance as well as style — and style counts in the cosmopolitan economy of Sidney's poetic universe. Self-love can corrupt English poetry too, not just the scholarly disciplines, as happens when a surfeit of "similitudes in certain printed discours es" spawns "a most tedious prattling," the exaggerated artificiality exercised by the native writer who "more careful to speak curiously than to speak truly... doth dance to his own music". Dancing to one's own music is precisely what poetic imitation, properly understood, is designed to inhibit.

The liberal art serves the liberal mind. As Sidney learned from Johann Sturm, his one-time teacher at the Strasbourg academy and subsequently his lifelong friend, the always cosmopolitan goal of imitation (the comparatio of great literary models) is to eliminate what this republic of letters universally regarded as the most tyrannical of vices, the sin of self-love: "Imitatia ingenium ultra naturae ducit terminos: ut se amare desinat: & meliores admirari incipiat." (Imitation leads his genius beyond the boundaries of nature: so that he ceases to love himself: and begins to admire better things.)

The comprehensiveness of Sidney's concerns is striking. Pugliano's artistic folly, the philosopher's and the historian's disciplinary arrogance, the writer's stylistic solipsism — all are linked as variations on the theme of self-love. In turn, all shadow that darker political tyranny of Phalaris, who, roasting his victims alive for the pleasure of hearing their screams, himself (Cecropia-wise) seems like a beastly parody of the poet. Such comprehensiveness is especially revealing, in turn, about Sidney's conceptual predisposition: his deeply cultivated aversion for the narrowly partisan, whether that partisanship manifests itself as the product of English literary provincialism, and its quirky self-pleasing rhetoric, the disciplinary narrowness of arrogant scholars, or the brutal fanaticism of contemporary confessional politics.

Against the provincialism of the English tradition, the Defence persistently illustrates its arguments from a cosmopolitan canon of continental works, ancient and modern. Again st disciplinary narrowness, it asserts the claims of poetry as a kind of master-science, superior to history and philosophy, because it performs inclusively (moving and teaching) the work of both. Against the partisanship of confessionalism, it refuses theological disputation or indulging even a hint of partisan name-calling (no anti-papist banter troubles its pages), and when it proceeds in a climactic moment to celebrate a pageant of worthies — those great men who have also been great poets — it embraces ecumenically Hebrews and pagans (David and Sophocles) as well as Catholics and Protestants, Calvinists and Lutherans, with its praise for "Such cardinals as Bembus and Bibiena" (Pietro Bembo and Bernardo Dovizi, humanists and poets) in parallel to such "preachers and teachers" as Beza and Melanchthon. Conceived in this light, then, Sidney's apology for poetry emerges as a sort of "cosmopology," as a defence of fiction-making in the service of freedom.

The right poet rescues poetry and learning, church and state, from the always partisan, always divisive tyranny of self-love. The comprehensiveness of this cosmopology's concerns, in turn, is revealing about Sidney's own deep commitment to the "intellectualism" of this circle of humanist allies, and to his own belief that the high-flying liberty of the poet is exercised most vitally in the liberation of the mind.

Nothing shows more profoundly Sidney's debts to the natural law theorists of his circle than the weight his Defence places upon the anthropological arguments at its core. Wonderful as the making of golden worlds may be, in their superiority to nature's brazen one, Sidney carefully structures the conceptual centre of his aggressively optimistic poetics to highlight the consequences of the poet's making for man, for whom the poet's "uttermost cunning" is employed. Our natural condition is a fallen one. Because of Adam's sin, "our erected wit maketh us know what perfection is and yet our infected will keepeth us from reaching unto it".

Poetry works by attempting to restore that now corrupted will to goodness, freeing the individual from the brazen world of history—and the sins "natural" to it—as it recreates that natural harmony between wit and will enjoyed in the golden world of the garden. Sidney here reaps the traditional advantages of the natural law theorist's argument in Christian form: the appeal simultaneously to nature (created nature) as corrupt and to Nature (creating Nature) as a vehicle for securing freedom from corruption. Consider how that freedom is gained. As the Defence makes clear, the superiority of the poet's world to history's (the explanation for its golden quality) consists "not in the work itself," but in "that Idea or fore-conceit" represented, counterfeited or figured forth by the poet's still-erect wit. His Idea is a universal truth about experience—a representation of virtue or vice—which stands at the foundation of the fiction, generating speaking pictures and providing unity to the whole.

In this context, what is especially noteworthy about those Ideas whenever they are specifically illustrated in the Defence—the chastity of Lucretia, the piety of Aeneas Aeneas, in the Bible Aeneas (ç`nçYs, -nç`-), palsied man whom Peter cured in the Acts of the Apostles.

Aeneas, in Greek mythology Aeneas, the courage of Turnus—is their invariable representation as the commonplaces of Sidney's own education in moral philosophy, in reading, that is, natural law.

Once more, not only does Sidney clearly associate those Ideas given substance by right poets with the moral principles of natural law theory, but also he appears to account for their "rightness" (legitimacy) on the basis of shared philosophical assumptions. The Defence assumes both the autonomy of the Idea and its legitimacy (its authority as an instance of true knowledge).

It is possible to identify the poem's generative Idea (its "stuff') as the creation of the poet's own "erected" wit, but Sidney never writes about the poet as a maker of Ideas. Hence, such an identification appears improbable. More likely, Sidney conceives of the Idea as innate to that same erected wit, an impression remaining from his Maker inscribed within (hence, innate to) what the Defence refers to as the mind's own divine essence. When he agrees with those "learned men who have learnedly thought" that "in Nature we know it is well to doe well, and what is well and what is evil," he does so by appealing to belief in natural law w ritten in the heart of man that teaches him, as a body of innate knowledge, truths that extend from basic tenets of moral philosophy to the recognition of the soul's immortality and the existence of a providential God — precisely the recognition provided, for instance, to his "pagan" Arcadian princes on the eve of their trial and feared death. In a sixteenth-century context, most prominent among those "learned men" who espoused a theory of innate ideas as the cornerstone both of moral and natural philosophy was Philip Melanchthon.

Sidney draws upon the intellectual assumptions of his circle in specific ways: by adopting an anthropological framework to explain the poet's "scope" or purpose; by associating the poet's Ideas with the commonplaces of moral philosophy; and by assuming, as deep structure for his own arguments on behalf of poetic authority, a theory of innate ideas divinely scripted in the mind as natural law. His debts are evident, and all the more explicit with the reminder that what this argument has termed the anthropology of the Defence is given a specific authorial source in a poem whose real subject is also tyrannicide, the beast fable from the wedding celebrations of The Old Arcadia's third book.

At the wedding of Lalus and Kala, Sidney's fictive double, Philisides, recounts a musical fable that he reports to have learned from "old Languet," whom he calls affectionately "the shepherd best swift Ister knew." As fictions multiply inside fictions, with Sidney writing about Philisides performing a song remembe red from the teacher of his youth, paradoxically the poem moves closer to the world of real events: Languet is the only contemporary ever explicitly named in Sidney's poetry. Philisides attributes to him both his piety and his moral education:

He said the music best thilke powers pleased
Was jump concord between our wit and will,
Where highest notes to godliness are raised,
And lowest sink not down to jot of ill.
With old true tales he wont mine ears to fill:
How shepherds did of yore, how now, they thrive,
Spoiling their flock, or while twixt them they strive.

Principles of faculty psychology secure the foundation of Philisides' political fable about the origins of monarchy: the concord between wit and will that Languet praises as a tenet of natural law (and he is "shepherd best" because he best knows the laws of nature) corresponds exactly to the balance celebrated between sovereign and subjects in the state. 'When that concord is violated, with the emergence of self-loving sovereigns who "think all things... made them to please," golden-world harmony is undone by brazen-world tyranny. The same division between wit and will that motivates Sidney's aggressively optimistic poetics in the Defence achieves in his beast fable an explicitly political focus: Philisides ends by counseling his "poor beasts" either "in patience to bide your hell, Or know your strengths, and then you shall do well". There is no real mystery about Philisides' advice or Sidney's meaning.

His Arcadias take for granted, as readily as his Defence, the necessity and virtue of tyrannicide. What matters here to the present argument is the clarification that the beast fable supplies about the relationship between the Defence and the natural law theory of Sidney's intellectual circle. Sidney's golden world poetic is so frequently couched in the language of natural law, and so persistently motivated by fears of self-love and tyranny, not by virtue of some loose correspondence between friend and mentor, but rather — as Philisides' fable makes clear — as the authorially explicit debt of a student to a teacher. Sidney inherited an anthropology of self-love and a politics of tyrannicide from his Philippist mentor, Hubert Languet. Sidney associates the Ideas of his right poet with the commonplaces of moral philosophy, this essay has argued, because he was inspired by an old shepherd whose chief vehicle of teaching appears to have been history: "With old true tales he won't mine ears to fill." Sidney acknowledged profound debts, especially to Languet, even while he was at work importantly in his Defence in contesting related intellectual assumptions. Associations do not constitute identities, and however alike Sidney's Ideas are to those of the moral philosopher, a crucial distinction exists between their deployment.

The distinction is crucial because that difference in deployment of the Idea explains why and how Sidney both borrows crucial intellectual assumptions of his circle and simultaneously contests them—explains why, in short, such shared assumptions could supply Sidney with a motive for writing poetry rather than history or philosophy. In history, the Idea is always conditioned by the contaminating circumstances of an imperfect world of events: Phalaris dies quietly in bed, and tyranny goes unchastened. In philosophy, Ideas remain abstractions, too remote and insubstantial either to achieve clarity or to carry affective force. By contrast, the poet's Ideas are substantive images exemplified as pictures of his own making. The figuring-forth of the Sidneian poet works "substantially" in his creation of a "perfect picture... of a true and lively knowledge" — knowledge that makes a reality available for the reader.

It is crucial to emphasize the important activity of the poem in presenting a "reality" in order to foreground the extraordinary intellectual and affective power that Sidney attributes to the Idea as it is figured forth — the capacity of the poet's "perfect" pictures to unleash real powers that exist at once in Nature and in the mind. This is a distinction worth maintaining because it highlights Sidney's decision to liberate the Idea from its purely conceptual locus in philosophy and its conditional status in history and to return it to its origins in rhetoric — a liberation that he achieves without sacrificing the exemplary power of Languet's "old true tales" or capitulating to history's sad capitivity to the brazen world of events. Thus, in the Defence, Sidney's poet "goeth hand in hand with Nature" because that cooperation secures for his Ideas a whole separate order of persuasiveness related to, but distinct from their logical power. It secures the added dimension of existential effectiveness, the persuasiveness of the Ideas depicted by fictions — persuasiveness that derives from their power to speak to the needs of human nature.

We respond to fictions — especially to the characters represented by narrative fictions — because we see ourselves mirrored in them, "ourselves" as teleologically considered beings we naturally are or should be. Ideas have, therefore, a rhetorical, rather than just a conceptual power, rendering them superior both to the always conditioned examples of unsatisfying history and to the abstractions of philosophical thought. Such insight suggests, in turn, some key assumptions about what it means for the poet "to deliver forth in such excellency" Ideas just "as he hath imagined them".

Sidney attributes to Nature in the Defence extraordinary power, not just as that great creating force with which the poet walks hand in hand — itself a speaking picture of the cooperation of the maker and his Maker, the human and the divine — but also the motivating impulse attributed to human nature in its appetite for goodness.

The Ideas figured forth by poets have power, Sidney argues repeatedly, because "poetry ever setteth virtue so out in her best colours... that one must needs be enamoured of her". When the reader is led to imagine Aeneas carrying old Anchises Anchises (ãnkî`sçz), in Greek mythology, member of the ruling family of Troy; father of Aeneas by Aphrodite. When Anchises boasted of the goddess's love, Zeus crippled or, in some versions of the legend, blinded him. When Troy fell, Aeneas rescued his father in a scene often depicted by later painters, including Bernini. on his back, the "form of goodness" poetically depicted, "cannot but" be loved. So similarly, in his discussion of heroic characters like Cyrus, Turnus, and Achilles, Sidney cites Plato and Cicero's opinion "that who could see virtue would be wonderfully ravished with the love of her beauty".

Poetry has such power to "plant goodness even in the secretest cabinet of our souls" because of the human appetite for virtue and becaus e of that substantive form (the imagined hero himself!) in which the Idea of virtue is made real — its substantiality at once moving and teaching, freeing the will from the tyranny of its own self-serving appetites as it recalls to the mind the goods of Nature. Sidney is not naive, and he scarcely thinks poetry always effective. Bartholomew's Day 1572 and the failures of Pibrac were far too potent memories to allow him to sustain idealizations unreflectively.

The tyrant Alexander Pheraeus, as Plutarch relates, was moved to tears by tragedy, but "in despite of himself" continued to perpetrate tragedies.The phrase "in despite of himself" makes Sidney's point for him; Pheraeus acted against his nature. By natural law, what the will wills is virtue.

Sidney draws upon the anthropology of natural law theorists in order to contest the very adequacy of history and philosophy as disciplines. Or more concretely, what Sidney learned about human nature from Languet and Mornay also persuaded him — given the zodiacal powers of the wit, and the infected condition of the will — that only poetry could have the power to undo the tyranny of self-love over the soul and self-loving sovereigns in the state. Given that anthropology; the wit must be instructed, and (even more importantly) the will moved: both requirements demand a discipline beyond history and philosophy, one that including both, transcends both. In a golden world set free from the contaminations of history — of a past that too often records the triumph of vice over virtue, or a present that too often divides Christian from Christian in endless confessional debate — the poet takes aim against the Idea of tyranny, realized as a substantial image in a fictive world beyond partisan politics, in order to ch asten history — to purge the body politic from the contaminations of self-love.

Just as Sidney begins the important work of the Defence by illustrating imitation with the example of Tarquin's tyranny over Lucretia, so later in the text he highlights two more tales of tyranny, the stories of Menenius Agrippa and the biblical Nathan. The first narrates Agrippa's success in quelling a rebellion in ancient Rome by means of a story about the interdependence of the various parts of the human body: populist anger against what appears patrician greed is alleviated as the working limbs of the polity (the plebeians) are made to understand the necessary function of the belly. While the belly (the patrician class) may consume, such consumption nourishes (Menenius' exemplum insists) the whole of the body politic. Sidney's second story narrates Nathan's success in devising a tale for David in the wake of his adultery with Bathsheba and his culpability in the death of her husband.

Nathan's fictive account of "a man whose beloved lamb was ungratefully taken from him" quickly shames David into repentance. The two stories are introduced at a crucial juncture of Sidney's argument. They are placed at the climactic moment of the Defense's demonstration of poetry's "most excellent work" – the "high argument" of its confirmatio – just before the turn to justify poetry by an examination of its parts. So situated, the tales supply summary proofs of the main burden of Sidney's claim on behalf of the superiority of the poet's "works" – its effects upon the reader – over those of his chief rivals for cultural authority, the historian and the philosopher.

The tales of Agrippa and Nathan supply a complementary pair of proof texts. One is drawn from classical history, the other from sacred. One illustrates the power of a fable to provide "a perfect reconcilement" in the public sphere, as Agrippa's tale of the belly heals the divisions in Rome's body politic; the other illustrates the power of fiction-making in the private sphere, as David is shamed by Nathan's story of the lamb "as in a glass [to]see his own filthiness," to repent for adultery and murder, and reclaim ("as that psalm of mercy well testifieth") his role as God's chosen servant. One illustrates the power of a feigned tale over the people, one over the prince.

In both, Sidney dramatizes the tyranny of self-love as a universal condition afflicting individuals and the state. In

Agrippa's fable, we see the tyranny of mob violence — one of the principal forms of tyranny analyzed in Buchanan's De jure; in Nathan's tale, the tyranny of lust over the sovereign — one of Melanchthon's favourite pro of texts about tyrannical self-love. Paired in this manner, the twin tales seem deliberately chosen in order to illustrate comprehensively, across the domains of pagan and sacred history, public and private life, among the low and the high, the superior effects of poetry's "most excellent work" in teaching and persuading.

As a preface to his illustrations of that work, in the paragraph immediately preceding, Sidney recalls approvingly Aristotle's claim on behalf of poetry's "conveniency to Nature" as a way of highlighting those powerfully persuasive acts of identification that make readers want to see themselves as Turnus courageously preferring death to dishonor, as Aeneas piously bearing old Anchises on his back, or as Lucretia chastely resisting the tyranny of lust. Both "the whole people of Rome" collectively and David individually are brought to an architectonic knowledge of themselves; they are taught fictions that heighten understanding about their natures and that move them by reason of such knowledge to virtuous action. In both cases, that architectonic knowledge is liberating, since knowledge about their real natures (the nature of the body politic's necessary interdependence of parts, the nature of the self's dependence on God) sparks change that frees them from self-love and renders them what they truly are (a whole people, a chosen servant). Poetry's "most excellent work," Sidney's speaking pictures eloquently declare, is liberty.

Freeing the Defence

"Liberty" seems just the right word with which to conclude a discussion about the politics of Sidney's poetics because it points to the need to rewrite the revisionary critical history imposed upon it by recent critics generally and by Alan Sinfield especially. In particular, it seems high time to liberate the Defence of Poesy from its guilty association with Soviet-style absolutism.

There can be no question about Sidney's intellectual

commitments to a universalizing epistemology: the poet's golden world achieves its legitimacy and power only because the Ideas to which it lends rhetorical substance have the status of natural law. However, as this essay has argued in some detail, Sidney had recourse to the language and logic of natural law precisely in order to contest the claims of what appeared to his understanding and to his experience of the international landscape as politically abhorrent absolutism.

Sidney's natural law arguments are drawn from the rhetorical arsenal of Protestant tyrannomachists waging campaigns against the AntiChrist of post-Tridentine Catholicism, dating from Melanchthon's appeals against the emperor in the War of the League of the Schmalkaldan to Languet's assaults against Philip II during the Dutch wars of liberation. Derived from political theorists who espoused a theory of limited monarchy, such rhetoric unsurprisingly was anathema to Tudor absolutists — the exponents of a pious orthodoxy with its own very real absolutist ideology of obedience. In light of which circumstance, assertions about Sidney's complicity in Elizabethan absolutism seem peculiarly unhistorical, especially when unsupported by analysis. By advancing natural law arguments, Sidney and his circle hoped to have discovered a vehicle for securing reasoned political agreements beyond the partisan rhetoric of confessional debate, the "universalizing" force of its ideas most important for their putative power to reconstruct universal agreement among civil communities.

If that hope seems at this historical juncture theoret ically naive and pragmatically bankrupt, as the product of intellectually elite humanists who never secured the institutional authority to put purpose into practice, such a hope seems no more dismissable as the product of factional politics than it does as absolutist propagandizing.

The community that matters most for understanding the politics of the Defence is not a faction at the Elizabethan court (vaguely characterizable as earnest puritan" by Sinfield or "forward Protestant" by Worden), but an identifiable network of cosmopolitan Protestant humanists reaching from Languet to Mornay to Rogers to Buchanan to Sidney, one which found its most important "commonplace" agreements in that distinctive version of Protestantism that derives from Philip Melanchthon's vastly influential and still-obscured labors.

It is to that community that Sidney owes his tyrannomachist politics, his natural law theory, his intellectualist assumptions, and his anthropology, as well as his identification of tyranny with self-love. His was a community, an active "republic of letters," if one likes, but never powerful enough in institutional terms to rise to level of a faction. Recovering a history of ideas from that network of intellectually elite humanists with whom Sidney associated intimately throughout his a dult life and from which he derived so much of his political and poetic thought has a special urgency, it might be well to conclude, because we still know so little about it.

Chapter 7

Literature and Virtue in Sidney's "Apology for Poetry"

In "An Apology for Poetry" Sir Philip Sidney attempts to reassert the fundamental importance of literature to society in general as well as to other creative and intellectual endeavors. Though Sidney's work does provide a synthesis (and in some cases an aberration) of much Greek and Roman literary theory, his argument aspires to go beyond an esoteric academic debate. Literature can "teach and delight" in a manner which other methods of communication do not possess. The moralethical impact any literary text has upon a reader is of paramount importance to Sidney. The argument Sidney presents and develops is built around the assumption that literature has the capacity to teach most effectively and to demonstrate virtue. Perhaps in better understanding how Sidney specifically supports this claim, we can better assess its strength or validity.

Sidney places literature in an hierarchical relationship with all other forms of learning; literature inhabits the highest and most influential tier. Literature is "the first light-giver to ignorance", and from it all other sources of knowledge have been nurtured. As the first use of language beyond the completely utilitarian, literature stretches and expands language to accommodate broader and more conceptual inquiries. Though an ardent admirer of Platonic philosophy, Sydney, in order to serve his intellectual exercise, rewrites or rehabilitates Plato's harsh stance on the worthlessness of literature. Unlike Plato's poet who perpetuates images far removed from the Truth, Sidney's poet can dip into the world of Forms, the Ideal, and provide us with knowledge of virtue. While the tangible world of appearances "is brazen, the poets only deliver a golden".

Against the established disciplines of history and philosophy, Sidney also uses a revision of Aristotle's Poetics to help demonstrate how literature mediates the interests of both forms of knowledge in order to teach virtue. Where philosophy deals solely with the universal, history is consumed with the particular. Literature is able to deal with the same abstract moralethical (universal) concepts with which philosophy grapples by providing examples rooted in concrete, albeit fictionalized, details. History is too concerned with the accurate recording of facts to make any conjectures on such broad, less substantiated concepts. Literature exists between and above history and philosophy because the knowledge it conveys (knowledge of the good) is the best and most useful knowledge that exists. As Sidney states, "no learning is so good as that which teacheth and moveth to virtue, and that none can both teach and move thereto so much as poetry".

Sidney attempts to provide an utterly rational foundation for his claims, however. He develops a systematic analysis of the mechanisms employed by literature to teach virtue. He sorts literature according to its works and its parts. The works of a literary text can be seen in four specific ethical effects which it should seek to elicit in a reader. Sidney defines these four as: the purifying of wit, enriching of memory, enabling of judgement, and enlarging of conceit.

In order to purify the wit, literature must engage the intellect in new and different ways. By allowing the reader to view a particular idea, character, or situation from a new or novel vantage point, literature is able to provide a vicarious, condensed education available through no other medium. Memories gathered from these fictional experiences provide a common frame of reference between otherwise disparate individuals. Fictional examples become touchstones which can be understood and experienced more easily by others. Literary memories point toward a more universal experience and invite the reader to find new and possibly profound meanings in personal experiences as well. Sidney implies that a life without such memories would surely be impoverished. Building upon the first two works, literature also provides a reader with ample and necessary practise in making moralethical judgments.

A literary text provides a safe outlet for such judgments to be made, discussed, and re-examined. Personal and societal codes of behaviour are shaped, both strengthened and challenged, by this practise. Literature engages the reader actively with virtue as a part of this decision making process. To enlarge the conceit, literature also expands a reader's knowledge and understanding of language (in terms of style, structure, form) as well. This, in turn, opens new modes of expression, new metaphors, to a reader. The ability to create new and different texts is stamped into the very nature of literature.

The ability to articulate and teach virtue effectively is constantly in flux from generation to generation. Literature is constantly in demand of new metaphors in order to remain resilient and relevant. Each narrative, housing the potential to fundamentally redefine and reevaulate itself, represents a metaphor for the world. Thus it is vital that literature possess this self perpetuating but continually evolving quality.

To discuss literature in its various parts, Sidney develops a series of stylistic, structural, and thematic categories: pastoral, elegiac, iambic, satiric, comic, tragic, lyric, and heroic. Each category (part) of literature also attempts to elicit a specific ethical response from the reader. The parts themselves are arranged hierarchically as well, with the heroic being placed at the top. Though an interesting (if historically outdated) method of division, Sidney's categories seem to elaborate more than advance his general argument, however. He places more emphasis on the ethical questions posed by the works of a literary text, rather than its parts.

Sidney concludes his comprehensive defence of literature by attempting to answer various challenges to its merit and continued support. The most serious of these allegations, that literature is "the nurse of abuse, infecting us with pestilent desires", Sidney is forced to acknowledge as true to a greater or lesser extent. This might seem, at first glance, to refute or undermine the argument he has labored so long to create. Sidney, however, has qualified his praise of literature from the onset. Literature can contribute to learning virtue but does not ensure virtuous action.

Because he is aware of the fact that literature can and is abused by some, Sidney describes literature as a tool with the greatest potential for good, but not an inherently virtuous invention in and of itself. The destructive qualities evoked by literature are products of the fallible fragile human beings who created it, rather than an indictment of the evil nature of all literature in general. Do not, as Sidney states, "say that poetry abuseth man's wit, but that man's wit abuseth poetry".

Sidney's responses have become the mainstay of the supporters of a liberal arts education. Unfortunately, literature has become sanctified to the extent that knowledge of literature has become practically synonymous with virtuous action. Such modern interpretations of Sidney's defence of literature seem to strike against the very heart of his argument. Sidney seems to understand all too well that human beings house both virtuous and vicious impulses; it is within our power to infuse our creations with both the sinister and the sublime. Because this is true of any human invention, Sidney counsels that the potential of literature for good or ill should not be easily discounted or dismissed.

Chapter 8

Sidney to Macaulay

WHEN the right virtuous Edward Wotton and I were at the Emperor's 1 court together, we gave ourselves to learn horsemanship of John Pietro Pugliano, one that with great commendation had the place of an esquire in his stable; and he, according to the fertileness of the Italian wit, did not only afford us the demonstration of his practice, but sought to enrich our minds with the contemplations therein which he thought most precious. But with none I remember mine ears were at any time more loaden, than when—either angered with slow payment, or moved with our learner-like admiration—he exercised his speech in the praise of his faculty. He said soldiers were the noblest estate of mankind, and horsemen the noblest of soldiers. He said they were the masters of war and ornaments of peace, speedy goers and strong abiders, triumphers both in camps and courts.

Nay, to so unbelieved a point he proceeded, as that no earthly thing bred such wonder to a prince as to be a good horseman; skill of government was but a pedanteria in comparison. Then would he add certain praises, by telling what a peerless beast the horse was, the only serviceable courtier without flattery, the beast of most beauty, faithfulness, courage, and such more, that if I had not been a piece of a logician before I came to him, I think he would have persuaded me to have wished myself a horse. But thus much at least with his no few words he drave into me, that self-love is better than any gilding to make that seem gorgeous wherein ourselves be parties.

Wherein if Pugliano's strong affection and weak

arguments will not satisfy you, I will give you a nearer example of myself, who, I know not by what mischance, in these my not old years and idlest times, having slipped into the title of a poet, am provoked to say something unto you in the defence of that my unelected vocation, which if I handle with more good will than good reasons, bear with me, since the scholar is to be pardoned that followeth the steps of his master.

And yet I must say that, as I have just cause to make a pitiful defence of poor poetry, which from almost the highest estimation of learning is fallen to be the laughing-stock of children, so have I need to bring some more available proofs, since the former is by no man barred of his deserved credit, the silly 3 latter hath had even the names of philosophers used to the defacing of it, with great danger of civil war among the Muses. And first, truly, to all them that, professing learning, inveigh against poetry, may justly be objected that they go very near to ungratefulness, to seek to deface that which, in the noblest nations and languages that are known, hath been the first light-giver to ignorance, and first nurse, whose milk by little and little enabled them to feed afterwards of tougher knowledges. And will they now play the hedgehog, that, being received into the den, drave out his host? Or rather the vipers, that with their birth kill their parents? Let learned Greece in any of her manifold sciences be able to show me one book before Musæus, Homer, and Hesiod, all three nothing else but poets.

Nay, let any history be brought that can say any writers were there before them, if they were not men of the same skill, as Orpheus, Linus, and some other are named, who, having been the first of that country that made pens deliver of their knowledge to their posterity, may justly challenge to be called their fathers in learning. For not only in time they had this priority—although in itself antiquity be venerable—but went before them as causes, to draw with their charming sweetness the wild untamed wits to an admiration of knowledge. So as Amphion was said to move stones with his poetry to build Thebes, and Orpheus to be listened to by beasts,—indeed stony and beastly people. So among the Romans were Livius

Andronicus and Ennius; so in the Italian language the first that made it aspire to be a treasure-house of science were the poets Dante, Boccace, and Petrarch; so in our English were Gower and Chaucer, after whom, encouraged and delighted with their excellent foregoing, others have followed to beautify our mother-tongue, as well in the same kind as in other arts. This did so notably show itself, that the philosophers of Greece durst not a long time appear to the world but under the masks of poets. So Thales, Empedocles, and Parmenides sang their natural philosophy in verses; so did Pythagoras and Phocylides their moral counsels; so did Tyrtæus in war matters, and Solon in matters of policy; or rather they, being poets, did exercise their delightful vein in those points of highest knowledge which before them lay hidden to the world. For that wise Solon was directly a poet it is manifest, having written in verse the notable fable of the Atlantic Island which was continued by Plato. And truly even Plato whosoever well considereth, shall find that in the body of his work though the inside and strength were philosophy, the skin as it were and beauty depended most of poetry.

For all standeth upon dialogues; wherein he feigneth many honest burgesses of Athens to speak of such matters that, if they had been set on the rack, they would never have confessed them; besides his poetical describing the circumstances of their meetings, as the well-ordering of a banquet, the delicacy of a walk, with interlacing mere tales, as Gyges' Ring and others, which who knoweth not to be flowers of poetry did never walk into Apollo's garden.

And even historiographers, although their lips sound of things done, and verity be written in their foreheads, have been glad to borrow both fashion and perchance weight of the poets.

So Herodotus entitled his history by the name of the nine Muses; and both he and all the rest that followed him either stole or usurped of poetry their passionate describing of passions, the many particularities of battles which no man could affirm, or, if that be denied me, long orations put in the mouths of great kings and captains, which it is certain they never pronounced.

So that truly neither philosopher nor historiographer could at the first have entered into the gates of popular judgments, if they had not taken a great passport of poetry, which in all nations at this day, where learning flourisheth not, is plain to be seen; in all which they have some feeling of poetry. In Turkey, besides their lawgiving divines they have no other writers but poets.

In our neighbour country Ireland, where truly learning goeth very bare, yet are their poets held in a devout reverence. Even among the most barbarous and simple Indians, where no writing is, yet have they their poets, who make and sing songs (which they call areytos), both of their ancestors' deeds and praises of their gods,—a sufficient probability that, if ever learning come among them, it must be by having their hard dull wits softened and sharpened with the sweet delights of poetry; for until they find a pleasure in the exercise of the mind, great promises of much knowledge will little persuade them that know not the fruits of knowledge.

In Wales, the true remnant of the ancient Britons, as there are good authorities to show the long time they had poets which they called bards, so through all the conquests of Romans, Saxons, Danes, and Normans, some of whom did seek to ruin all memory of learning from among them, yet do their poets even to this day last; so as it is not more notable in soon beginning, than in long continuing.

But since the authors of most of our sciences were the Romans, and before them the Greeks, let us a little stand upon their authorities, but even 4 so far as to see what names they have given unto this now scorned skill. Among the Romans a poet was called vates, which is as much as a diviner, foreseer, or prophet, as by his conjoined words, vaticinium and vaticinari, is manifest; so heavenly a title did that excellent people bestow upon this heart-ravishing knowledge. And so far were they carried into the admiration thereof, that they thought in the chanceable hitting upon any such verses great fore-tokens of their following fortunes were placed; whereupon grew the word of Sortes Virgilianæ, when by sudden opening Virgil's book they lighted upon some verse of his making. Whereof the Histories of the Emperors' Lives are full: as of Albinus, the governor of our island, who in his childhood met with this verse, Arma amens capio, nec sat rationis in armis,

and in his age performed it. Although it were a very vain and godless superstition, as also it was to think that spirits were commanded by such verses—whereupon this word charms, derived of carmina, cometh—so yet serveth it to show the great reverence those wits were held in, and altogether not 5 without ground, since both the oracles of Delphos and Sibylla's prophecies were wholly delivered in verses; for that same exquisite observing of number and measure in words, and that high-flying liberty of conceit, 6 proper to the poet, did seem to have some divine force in it.

And may not I presume a little further to show the reasonableness of this word vates, and say that the holy David's Psalms are a divine poem? If I do, I shall not do it without the testimony of great learned men, both ancient and modern. But even the name of Psalms will speak for me, which, being interpreted, is nothing but Songs; then, that it is fully written in metre, as all learned Hebricians agree, although the rules be not yet fully found; lastly and principally, his handling his prophecy, which is merely poetical.

For what else is the awaking his musical instruments, the often and free changing of persons, his notable prosopopoeias, when he maketh you, as it were, see God coming in His majesty, his telling of the beasts' joyfulness and hills' leaping, but a heavenly poesy, wherein almost he showeth himself a passionate lover of that unspeakable and everlasting beauty to be seen by the eyes of the mind, only cleared by faith? But truly now having named him, I fear I seem to profane that holy name, applying it to poetry, which is among us thrown down to so ridiculous an estimation.

But they that with quiet judgments will look a little deeper into it, shall find the end and working of it such as, being rightly applied, deserveth not to be scourged out of the church of God. But now let us see how the Greeks named it and how they deemed of it. The Greeks called him, which name hath, as the most excellent, gone through other languages. It cometh of this word, which is "to make"; wherein I know not whether by luck or wisdom we Englishmen have met with the Greeks in calling him a maker. Which name how high and incomparable a title it is, I had rather were known by marking the scope of other sciences than by any partial allegation.

There is no art delivered unto mankind that hath not the works of nature for his principal object, without which they could not consist, and on which they so depend as they become actors and players, as it were, of what nature will have set forth. So doth the astronomer look upon the stars, and, by that he seeth, set down what order nature hath taken therein. So do the geometrician and arithmetician in their divers sorts of quantities. So doth the musician in times tell you which by nature agree, which not.

The natural philosopher thereon hath his name, and the moral philosopher standeth upon the natural virtues, vices, and passions of man; and "follow nature," saith he, "therein, and thou shalt not err." The lawyer saith what men have determined, the historian what men have done. The grammarian speaketh only of the rules of speech, and the rhetorician and logician, considering what in nature will soonest prove and persuade, thereon give artificial rules, which still are compassed within the circle of a question, according to the proposed matter.

The physician weigheth the nature of man's body, and the nature of things helpful or hurtful unto it. And the metaphysic, though it be in the second and abstract notions, and therefore be counted supernatural, yet doth he, indeed, build upon the depth of nature.

Only the poet, disdaining to be tied to any such subjection, lifted up with the vigour of his own invention, doth grow, in effect, into another nature, in making things either better than nature bringeth forth, or, quite anew, forms such as never were in nature, as the heroes, demi-gods, cyclops, chimeras, furies, and such like; so as he goeth hand in hand with nature, not enclosed within the narrow warrant of her gifts, but freely ranging within the zodiac of his own wit. Nature never set forth the earth in so rich tapestry as divers poets have done; neither with pleasant rivers, fruitful trees, sweet-smelling flowers, nor whatsoever else may make the too-much-loved earth more lovely; her world is brazen, the poets only deliver a golden.

But let those things alone, and go to man—for whom as the other things are, so it seemeth in him her uttermost cunning is employed—and know whether she have brought forth so true a lover as Theagenes; so constant a friend as Pylades; so valiant a man as Orlando; so right a prince as Xenophon's Cyrus; so excellent a man every way as Virgil's Æneas? Neither let this be jestingly conceived, because the works of the one be essential, the other in imitation or fiction; for any understanding knoweth the skill of each artificer standeth in that idea, or fore-conceit of the work, and not in the work itself.

And that the poet hath that idea is manifest, by delivering them forth in such excellency as he hath imagined them. Which delivering forth, also, is not wholly imaginative, as we are wont to say by them that build castles in the air; but so far substantially it worketh, not only to make a Cyrus, which had been but a particular excellency, as nature might have done, but to bestow a Cyrus upon the world to make many Cyruses, if they will learn aright why and how that maker made him.

Neither let it be deemed too saucy a comparison to balance the highest point of man's wit with the efficacy of nature; but rather give right honour to the Heavenly Maker of that maker, who, having made man to His own likeness, set him beyond and over all the works of that second nature. Which in nothing he showeth so much as in poetry, when with the force of a divine breath he bringeth things forth far surpassing her doings, with no small argument to the incredulous of that first accursed fall of Adam,—since our erected wit maketh us know what perfection is, and yet our infected will keepeth us from reaching unto it. But these arguments will by few be understood, and by fewer granted; thus much I hope will be given me, that the Greeks with some probability of reason gave him the name above all names of learning.

Now let us go to a more ordinary opening of him, that

the truth may be the more palpable; and so, I hope, though we get not so unmatched a praise as the etymology of his names will grant, yet his very description, which no man will deny, shall not justly be barred from a principal commendation. Poesy, therefore, is an art of imitation, for so Aristotle termeth it in his word, that is to say, a representing, counterfeiting, or figuring forth; to speak metaphorically, a speaking picture, with this end,—to teach and delight.

Of this have been three general kinds. The chief, both in antiquity and excellency, were they that did imitate the inconceivable excellencies of God. Such were David in his Psalms; Solomon in his Song of Songs, in his Ecclesiastes and Proverbs; Moses and Deborah in their Hymns; and the writer of Job; which, beside other, the learned Emanuel Tremellius and Franciscus Junius do entitle the poetical part of the Scripture. Against these none will speak that hath the Holy Ghost in due holy reverence. In this kind, though in a full wrong divinity, were Orpheus, Amphion, Homer in his Hymns, and many other, both Greeks and Romans. And this poesy must be used by whosoever will follow St. James' counsel in singing psalms when they are merry; and I know is used with the fruit of comfort by some, when, in sorrowful pangs of their death-bringing sins, they find the consolation of the never-leaving goodness.

The second kind is of them that deal with matters philosophical, either moral, as Tyrtæus, Phocylides, and Cato; or natural, as Lucretius and Virgil's Georgics; or astronomical, as Manilius and Pontanus; or historical, as Lucan; which who mislike, the fault is in their judgment quite out of taste, and not in the sweet food of sweetly uttered knowledge.

But because this second sort is wrapped within the fold of the proposed subject, and takes not the free course of his own invention, whether they properly be poets or no let grammarians dispute, and go to the third, indeed right poets, of whom chiefly this question ariseth. Betwixt whom and these second is such a kind of difference as betwixt the meaner sort of painters, who counterfeit only such faces as are set before them, and the more excellent, who having no law but wit, bestow that in colors upon you which is fittest for the eye to see,—as the constant though lamenting look of Lucretia, when she punished in herself another's fault; wherein he painteth not Lucretia, whom he never saw, but painteth the outward beauty of such a virtue. For these third be they which most properly do imitate to teach and delight; and to imitate borrow nothing of what is, hath been, or shall be; but range, only reined with learned discretion, into the divine consideration of what may be and should be.

These be they that, as the first and most noble sort may justly be termed vates, so these are waited on in the excellentest languages and best understandings with the fore-described name of poets. For these, indeed, do merely make to imitate, and imitate both to delight and teach, and delight to move men to take that goodness in hand, which without delight they would fly as from a stranger; and teach to make them know that goodness whereunto they are moved:—which being the noblest scope to which ever any learning was directed, yet want there not idle tongues to bark at them.

These be subdivided into sundry more special denominations. The most notable be the heroic, lyric, tragic, comic, satiric, iambic, elegiac, pastoral, and certain others, some of these being termed according to the matter they deal with, some by the sort of verse they liked best to write in,—for indeed the greatest part of poets have apparelled their poetical inventions in that numberous kind of writing which is called verse. Indeed but apparelled, verse being but an ornament and no cause to poetry, since there have been many most excellent poets that never versified, and now swarm many versifiers that need never answer to the name of poets. For Xenophon, who did imitate so excellently as to give us effigiem justi imperii—the portraiture of a just empire under the name of Cyrus (as Cicero saith of him)—made therein an absolute heroical poem; so did Heliodorus in his sugared invention of that picture of love in Theagenes and Chariclea; and yet both these wrote in prose.

Which I speak to show that it is not riming and versing that maketh a poet—no more than a long gown maketh an advocate, who, though he pleaded in armor, should be an advocate and no soldier—but it is that feigning notable images of virtues, vices, or what else, with that delightful teaching, which must be the right describing note to know a poet by. Although indeed the senate of poets hath chosen verse as their fittest raiment, meaning, as in matter they passed all in all, so in manner to go beyond them; not speaking, table-talk fashion, or like men in a dream, words as they chanceably fall from the mouth, but peizing 7 each syllable of each word by just proportion, according to the dignity of the subject.

Now, therefore, it shall not be amiss, first to weigh this latter sort of poetry by his works, and then by his parts; and if in neither of these anatomies he be condemnable, I hope we shall obtain a more favorable sentence. This purifying of wit, this enriching of memory, enabling of judgment, and enlarging of conceit, which commonly we call learning, under what name soever it come forth or to what immediate end soever it be directed, the final end is to lead and draw us to as high a perfection as our degenerate souls, made worse by their clay lodgings, can be capable of.

This, according to the inclination of man, bred many-formed impressions. For some that thought this felicity principally to be gotten by knowledge, and no knowledge to be so high or heavenly as acquaintance with the stars, gave themselves to astronomy; others, persuading themselves to be demi-gods if they knew the causes of things, became natural and supernatural philosophers. Some an admirable delight drew to music, and some the certainty of demonstration to the mathematics; but all, one and other, having this scope:—to know, and by knowledge to lift up the mind from the dungeon of the body to the enjoying his own divine essence. But when by the balance of experience it was found that the astronomer, looking to the stars, might fall into a ditch, that the inquiring philosopher might be blind in himself, and the mathematician might draw forth a straight line with a crooked heart; then lo! did proof, the overruler of opinions, make manifest, that all these are but serving sciences, which, as they have each a private end in themselves, so yet are they all directed to the highest end of the mistress knowledge, by the Greeks called, which stands, as I think, in the knowledge of a man's self, in the ethic and politic consideration, with the end of well-doing, and not of well-knowing only:—even as the saddler's next end is to make a good saddle, but his further end to serve a nobler faculty, which is horsemanship; so the horseman's to soldiery; and the soldier not only to have the skill, but to perform the practice of a soldier.

So that the ending end of all earthly learning being virtuous action, those skills that most serve to bring forth that have a most just title to be princes over all the rest; wherein, if we can show, the poet is worthy to have it before any other competitors. Among whom as principal challengers step forth the moral philosophers; whom, me thinketh, I see coming toward me with a sullen gravity, as though they could not abide vice by daylight; rudely clothed, for to witness outwardly their contempt of outward things; with books in their hands against glory, whereto they set their names; sophistically speaking against subtility; and angry with any man in whom they see the foul fault of anger.

These men, casting largess as they go of definitions, divisions, and distinctions, with a scornful interrogative do soberly ask whether it be possible to find any path so ready to lead a man to virtue, as that which teacheth what virtue is, and teacheth it not only by delivering forth his very being, his causes and effects, but also by making known his enemy, vice, which must be destroyed, and his cumbersome servant, passion, which must be mastered; by showing the generalities that contain it, and the specialities that are derived from it; lastly, by plain setting down how it extendeth itself out of the limits of a man's own little world, to the government of families, and maintaining of public societies?

The historian scarcely giveth leisure to the moralist to say so much, but that he, loaden with old mouse-eaten records, authorizing himself for the most part upon other histories, whose greatest authorities are built upon the notable foundation of hearsay; having much ado to accord differing writers, and to pick truth out of partiality; better acquainted with a thousand years ago than with the present age, and yet better knowing how this world goeth than how his own wit runneth; curious for antiquities and inquisitive of novelties, a wonder to young folks and a tyrant in table-talk; denieth, in a great chafe, 8 that any man for teaching of virtue and virtuous actions is comparable to him. "I am testis temporum, lux veritatis, vita memoriæ, magistra vitæ, nuntia vetustatis.

The philosopher," saith he, "teacheth a disputative virtue, but I do an active. His virtue is excellent in the dangerless Academy of Plato, but mine showeth forth her honorable face in the battles of Marathon, Pharsalia, Poitiers, and Agincourt. He teacheth virtue by certain abstract considerations, but I only bid you follow the footing of them that have gone before you. Old-aged experience goeth beyond the fine-witted philosopher; but I give the experience of many ages.

Lastly, if he make the songbook, I put the learner's hand to the lute; and if he be the guide, I am the light." Then would he allege you innumerable examples, confirming story by story, how much the wisest senators and princes have been directed by the credit of history, as Brutus, Alphonsus of Aragon—and who not, if need be? At length the long line of their disputation maketh a point in this,—that the one giveth the precept, and the other the example.

Now whom shall we find, since the question standeth for the highest form in the school of learning, to be moderator? Truly, as me seemeth, the poet; and if not a moderator, even the man that ought to carry the title from them both, and much more from all other serving sciences. Therefore compare we the poet with the historian and with the moral philosopher; and if he go beyond them both, no other human skill can match him. For as for the divine, with all reverence it is ever to be excepted, not only for having his scope as far beyond any of these as eternity exceedeth a moment, but even for passing each of these in themselves.

And for the lawyer, though Jus be the daughter of Justice, and Justice the chief of virtues, yet because he seeketh to make men good rather formidine poeœnæ than virtutis amore 12 or, to say righter, doth not endeavour to make men good, but that their evil hurt not others; having no care, so he be a good citizen, how bad a man he be; therefore, as our wickedness maketh him necessary, and necessity maketh him honorable, so is he not in the deepest truth to stand in rank with these, who all endeavor to take naughtiness away, and plant goodness even in the secretest cabinet of our souls. And these four are all that any way deal in that consideration of men's manners, which being the supreme knowledge, they that best breed it deserve the best commendation.

The philosopher therefore and the historian are they which would win the goal, the one by precept, the other by example; but both not having both, do both halt. For the philosopher, setting down with thorny arguments the bare rule, is so hard of utterance and so misty to be conceived, that one that hath no other guide but him shall wade in him till he be old, before he shall find sufficient cause to be honest. For his knowledge standeth so upon the abstract and general that happy is that man who may understand him, and more happy that can apply what he doth understand. On the other side, the historian, wanting the precept, is so tied, not to what should be but to what is, to the particular truth of things, and not to the general reason of things, that his example draweth no necessary consequence, and therefore a less fruitful doctrine.

Now doth the peerless poet perform both; for whatsoever the philosopher saith should be done, he giveth a perfect picture of it in some one by whom he presupposeth it was done, so as he coupleth the general notion with the particular example. A perfect picture, I say; for he yieldeth to the powers of the mind an image of that whereof the philosopher bestoweth but a wordish description, which doth neither strike, pierce, nor possess the sight of the soul so much as that other doth.

For as, in outward things, to a man that had never seen an elephant or a rhinoceros, who should tell him most exquisitely all their shapes, colour, bigness, and particular marks; or of a gorgeous palace, an architector, with declaring the full beauties, might well make the hearer able to repeat, as it were by rote, all he had heard, yet should never satisfy his inward conceit with being witness to itself of a true lively knowledge; but the same man, as soon as he might see those beasts well painted, or that house well in model, should straightways grow, without need of any description, to a judicial comprehending of them; so no doubt the philosopher, with his learned definitions, be it of virtues or vices, matters of public policy or private government, replenisheth the memory with many infallible grounds of wisdom, which notwithstanding lie dark before the imaginative and judging power, if they be not illuminated or figured forth by the speaking picture of poesy.

Tully taketh much pains, and many times not without poetical helps, to make us know the force love of our country hath in us. Let us but hear old Anchises speaking in the midst of Troy's flames, or see Ulysses, in the fulness of all Calypso's delights, bewail his absence from barren and beggarly Ithaca. Anger, the Stoics said, was a short madness. Let but Sophocles bring you Ajax on a stage, killing and whipping sheep and oxen, thinking them the army of Greeks, with their chieftains Agamemnon and Menelaus, and tell me if you have not a more familiar insight into anger, than finding in the schoolmen his genus and difference.

See whether wisdom and temperance in Ulysses and Diomedes, valor in Achilles, friendship in Nisus and Euryalus, even to an ignorant man carry not an apparent shining. And, contrarily, the remorse of conscience, in Oedipus; the soon-repenting pride of Agamemnon; the self-devouring cruelty in his father Atreus; the violence of ambition in the two Theban brothers; the sour sweetness of revenge in Medea; and, to fall lower, the Terentian Gnatho and our Chaucer's Pandar so expressed that we now use their names to signify their trades; and finally, all virtues, vices, and passions so in their own natural states laid to the view, that we seem not to hear of them, but clearly to see through them.

But even in the most excellent determination of goodness, what philosopher's counsel can so readily direct a prince, as the feigned Cyrus in Xenophon? Or a virtuous man in all fortunes, as Æneas in Virgil? Or a whole commonwealth, as the way of Sir Thomas More's Utopia? I say the way, because where Sir Thomas More erred, it was the fault of the man, and not of the poet; for that way of patterning a commonwealth was most absolute, though he, perchance, hath not so absolutely performed it. For the question is, whether the feigned image of poesy, or the regular instruction of philosophy, hath the more force in teaching. Wherein if the philosophers have more rightly showed themselves philosophers than the poets have attained to the high top of their profession,—as in truth,

Mediocribus esse poetis
Non Dii, non homines, non concessere columnæ,
it is, I say again, not the fault of the art, but that by few men that art can be accomplished.

Certainly, even our Saviour Christ could as well have given the moral commonplaces of uncharitableness and humbleness as the divine narration of Dives and Lazarus; or of disobedience and mercy, as that heavenly discourse of the lost child and the gracious father; but that his thorough-searching wisdom knew the estate of Dives burning in hell, and of Lazarus in Abraham's bosom, would more constantly, as it were, inhabit both the memory and judgment. Truly, for myself, me seems I see before mine eyes the lost child's disdainful prodigality, turned to envy a swine's dinner; which by the learned divines are thought not historical acts, but instructing parables.

For conclusion, I say the philosopher teacheth, but he teacheth obscurely, so as the learned only can understand him; that is to say, he teacheth them that are already taught. But the poet is the food for the tenderest stomachs; the poet is indeed the right popular philosopher. Whereof Æsop's tales give good proof; whose pretty allegories, stealing under the formal tales of beasts, make many, more beastly than beasts, begin to hear the sound of virtue from those dumb speakers.

But now it may be alleged that if this imagining of matters be so fit for the imagination, then must the historian needs surpass, who bringeth you images of true matters, such as indeed were done, and not such as fantastically or falsely may be suggested to have been done. Truly, Aristotle himself, in his Discourse of Poesy, plainly determineth this question, saying that poetry is and, that is to say, it is more philosophical and more studiously serious than history. His reason is, because poesy dealeth with, that is to say with the universal consideration, and the history with, the particular.

"Now," saith he, "the universal weighs what is fit to be said or done, either in likelihood or necessity—which the poesy considereth in his imposed names; and the particular only marketh whether Alcibiades did, or suffered, this or that:" thus far Aristotle. Which reason of his, as all his, is most full of reason. For, indeed, if the question were whether it were better to have a particular act truly or falsely set down, there is no doubt which is to be chosen, no more than whether you had rather have Vespasian's picture right as he was, or, at the painter's pleasure, nothing resembling.

But if the question be for your own use and learning, whether it be better to have it set down as it should be or as it was, then certainly is more doctrinable 16 the feigned Cyrus in Xenophon than the true Cyrus in Justin; and the feigned Æneas in Virgil than the right Æneas in Dares Phrygius; as to a lady that desired to fashion her countenance to the best grace, a painter should more benefit her to portrait a most sweet face, writing Canidia upon it, than to paint Canidia as she was, who, Horace sweareth, was foul and ill-favored.

If the poet do his part aright, he will show you in Tantalus, Atreus, and such like, nothing that is not to be shunned; in Cyrus, Æneas, Ulysses, each thing to be followed. Where the historian, bound to tell things as things were, cannot be liberal—without he will be poetical—of a perfect pattern; but, as in Alexander, or Scipio himself, show doings, some to be liked, some to be misliked; and then how will you discern what to follow but by your own discretion, which you had without reading Quintus Curtius? And whereas a man may say, though in universal consideration of doctrine the poet prevaileth, yet that the history, in his saying such a thing was done, doth warrant a man more in that he shall follow,—the answer is manifest: that if he stand upon that was, as if he should argue, because it rained yesterday therefore it should rain to-day, then indeed it hath some advantage to a gross conceit.

But if he know an example only informs a conjectured likelihood, and so go by reason, the poet doth so far exceed him as he is to frame his example to that which is most reasonable, be it in warlike, politic, or private matters; where the historian in his bare was hath many times that which we call fortune to overrule the best wisdom. Many times he must tell events whereof he can yield no cause; or if he do, it must be poetically.

For, that a feigned example hath as much force to teach as a true example—for as for to move, it is clear, since the feigned may be tuned to the highest key of passion—let us take one example wherein a poet and a historian do concur. Herodotus and Justin do both testify that Zopyrus, king Darius' faithful servant, seeing his master long resisted by the rebellious Babylonians, feigned himself in extreme disgrace of his king; for verifying of which he caused his own nose and ears to be cut off, and so flying to the Babylonians, was received, and for his known valor so far credited, that he did find means to deliver them over to Darius. Muchlike matter doth Livy record of Tarquinius and his son.

Xenophon excellently feigneth such another stratagem, performed by Abradatas in Cyrus' behalf. Now would I fain know, if occasion be presented unto you to serve your prince by such an honest dissimulation, why do you not as well learn it of Xenophon's fiction as of the other's verity? and, truly, so much the better, as you shall save your nose by the bargain; for Abradatas did not counterfeit so far.

So, then, the best of the historian is subject to the poet; for whatsoever action or faction, whatsoever counsel, policy, or war-stratagem the historian is bound to recite, that may the poet, if he list, with his imitation make his own, beautifying it both for further teaching and more delighting, as it pleaseth him; having all, from Dante's Heaven to his Hell, under the authority of his pen. Which if I be asked what poets have done? so as I might well name some, yet say I, and say again, I speak of the art, and not of the artificer.

Now, to that which is commonly attributed to the praise of history, in respect of the notable learning is gotten by marking the success, as though therein a man should see virtue exalted and vice punished,—truly that commendation is peculiar to poetry and far off from history. For, indeed, poetry ever setteth virtue so out in her best colors, making Fortune her well-waiting handmaid, that one must needs be enamored of her. Well may you see Ulysses in a storm, and in other hard plights; but they are but exercises of patience and magnanimity, to make them shine the more in the near following prosperity. And, of the contrary part, if evil men come to the stage, they ever go out—as the tragedy writer answered to one that misliked the show of such persons—so manacled as they little animate folks to follow them.

But the historian, being captived to the truth of a foolish world, is many times a terror from well-doing, and an encouragement to unbridled wickedness. For see we not valiant Miltiades rot in his fetters? The just Phocion and the accomplished Socrates put to death like traitors? The cruel Severus live prosperously? The excellent Severus miserably murdered? Sylla and Marius dying in their beds? Pompey and Cicero slain then, when they would have thought exile a happiness? See we not virtuous Cato driven to kill himself, and rebel Cæsar so advanced that his name yet, after sixteen hundred years, lasteth in the highest honour? And mark but even Cæsar's own words of the forenamed Sylla—who in that only did honestly, to put down his dishonest tyranny—literas nescivit: as if want of learning caused him to do well.

He meant it not by poetry, which, not content with earthly plagues, deviseth new punishments in hell for tyrants; nor yet by philosophy, which teacheth occidendos esse; but, no doubt, by skill in history, for that indeed can afford you Cypselus, Periander, Phalaris, Dionysius, and I know not how many more of the same kennel, that speed well enough in their abominable injustice or usurpation.

I conclude, therefore, that he excelleth history, not only in furnishing the mind with knowledge, but in setting it forward to that which deserveth to be called and accounted good; which setting forward, and moving to well-doing, indeed setteth the laurel crown upon the poet as victorious, not only of the historian, but over the philosopher, howsoever in teaching it may be questionable. For suppose it be granted—that which I suppose with great reason may be denied—that the philosopher, in respect of his methodical proceeding, teach more perfectly than the poet, yet do I think that no man is so much as to compare the philosopher in moving with the poet.

And that moving is of a higher degree than teaching, it may by this appear, that it is well nigh both the cause and the effect of teaching; for who will be taught, if he be not moved with desire to be taught? And what so much good doth that teaching bring forth—I speak still of moral doctrine—as that it moveth one to do that which it doth teach? For, as Aristotle saith, it is but must be the fruit; and how cannot be, without being moved to practise, it is no hard matter to consider.

The philosopher showeth you the way, he informeth you of the particularities, as well of the tediousness of the way, as of the pleasant lodging you shall have when your journey is ended, as of the many by-turnings that may divert you from your way; but this is to no man but to him that will read him, and read him with attentive, studious painfulness; which constant desire whosoever hath in him, hath already passed half the hardness of the way, and therefore is beholding to the philosopher but for the other half. Nay, truly, learned men have learnedly thought, that where once reason hath so much overmastered passion as that the mind hath a free desire to do well, the inward light each mind hath in itself is as good as a philosopher's book; since in nature we know it is well to do well, and what is well and what is evil, although not in the words of art which philosophers bestow upon us; for out of natural conceit the philosophers drew it. But to be moved to do that which we know, or to be moved with desire to know, hoc opus, hic labor est.

Now therein of all sciences—I speak still of human, and according to the human conceit—is our poet the monarch. For he doth not only show the way, but giveth so sweet a prospect into the way as will entice any man to enter into it. Nay, he doth, as if your journey should lie through a fair vineyard, at the very first give you a cluster of grapes, that full of that taste you may long to pass further.

He beginneth not with obscure definitions, which must blur the margent with interpretations, and load the memory with doubtfulness. But he cometh to you with words set in delightful proportion, either accompanied with, or prepared for, the well-enchanting skill of music; and with a tale, forsooth, he cometh unto you, with a tale which holdeth children from play, and old men from the chimney-corner, and, pretending no more, doth intend the winning of the mind from wickedness to virtue; even as the child is often brought to take most wholesome things, by hiding them in such other as to have a pleasant taste,—which, if one should begin to tell them the nature of the aloes or rhubarb they should receive, would sooner take their physic at their ears than at their mouth.

So is it in men, most of which are childish in the best things, till they be cradled in their graves,—glad they will be to hear the tales of Hercules, Achilles, Cyrus, Æneas; and, hearing them, must needs hear the right description of wisdom, valor, and justice; which, if they had been barely, that is to say philosophically, set out, they would swear they be brought to school again. That imitation whereof poetry is, hath the most conveniency to nature of all other; insomuch that, as Aristotle saith, those things which in themselves are horrible, as cruel battles, unnatural monsters, are made in poetical imitation delightful. Truly, I have known men, that even with reading Amadis de Gaule, which, God knoweth, wanteth much of a perfect poesy, have found their hearts moved to the exercise of courtesy, liberality, and especially courage. Who readeth Æneas carrying old Anchises on his back, that wisheth not it were his fortune to perform so excellent an act? Whom do not those words of Turnus move, the tale of Turnus having planted his image in the imagination?

Fugientem haec terra videbit?
Usque adeone mori miserum est?

Where the philosophers, as they scorn to delight, so must they be content little to move—saving wrangling whether virtue be the chief or the only good, whether the contemplative or the active life do excel—which Plato and Boethius well knew, and therefore made Mistress Philosophy very often borrow the masking raiment of Poesy. For even those hard-hearted evil men who think virtue a school-name, and know no other good but indulgere genio, 25 and therefore despise the austere admonitions of the philosopher, and feel not the inward reason they stand upon, yet will be content to be delighted, which is all the good-fellow poet seemeth to promise; and so steal to see the form of goodness—which seen, they cannot but love—ere themselves be aware, as if they took a medicine of cherries.

Infinite proofs of the strange effects of this poetical invention might be alleged; only two shall serve, which are so often remembered as I think all men know them. The one of Menenius Agrippa, who, when the whole people of Rome had resolutely divided themselves from the senate, with apparent show of utter ruin, though he were, for that time, an excellent orator, came not among them upon trust either of figurative speeches or cunning insinuations, and much less with far-fetched maxims of philosophy, which, especially if they were Platonic, they must have learned geometry before they could well have conceived; but, forsooth, he behaves himself like a homely and familiar poet. He telleth them a tale, that there was a time when all parts of the body made a mutinous conspiracy against the belly, which they thought devoured the fruits of each other's labor; they concluded they would let so unprofitable a spender starve.

In the end, to be short—for the tale is notorious, and as notorious that it was a tale—with punishing the belly they plagued themselves. This, applied by him, wrought such effect in the people, as I never read that ever words brought forth but then so sudden and so good an alteration; for upon reasonable conditions a perfect reconcilement ensued.

The other is of Nathan the prophet, who, when the holy David had so far forsaken God as to confirm adultery with murder, when he was to do the tenderest office of a friend, in laying his own shame before his eyes,—sent by God to call again so chosen a servant, how doth he it but by telling of a man whose beloved lamb was ungratefully taken from his bosom? The application most divinely true, but the discourse itself feigned; which made David (I speak of the second and instrumental cause) as in a glass to see his own filthiness, as that heavenly Psalm of Mercy well testifieth.

By these, therefore, examples and reasons, I think it may be manifest that the poet, with that same hand of delight, doth draw the mind more effectually than any other art doth. And so a conclusion not unfitly ensueth: that as virtue is the most excellent resting-place for all wordly learning to make his end of, so poetry, being the most familiar to teach it, and most princely to move towards it, in the most excellent work is the most excellent workman.

But I am content not only to decipher him by his works—although works in commendation or dispraise must ever hold a high authority—but more narrowly will examine his parts; so that, as in a man, though all together may carry a presence full of majesty and beauty, perchance in some one defectious piece we may find a blemish.

Now in his parts, kinds, or species, as you list to term them, it is to be noted that some poesies have coupled together two or three kinds,—as tragical and comical, whereupon is risen the tragi-comical; some, in the like manner, have mingled prose and verse, as Sannazzaro and Boethius; some have mingled matters heroical and pastoral; but that cometh all to one in this question, for, if severed they be good, the conjunction cannot be hurtful. Therefore, perchance forgetting some, and leaving some as needless to be remembered, it shall not be amiss in a word to cite the special kinds, to see what faults may be found in the right use of them.

Is it then the pastoral poem which is misliked?—for perchance where the hedge is lowest they will soonest leap over. Is the poor pipe disdained, which sometimes out of Meliboeœus' mouth can show the misery of people under hard lords and ravening soldiers, and again, by Tityrus, what blessedness is derived to them that lie lowest from the goodness of them that sit highest? sometimes, under the pretty tales of wolves and sheep, can include the whole considerations of wrong-doing and patience; sometimes show that contention for trifles can get but a trifling victory; where perchance a man may see that even Alexander and Darius, when they strave who should be cock of this world's dunghill, the benefit they got was that the after-livers may say:

Hæc memini et victum frustra contendere Thyrsim;
Ex illo Corydon, Corydon est tempore nobis.

Or is it the lamenting elegiac, which in a kind heart would move rather pity than blame; who bewaileth, with the great philosopher Heraclitus, the weakness of mankind and the wretchedness of the world; who surely is to be praised, either for compassionate accompanying just causes of lamentation, or for rightly painting out how weak be the passions of wofulness?

Is it the bitter and wholesome iambic, who rubs the galled mind, in making shame the trumpet of villainy with bold and open crying out against naughtiness?

Or the satiric? who

Omne vafer vitium ridenti tangit amico;

who sportingly never leaveth till he make a man laugh at folly, and at length ashamed to laugh at himself, which he cannot avoid without avoiding the folly; who, while circum præcordia ludit, giveth us to feel how many headaches a passionate life bringeth us to,—how, when all is done,

Est Ulubris, animus si nos non deficit æquus.

No, perchance it is the comic; whom naughty play-makers and stage—keepers have justly made odious. To the argument of abuse I will answer after. Only thus much now is to be said, that the comedy in an imitation of the common errors of our life, which he representeth in the most ridiculous and scornful sort that may be, so as it is impossible that any beholder can be content to be such a one. Now, as in geometry the oblique must be known as well as the right, and in arithmetic the odd as well as the even; so in the actions of our life who seeth not the filthiness of evil, wanteth a great foil to perceive the beauty of virtue. This doth the comedy handle so, in our private and domestical matters, as with hearing it we get, as it were, an experience what is to be looked for of a niggardly Demea, of a crafty Davus, of a flattering Gnatho, of a vain-glorious Thraso; and not only to know what effects are to be expected, but to know who be such, by the signifying badge given them by the comedian. And little reason hath any man to say that men learn evil by seeing it so set out; since, as I said before, there is no man living, but by the force truth hath in nature, no sooner seeth these men play their parts, but wisheth them in pistrinum, although perchance the sack of his own faults lie so behind his back, that he seeth not himself to dance the same measure,—whereto yet nothing can more open his eyes than to find his own actions contemptibly set forth.

So that the right use of comedy will, I think, by nobody be blamed, and much less of the high and excellent tragedy, that openeth the greatest wounds, and showeth forth the ulcers that are covered with tissue; that maketh kings fear to be tyrants, and tyrants manifest their tyrannical humors; that with stirring the effects of admiration and commiseration teacheth the uncertainty of this world, and upon how weak foundations gilden roofs are builded; that maketh us know:

Qui sceptra sævus duro imperio regit,
Timet timentes, metus in auctorem redit.

But how much it can move, Plutarch yieldeth a notable testimony of the abominable tyrant Alexander Pheræus; from whose eyes a tragedy, well made and represented, drew abundance of tears, who without all pity had murdered infinite numbers, and some of his own blood; so as he that was not ashamed to make matters for tragedies, yet could not resist the sweet violence of a tragedy. And if it wrought no further good in him, it was that he, in despite of himself, withdrew himself from hearkening to that which might mollify his hardened heart. But it is not the tragedy they do mislike, for it were too absurd to cast out so excellent a representation of whatsoever is most worthy to be learned.

Is it the lyric that most displeaseth, who with his tuned lyre and well accorded voice, giveth praise, the reward of virtue, to virtuous acts; who giveth moral precepts and natural problems; who sometimes raiseth up his voice to the height of the heavens, in singing the lauds of the immortal God? Certainly I must confess mine own barbarousness; I never heard the old song of Percy and Douglas that I found not my heart moved more than with a trumpet; and yet it is sung but by some blind crowder, with no rougher voice than rude style; which being so evil apparelled in the dust and cobwebs of that uncivil age, what would it work, trimmed in the gorgeous eloquence of Pindar? In Hungary I have seen it the manner of all feasts, and other such meetings, to have songs of their ancestors' valor, which that right soldierlike nation think the chiefest kindlers of brave courage.

The incomparable Lacedæmonians did not only carry that kind of music ever with them to the field, but even at home, as such songs were made, so were they all content to be singers of them; when the lusty men were to tell what they did, the old men what they had done, and the young men what they would do. And where a man may say that Pindar many times praiseth highly victories of small moment, matters rather of sport than virtue; as it may be answered, it was the fault of the poet, and not of the poetry, so indeed the chief fault was in the time and custom of the Greeks, who set those toys at so high a price that Philip of Macedon reckoned a horserace won at Olympus among his three fearful felicities. But as the unimitable Pindar often did, so is that kind most capable and most fit to awake the thoughts from the sleep of idleness, to embrace honorable enterprises.

There rests the heroical, whose very name, I think, should daunt all backbiters. For by what conceit can a tongue be directed to speak evil of that which draweth with it no less champions than Achilles, Cyrus, Æneas, Turnus Tydeus, Rinaldo? who doth not only teach and move to a truth, but teacheth and moveth to the most high and excellent truth; who maketh magnanimity and justice shine through all misty fearfulness and foggy desires; who, if the saying of Plato and Tully be true, that who could see virtue would be wonderfully ravished with the love of her beauty, this man setteth her out to make her more lovely, in her holiday apparel, to the eye of any that will deign not to disdain until they understand. But if anything be already said in the defence of sweet poetry, all concurreth to the maintaining the heroical, which is not only a kind, but the best and most accomplished kind of poetry. For, as the image of each action stirreth and instructeth the mind, so the lofty image of such worthies most inflameth the mind with desire to be worthy, and informs with counsel how to be worthy.

Only let Æneas be worn in the tablet of your memory, how he governeth himself in the ruin of his country; in the preserving his old father, and carrying away his religious ceremonies; in obeying the god's commandment to leave Dido, though not only all passionate kindness, but even the human consideration of virtuous gratefulness, would have craved other of him; how in storms, how in sports, how in war, how in peace, how a fugitive, how victorious, how besieged, how besieging, how to strangers, how to allies, how to enemies, how to his own; lastly, how in his inward self, and how in his outward government; and I think, in a mind most prejudiced with a prejudicating humour, he will be found in excellency fruitful,—yea, even as Horace saith, melius Chrysippo et Crantore. But truly I imagine if falleth out with these poet-whippers as with some good women who often are sick, but in faith they cannot tell where. So the name of poetry is odious to them, but neither his cause nor effects, neither the sum that contains him nor the particularities descending from him, give any fast handle to their carping dispraise.

Since, then, poetry is of all human learnings the most ancient and of most fatherly antiquity, as from whence other learnings have taken their beginnings; since it is so universal that no learned nation doth despise it, nor barbarous nation is without it; since both Roman and Greek gave divine names unto it, the one of "prophesying," the other of "making," and that indeed that name of "making" is fit for him, considering that whereas other arts retain themselves within their subjects, and receive, as it were, their being from it, the poet only bringeth his own stuff, and doth not learn a conceit out of a matter, but maketh matter for a conceit; since neither his description nor his end containeth any evil, the thing described cannot be evil; since his effects be so good as to teach goodness, and delight the learners of it; since therein—namely in moral doctrine, the chief of all knowledges—he doth not only far pass the historian, but for instructing is well nigh comparable to the philosopher, and for moving leaveth him behind him; since the Holy Scripture, wherein there is no uncleanness, hath whole parts in it poetical, and that even our Saviour Christ vouchsafed to use the flowers of it; since all his kinds are not only in their united forms, but in their several dissections fully commendable; I think, and think I think rightly, the laurel crown appointed for triumphant captains doth worthily, of all other learnings, honour the poet's triumph.

But because we have ears as well as tongues, and that the lightest reasons that may be will seem to weigh greatly, if nothing be put in the counter-balance, let us hear, and, as well as we can, ponder, what objections be made against this art, which may be worthy either of yielding or answering.

First, truly, I note not only in these, poet-haters, but in all that kind of people who seek a praise by dispraising others, that they do prodigally spend a great many wandering words in quips and scoffs, carping and taunting at each thing which, by stirring the spleen, may stay the brain from a through-beholding the worthiness of the subject. Those kind of objections, as they are full of a very idle easiness—since there is nothing of so sacred a majesty but that an itching tongue may rub itself upon it—so deserve they no other answer, but, instead of laughing at the jest, to laugh at the jester. We know a playing wit can praise the discretion of an ass, the comfortableness of being in debt, and the jolly commodity of being sick of the plague. So of the contrary side, if we will turn Ovid's verse,

Ut lateat virtus proximitate mali,

"that good lie hid in nearness of the evil," Agrippa will be as merry in showing the vanity of science, as Erasmus was in commending of folly; neither shall any man or matter escape some touch of these smiling railers. But for Erasmus and Agrippa, they had another foundation than the superficial part would promise. Marry, these other pleasant fault-finders, who will correct the verb before they understand the noun, and confute others' knowledge before they confirm their own, I would have them only remember that scoffing cometh not of wisdom; so as the best title in true English they get with their merriments is to be called good fools,—for so have our grave forefathers ever termed that humorous kind of jesters.

But that which giveth greatest scope to their scorning humour is riming and versing. It is already said, and as I think truly said, it is not riming and versing that maketh poesy. One may be a poet without versing, and a versifier without poetry. But yet presuppose it were inseparable—as indeed it seemeth Scaliger judgeth—truly it were an inseparable commendation. For if oratio next to ratio, speech next to reason, be the greatest gift bestowed upon mortality, that cannot be praiseless which doth most polish that blessing of speech; which considereth each word, not only as a man may say by his forcible quality, but by his best-measured quantity; carrying even in themselves a harmony,—without, perchance, number, measure, order, proportion be in our time grown odious.

But lay aside the just praise it hath by being the only fit speech for music—music, I say, the most divine striker of the senses—thus much is undoubtedly true, that if reading be foolish without remembering, memory being the only treasurer of knowledge, those words which are fittest for memory are likewise most convenient for knowledge. Now that verse far exceedeth prose in the knitting up of the memory, the reason is manifest; the words, besides their delight, which hath a great affinity to memory, being so set, as one cannot be lost but the whole work fails; which, accusing itself, calleth the remembrance back to itself, and so most strongly confirmeth it.

Besides, one word so, as it were, begetting another, as, be it in rime or measured verse, by the former a man shall have a near guess to the follower. Lastly, even they that have taught the art of memory have showed nothing so apt for it as a certain room divided into many places, well and thoroughly known; now that hath the verse in effect perfectly, every word having his natural seat, which seat must needs make the word remembered. But what needeth more in a thing so known to all men? Who is it that ever was a scholar that doth not carry away some verses of Virgil, Horace, or Cato, which in his youth he learned, and even to his old age serve him for hourly lessons? as:

Percontatorem fugito, nam garrulus idem est.
Dum sibi quisque placet, credula turba sumus.

But the fitness it hath for memory is notably proved by all delivery of arts, wherein, for the most part, from grammar to logic, mathematic, physic, and the rest, the rules chiefly necessary to be borne away are compiled in verses. So that verse being in itself sweet and orderly, and being best for memory, the only handle of knowledge, it must be in jest that any man can speak against it. Now then go we to the most important imputations laid to the poor poets; for aught I can yet learn they are these. First, that there being many other more fruitful knowledges, a man might better spend his time in them than in this.

Secondly, that it is the mother of lies.

Thirdly, that it is the nurse of abuse, infecting us with many pestilent desires, with a siren's sweetness drawing the mind to the serpent's tail of sinful fancies,—and herein especially comedies give the largest field to ear, as Chaucer saith; how, both in other nations and in ours, before poets did soften us, we were full of courage, given to martial exercises, the pillars of manlike liberty, and not lulled asleep in shady idleness with poets' pastimes. And, lastly and chiefly, they cry out with an open mouth, as if they had overshot Robin Hood, that Plato banished them out of his Commonwealth. Truly this is much, if there be much truth in it.

First, to the first, that a man might better spend his time is a reason indeed; but it doth, as they say, but petere principium. For if it be, as I affirm, that no learning is so good as that which teacheth and moveth to virtue, and that none can both teach and move thereto so much as poesy, then is the conclusion manifest that ink and paper cannot be to a more profitable purpose employed. And certainly, though a man should grant their first assumption, it should follow, methinks, very unwillingly, that good is not good because better is better. But I still and utterly deny that there is sprung out of earth a more fruitful knowledge.

To the second, therefore, that they should be the principal liars, I answer paradoxically, but truly, I think truly, that of all writers under the sun the poet is the least liar; and though he would, as a poet can scarcely be a liar. The astronomer, with his cousin the geometrician, can hardly escape when they take upon them to measure the height of the stars. How often, think you, do the physicians lie, when they aver things good for sicknesses, which afterwards send Charon a great number of souls drowned in a potion before they come to his ferry? And no less of the rest which take upon them to affirm. Now for the poet, he nothing affirmeth, and therefore never lieth.

For, as I take it, to lie is to affirm that to be true which is false; so as the other artists, and especially the historian, affirming many things, can, in the cloudy knowledge of mankind, hardly escape from many lies. But the poet, as I said before, never affirmeth. The poet never maketh any circles about your imagination, to conjure you to believe for true what he writeth. He citeth not authorities of other histories, but even for his entry calleth the sweet Muses to inspire into him a good invention; in troth, not laboring to tell you what is or is not, but what should or should not be.

And therefore though he recount things not true, yet because he telleth them not for true he lieth not; without we will say that Nathan lied in his speech, before alleged, to David; which, as a wicked man durst scarce say, so think I none so simple would say that Æsop lied in the tales of his beasts; for who thinketh that Æsop wrote it for actually true, were well worthy to have his name chronicled among the beasts he writeth of. What child is there that, coming to a play, and seeing Thebes written in great letters upon an old door, doth believe that it is Thebes? If then a man can arrive at that child's-age, to know that the poet's persons and doings are but pictures what should be, and not stories what have been, they will never give the lie to things not affirmatively but allegorically and figuratively written.

And therefore, as in history looking for truth, they may go away full-fraught with falsehood, so in poesy looking but for fiction, they shall use the narration but as an imaginative ground—plot of a profitable invention. But hereto is replied that the poets give names to men they write of, which argueth a conceit of an actual truth, and so, not being true, proveth a falsehood. And doth the lawyer lie then, when, under the names of John of the Stile, and John of the Nokes, he putteth his case? But that is easily answered: their naming of men is but to make their picture the more lively, and not to build any history. Painting men, they cannot leave men nameless. We see we cannot play at chess but that we must give names to our chess-men; and yet, me thinks, he were a very partial champion of truth that would say we lied for giving a piece of wood the reverend title of a bishop.

The poet nameth Cyrus and Æneas no other way than to show what men of their fames, fortunes, and estates should do. Their third is, how much it abuseth men's wit, training it to wanton sinfulness and lustful love. For indeed that is the principal, if not the only, abuse I can hear alleged. They say the comedies rather teach than reprehend amorous conceits. They say the lyric is larded with passionate sonnets, the elegiac weeps the want of his mistress, and that even to the heroical Cupid hath ambitiously climbed.

Alas! Love, I would thou couldst as well defend thyself as thou canst offend others! I would those on whom thou dost attend could either put thee away, or yield good reason why they keep thee! But grant love of beauty to be a beastly fault, although it be very hard, since only man, and no beast, hath that gift to discern beauty; grant that lovely name of Love to deserve all hateful reproaches, although even some of my masters the philosophers spent a good deal of their lamp-oil in setting forth the excellency of it; grant, I say, whatsoever they will have granted that not only love, but lust, but vanity, but, if they list, scurrility possesseth many leaves of the poets' books; yet think I when this is granted, they will find their sentence may with good manners put the last words foremost, and not say that poetry abuseth man's wit, but that man's wit abuseth poetry. For I will not deny, but that man's wit may make poesy, which should be, which some learned have defined, figuring forth good things, to be, which doth contrariwise infect the fancy with unworthy objects; as the painter that should give to the eye either some excellent perspective, or some fine picture fit for building or fortification, or containing in it some notable example, as Abraham sacrificing his son Isaac, Judith killing Holofernes, David fighting with Goliath, may leave those, and please an ill pleased eye with wanton shows of better-hidden matters.

But what! shall the abuse of a thing make the right use odious? Nay, truly, though I yield that poesy may not only be abused, but that being abused, by the reason of his sweet charming force, it can do more hurt than any other army of words, yet shall it be so far from concluding that the abuse should give reproach to the abused, that contrariwise it is a good reason, that whatsoever, being abused, doth most harm, being rightly used—and upon the right use each thing receiveth his title—doth most good.

Do we not see the skill of physic, the best rampire to our often-assaulted bodies, being abused, teach poison, the most violent destroyer? Doth not knowledge of law, whose end is to even and right all things, being abused, grow the crooked fosterer of horrible injuries? Doth not, to go in the highest, God's word abused breed heresy, and his name abused become blasphemy? Truly a needle cannot do much hurt, and as truly—with leave of ladies be it spoken—it cannot do much good. With a sword thou mayst kill thy father, and with a sword thou mayst defend thy prince and country. So that, as in their calling poets the fathers of lies they say nothing, so in this their argument of abuse they prove the commendation.

They allege herewith, that before poets began to be in price our nation hath set their hearts' delight upon action, and not upon imagination; rather doing things worthy to be written, than writing things fit to be done. What that before-time was. I think scarcely Sphinx can tell; since no memory is so ancient that hath the precedence of poetry. And certain it is that, in our plainest homeliness, yet never was the Albion nation without poetry. Marry, this argument, though it be levelled against poetry, yet is it indeed a chainshot against all learning,—or bookishness, as they commonly term it. Of such mind were certain Goths, of whom it is written that, having in the spoil of a famous city taken a fair library, one hangman—belike fit to execute the fruits of their wits—who had murdered a great number of bodies, would have set fire in it. "No," said another very gravely, "take heed what you do; for while they are busy about these toys, we shall with more leisure conquer their countries."

This, indeed, is the ordinary doctrine of ignorance, and many words sometimes I have heard spent in it; but because this reason is generally against all learning, as well as poetry, or rather all learning but poetry; because it were too large a digression to handle, or at least too superfluous, since it is manifest that all government of action is to be gotten by knowledge, and knowledge best by gathering many knowledges, which is reading; I only, with Horace, to him that is of that opinion

Jubeo stultum esse libenter;

for as for poetry itself, it is the freest from this objection, for poetry is the companion of the camps. I dare undertake, Orlando Furioso or honest King Arthur will never displease a soldier; but the quiddity of ens, and prima materia, will hardly agree with a corselet. And therefore, as I said in the beginning, even Turks and Tartars are delighted with poets. Homer, a Greek, flourished before Greece flourished; and if to a slight conjecture a conjecture may be opposed, truly it may seem, that as by him their learned men took almost their first light of knowledge, so their active men received their first motions of courage. Only Alexander's example may serve, who by Plutarch is accounted of such virtue, that Fortune was not his guide but his footstool; whose acts speak for him, though Plutarch did not; indeed the phoenix of warlike princes.

This Alexander left his schoolmaster, living Aristotle, behind him, but took dead Homer with him. He put the philosopher Callisthenes to death for his seeming philosophical, indeed mutinous, stubbornness; but the chief thing he was ever heard to wish for was that Homer had been alive. He well found he received more bravery of mind by the pattern of Achilles, than by hearing the definition of fortitude. And therefore if Cato misliked Fulvius for carrying Ennius with him to the field, it may be answered that if Cato misliked it, the noble Fulvius liked it, or else he had not done it.

For it was not the excellent Cato Uticensis, whose authority I would much more have reverenced; but it was the former, in truth a bitter punisher of faults, but else a man that had never sacrificed to the Graces.

He misliked and cried out upon all Greek learning; and yet, being fourscore years old, began to learn it, belike fearing that Pluto understood not Latin. Indeed, the Roman laws allowed no person to be carried to the wars but he that was in the soldiers' roll. And therefore though Cato misliked his unmustered person, he misliked not his work. And if he had, Scipio Nasica, judged by common consent the best Roman, loved him. Both the other Scipio brothers, who had by their virtues no less surnames than of Asia and Afric, so loved him that they caused his body to be buried in their sepulchre. So as Cato's authority being but against his person, and that answered with so far greater than himself, is herein of no validity.

But now, indeed, my burthen is great, that Plato's name is laid upon me, whom I must confess, of all philosophers I have ever esteemed most worthy of reverence; and with great reason, since of all philosophers he is the most poetical; yet if he will defile the fountain out of which his flowing streams have proceeded, let us boldly examine with what reasons he did it. First, truly, a man might maliciously object that Plato, being a philosopher, was a natural enemy of poets.

For, indeed, after the philosophers had picked out of the sweet mysteries of poetry the right discerning true points of knowledge, they forthwith, putting it in method, and making a school—art of that which the poets did only teach by a divine delightfulness, beginning to spurn at their guides, like ungrateful prentices were not content to set up shops for themselves, but sought by all means to discredit their masters;

which by the force of delight being barred them, the less they could overthrow them the more they hated them.

For, indeed, they found for Homer seven cities strave who should have him for their citizen; where many cities banished philosophers, as not fit members to live among them. For only repeating certain of Euripides' verses, many Athenians had their lives saved of the Syracusans, where the Athenians themselves thought many philosophers unworthy to live. Certain poets as Simonides and Pindar, had so prevailed with Heiro the First, that of a tyrant they made him a just king; where Plato could do so little with Dionysius, that he himself of a philosopher was made a slave.

But who should do thus, I confess, should requite the objections made against poets with like cavillations against philosophers; as likewise one should do that should bid one read Phædrus or Symposium in Plato, or the Discourse of Love in Plutarch, and see whether any poet do authorize abominable filthiness, as they do. Again, a man might ask out of what commonwealth Plato doth banish them. In sooth, thence where he himself alloweth community of women. So as belike this banishment grew not for effeminate wantonness, since little should poetical sonnets be hurtful when a man might have what woman he listed. But I honour philosophical instructions, and bless the wits which bred them, so as they be not abused, which is likewise stretched to poetry.

Saint Paul himself, who yet, for the credit of poets, allegeth twice two poets, and one of them by the name of a prophet, setteth a watchword upon philosophy,—indeed upon the abuse. So doth Plato upon the abuse, not upon poetry. Plato found fault that the poets of his time filled the world with wrong opinions of the gods, making light tales of that unspotted essence, and therefore would not have the youth depraved with such opinions. Herein may much be said; let this suffice: the poets did not induce such opinions, but did imitate those opinions already induced. For all the Greek stories can well testify that the very religion of that time stood upon many and many-fashioned gods; not taught so by the poets, but followed according to their nature of imitation.

Who list may read in Plutarch the discourses of Isis and Osiris, of the Cause why Oracles ceased, of the Divine Providence, and see whether the theology of that nation stood not upon such dreams,—which the poets indeed superstitiously observed; and truly, since they had not the light of Christ, did much better in it than the philosophers, who, shaking off superstition, brought in atheism.

Plato therefore, whose authority I had much rather justly construe than unjustly resist, meant not in general of poets, in those words of which Julius Scaliger saith, Qua authoritate barbari quidam atque hispidi, abuti velint ad poetas e republica exigendos; but only meant to drive out those wrong opinions of the Deity, whereof now, without further law, Christianity hath taken away all the hurtful belief, perchance, as he thought, nourished by the then esteemed poets. And a man need go no further than to Plato himself to know his meaning; who, in his dialogue called Ion, giveth high and rightly divine commendation unto poetry.

So as Plato, banishing the abuse, not the thing, not banishing it, but giving due honour unto it, shall be our patron and not our adversary. For, indeed, I had much rather, since truly I may do it, show their mistaking of Plato, under whose lion's skin they would make an ass—like braying against poesy, than go about to overthrow his authority; whom, the wiser a man is, the more just cause he shall find to have in admiration; especially since he attributeth unto poesy more than myself do, namely to be a very inspiring of a divine force, far above man's wit, as in the forenamed dialogue is apparent.

Of the other side, who would show the honors have been by the best sort of judgments granted them, a whole sea of examples would present themselves: Alexanders, Cæsars, Scipios, all favorers of poets; Lælius, called the Roman Socrates, himself a poet, so as part of Heautontimoroumenos in Terence was supposed to be made by him. And even the Greek Socrates, whom Apollo confirmed to be the only wise man, is said to have spent part of his old time in putting Æsop's Fables into verses; and therefore full evil should it become his scholar, Plato, to put such words in his master's mouth against poets. But what needs more? Aristotle writes the Art of Poesy; and why, if it should not be written? Plutarch teacheth the use to be gathered of them; and how, if they should not be read? And who reads Plutarch's either history or philosophy, shall find he trimmeth both their garments with guards 39 of poesy. But I list not to defend poesy with the help of his underling historiography.

Let it suffice that it is a fit soil for praise to dwell upon; and what dispraise may set upon it, is either easily overcome, or transformed into just commendation. So that since the excellencies of it may be so easily and so justly confirmed, and the low-creeping objections so soon trodden down: it not being an art of lies, but of true doctrine; not of effeminateness, but of notable stirring of courage; not of abusing man's wit, but of strengthening man's wit; not banished, but honored by Plato; let us rather plant more laurels for to engarland our poets' heads—which honour of being laureate, as besides them only triumphant captains were, is a sufficient authority to show the price they ought to be held in—than suffer the ill-savored breath of such wrong speakers once to blow upon the clear springs of poesy.

But since I have run so long a career in this matter, methinks, before I give my pen a full stop, it shall be but a little more lost time to inquire why England, the mother of excellent minds, should be grown so hard a stepmother to poets; who certainly in wit ought to pass all others, since all only proceedeth from their wit, being indeed makers of themselves, not takers of others. How can I but exclaim,

Musa, mihi causas memora, quo numine læso?

Sweet poesy! that hath anciently had kings, emperors, senators, great captains, such as, besides a thousand others, David, Adrian, Sophocles, Germanicus, not only to favour poets, but to be poets; and of our nearer times can present for her patrons a Robert, King of Sicily; the great King Francis of France; King James of Scotland; such cardinals as Bembus and Bibbiena; such famous preachers and teachers as Beza and Melancthon; so learned philosophers as Fracastorius and Scaliger; so great orators as Pontanus and Muretus; so piercing wits as George Buchanan; so grave counsellors as—besides many, but before all—that Hospital of France, than whom, I think, that realm never brought forth a more accomplished judgement more firmly builded upon virtue; I say these, with numbers of others, not only to read others' poesies but to poetize for others' reading.

That poesy, thus embraced in all other places, should only find in our time a hard welcome in England, I think the very earth lamenteth it, and therefore decketh our soil with fewer laurels than it was accustomed. For heretofore poets have in England also flourished; and, which is to be noted, even in those time when the trumpet of Mars did sound loudest. And now that an over-faint quietness should seem to strew the house for poets, they are almost in as good reputation as the mountebanks at Venice. Truly even that, as of the one side it giveth great praise to poesy, which, li e Venus—but to better purpose—hath rather be troubled in the net with Mars, than enjoy the homely quiet of Vulcan; so serves it for a piece of a reason why they are less grateful to idle England, which now can scarce endure the pain of a pen. Upon this necessarily followeth, that base men with servile wits undertake it, who think it enough if they can be rewarded of the printer.

And so as Epaminondas is said, with the honour of his virtue to have made an office, by his exercising it, which before was contemptible, to become highly respected; so these men, no more but setting their names to it, by their own disgracefulness disgrace the most graceful poesy. For now, as if all the Muses were got with child to bring forth bastard poets, without any commission they do post over the banks of Helicon, till they make their readers more weary than posthorses; while, in the meantime, they, Queis meliore luto finxit præcordia Titan, are better content to suppress the outflowings of their wit, than by publishing them to be accounted knights of the same order.

But I that, before ever I dust aspire unto the dignity, am admitted into the company of the paper-blurrers, do find the very true cause of our wanting estimation is want of desert, taking upon us to be poets in despite of Pallas. Now wherein we want desert were a thank-worthy labor to express; but if I knew, I should have mended myself. But as I never desired the title, so have I neglected the means to come by it; only, overmastered by some thoughts, I yielded an inky tribute unto them. Marry, they that delight in poesy itself should seek to know what they do and how they do; and especially look themselves in an unflattering glass of reason, if they be inclinable unto it.

For poesy must not be drawn by the ears, it must be gently led, or rather it must lead; which was partly the cause that made the ancient learned affirm it was a divine gift, and no human skill, since all other knowledges lie ready for any that hath strength of wit, a poet no industry can make if his own genius be not carried into it. And therefore is it an old proverb: Orator fit, poeta nascitur. Yet confess I always that, as the fertilest ground must be manured, so must the highest-flying wit have a Dædalus to guide him.

That Dædalus, they say, both in this and in other, hath three wings to bear itself up into the air of due commendation: that is, art, imitation, and exercise. But these neither artificial rules nor imitative patterns, we much cumber ourselves withal. Exercise indeed we do, but that very fore-backwardly, for where we should exercise to know, we exercise as having known; and so is our brain delivered of much matter which never was begotten by knowledge. For there being two principal parts, matter to be expressed by words, and words to express the matter, in neither we use art or imitation rightly. Our matter is quodlibet indeed, though wrongly performing Ovid's verse, Quicquid conabar dicere, versus erat; never marshalling it into any assured rank, that almost the readers cannot tell where to find themselves.

Chaucer, undoubtedly, did excellently in his Troilus and Cressida; of whom, truly, I know not whether to marvel more, either that he in that misty time could see so clearly, or that we in this clear age walk so stumblingly after him. Yet had he great wants, fit to be forgiven in so revered antiquity. I account the Mirror of Magistrates meetly furnished of beautiful parts; and in the Earl of Surrey's lyrics many things tasting of a noble birth, and worthy of a noble mind. The Shepherd's Calendar hath much poetry in his eclogues, indeed worthy the reading, if I be not deceived.

That same framing of his style to an old rustic language I dare not allow, since neither Theocritus in Greek, Virgil in Latin, nor Sannazzaro in Italian did affect it. Besides these, I do not remember to have seen but few (to speak boldly) printed, that have poetical sinews in them. For proof whereof, let but most of the verses be put in prose, and then ask the meaning, and it will be found that one verse did but beget another, without ordering at the first what should be at the last; which becomes a confused mass of words, with a tinkling sound of rime, barely accompanied with reason.

Our tragedies and comedies not without cause cried out against, observing rules neither of honest civility nor of skilful poetry, excepting Gorboduc,—again I say of those that I have seen. Which notwithstanding as it is full of stately speeches and well-sounding phrases, climbing to the height of Seneca's style, and as full of notable morality, which it doth most delightfully teach, and so obtain the very end of poesy; yet in truth it is very defectious in the circumstances, which grieveth me, because it might not remain as an exact model of all tragedies. For it is faulty both in place and time, the two necessary companions of all corporal actions. For where the stage should always represent but one place, and the uttermost time presupposed in it should be, both by Aristotle's precept and common reason, but one day; there is both many days and many places inartificially imagined.

But if it be so in Gorboduc, how much more in all the rest? where you shall have Asia of the one side, and Afric of the other, and so many other under-kingdoms, that the player, when he cometh in, must ever begin with telling where he is, or else the tale will not be conceived. Now ye shall have three ladies walk to gather flowers, and then we must believe the stage to be a garden.

By and by we hear news of shipwreck in the same place, and then we are to blame if we accept it not for a rock. Upon the back of that comes out a hideous monster with fire and smoke, and then the miserable beholders are bound to take it for a cave. While in the mean time two armies fly in, represented with four swords and bucklers, and then what hard heart will not receive it for a pitched field?

Now of time they are much more liberal. For ordinary it is that two young princes fall in love; after many traverses she is got with child, delivered of a fair boy, he is lost, groweth a man, falleth in love, and is ready to get another child,—and all this in two hours' space; which how absurd it is in sense even sense may imagine, and art hath taught, and all ancient examples justified, and at this day the ordinary players in Italy will not err in. Yet will some bring in an example of Eunuchus in Terence, that containeth matter of two days, yet far short of twenty years. True it is, and so was it to be played in two days, and so fitted to the time it set forth. And though Plautus have in one place done amiss, let us hit with him, and not miss with him.

But they will say, How then shall we set forth a story which containeth both many places and many times? And do they not know that a tragedy is tied to the laws of poesy, and not of history; not bound to follow the story, but having liberty either to feign a quite new matter, or to frame the history to the most tragical conveniency? Again, many things may be told which cannot be showed,—if they know the difference betwixt reporting and representing. As for example I may speak, though I am here, of Peru, and in speech digress from that to the description of Calicut; but in action I cannot represent it without Pacolet's horse. And so was the manner the ancients took, by some Nuntius 46 to recount things done in former time or other place. Lastly, if they will represent a history, they must not, as Horace saith, begin ab ovo, but thee must come to the principal point of that one action which they will represent. By example this will be best expressed. I have a story of young Polydorus, delivered for safety's sake, with great riches, by his father Priamus to Polymnestor, King of Thrace, in the Trojan war time.

He, after some years, hearing the overthrow of Priamus, for to make the treasure his own murdereth the child; the body of the child is taken up by Hecuba; she, the same day, findeth a sleight to be revenged most cruelly of the tyrant. Where now would one of our tragedy writers begin, but with the delivery of the child? Then should he sail over into Thrace, and so spend I know not how many years, and travel numbers of places. But where doth Euripides? Even with the finding of the body, leaving the rest to be told by the spirit of Polydorus. This needs no further to be enlarged; the dullest wit may conceive it.

But, besides these gross absurdities, how all their plays be neither right tragedies nor right comedies, mingling kings and clowns, not because the matter so carrieth it, but thrust in the clown by head and shoulders to play a part in majestical matters, with neither decency nor discretion; so as neither the admiration and commiseration, nor the right sportfulness, is by their mongrel tragi-comedy obtained. I know Apuleius did somewhat so, but that is a thing recounted with space of time, not represented in one moment; and I know the ancients have one or two examples of tragi-comedies, as Plautus hath Amphytrio.

But, if we mark them well, we shall find that they never, or very daintily, match hornpipes and funerals. So falleth it out that, having indeed no right comedy in that comical part of our tragedy, we have nothing but scurrility, unworthy of any chaste ears, or some extreme show of doltishness, indeed fit to lift up a loud laughter, and nothing else; where the whole tract of a comedy should be full of delight, as the tragedy should be still maintained in a well-raised admiration.

But our comedians think there is no delight without laughter, which is very wrong; for though laughter may come with delight, yet cometh it not of delight, as though delight should be the cause of laughter; but well may one thing breed both together. Nay, rather in themselves they have, as it were, a kind of contrariety. For delight we scarcely do, but in things that have a conveniency to ourselves, or to the general nature; laughter almost ever cometh of things most disproportioned to ourselves and nature.

Delight hath a joy in it either permanent or present; laughter hath only a scornful tickling. For example, we are ravished with delight to see a fair woman, and yet are far from being moved to laughter. We laugh at deformed creatures, wherein certainly we cannot delight. We delight in good chances, we laugh at mischances. We delight to hear the happiness of our friends and country, at which he were worthy to be laughed at that would laugh. We shall, contrarily, laugh sometimes to find a matter quite mistaken and go down the hill against the bias, in the mouth of some such men, as for the respect of them one shall be heartily sorry he cannot choose but laugh, and so is rather pained than delighted with laughter. Yet deny I not but that they may go well together. For as in Alexander's picture well set out we delight without laughter, and in twenty mad antics we laugh without delight; so in Hercules, painted with his great beard and furious countenance, in woman's attire, spinning at Omphale's commandment, it breedeth both delight and laughter; for the representing of so strange a power in love, procureth delight, and the scornfulness of the action stirreth laughter.

But I speak to this purpose, that all the end of the comical part be not upon such scornful matters as stir laughter only, but mixed with it that delightful teaching which is the end of poesy. And the great fault, even in that point of laughter, and forbidden plainly by Aristotle, is that they stir laughter in sinful things, which are rather execrable than ridiculous; or in miserable, which are rather to be pitied than scorned. For what is it to make folks gape at a wretched beggar or a beggarly clown, or, against law of hospitality, to jest at strangers because they speak not English so well as we do? what do we learn? since it is certain:

Nil habet infelix paupertas durius in se,
Quam quod ridiculos homines facit.

But rather a busy loving courtier; a heartless threatening Thraso; a self-wise-seeming schoolmaster; a wry transformed traveller: these if we saw walk in stage-names, which we play naturally, therein were delightful laughter and teaching delightfulness,—as in the other, the tragedies of Buchanan do justly bring forth a divine admiration.

But I have lavished out too many words of this playmatter.

I do it, because as they are excelling parts of poesy, so is there none so much used in England, and none can be more pitifully abused; which, like an unmannerly daughter, showing a bad education, causeth her mother Poesy's honesty to be called in question. Other sorts of poetry almost have we none, but that lyrical kind of songs and sonnets, which, Lord if he gave us so good minds, how well it might be employed, and with how heavenly fruits both private and public, in singing the praises of the immortal beauty, the immortal goodness of that God who giveth us hands to write, and wits to conceive!—of which we might well want words, but never matter; of which we could turn our eyes to nothing, but we should ever have new-budding occasions.

But truly, many of such writings as come under the banner of unresistible love, if I were a mistress would never persuade me they were in love; so coldly they apply fiery speeches, as men that had rather read lovers' writings, and so caught up certain swelling phrases—which hang together like a man which once told me the wind was at north-west and by south, because he would be sure to name winds enough—than that in truth they feel those passions, which easily, as I think, may be bewrayed by that same forcibleness, or energia (as the Greeks call it) of the writer.

But let this be a sufficient, though short note, that we miss the right use of the material point of poesy. Now for the outside of it, which is words, or (as I may term it) diction, it is even well worse, so is that honey-flowing matron eloquence apparelled or rather disguised, in a courtesan-like painted affectation: one time with so farfet 49 words, that many seem monsters—but must seem strangers—to any poor Englishman; another time with coursing of a letter, 50 as if they were bound to follow the method of a dictionary; another time with figures and flowers extremely winter-starved.

But I would this fault were only peculiar to versifiers, and had not as large possession among prose-printers, and, which is to be marvelled, among many scholars, and, which is to be pitied, among some preachers. Truly I could wish—if at least I might be so bold to wish in a thing beyond the reach of my capacity—the diligent imitators of Tully and Demosthenes (most worthy to be imitated) did not so much keep Nizolian paper-books of their figures and phrases, as by attentive translation, as it were devour them whole, and make them wholly theirs. For now they cast sugar and spice upon every dish that is served to the table; like those Indians, not content to wear ear-rings at the fit and natural place of the ears, but they will thrust jewels through their nose and lips, because they will be sure to be fine. Tully, when he was to drive out Catiline as it were with a thunderbolt of eloquence, often used that figure of repetition, as Vivit. Vivit? Immo vero etiam in senatum venit, etc. Indeed, inflamed with a well-grounded rage, he would have his words, as it were, double out of his mouth; and so do that artificially, which we see men in choler do naturally.

And we, having noted the grace of those words, hale them in sometime to a familiar epistle, when it were too much choler to be choleric. How well store of similiter cadences doth sound with the gravity of the pulpit, I would but invoke Demosthenes' soul to tell, who with a rare daintiness useth them. Truly they have made me think of the sophister that with too much subtility would prove two eggs three, and though he might be counted a sophister, had none for his labor. So these men bringing in such a kind of eloquence, well may they obtain an opinion of a seeming fineness, but persuade few,—which should be the end of their fineness.

Now for similitudes in certain printed discourses, I think all herbarists, all stories of beasts, fowls, and fishes are rifled up, that they may come in multitudes to wait upon any of our conceits, which certainly is as absurd a surfeit to the ears as is possible. For the force of a similitude not being to prove any thing to a contrary disputer, but only to explain to a willing hearer; when that is done, the rest is a most tedious prattling, rather overswaying the memory from the purpose whereto they were applied, then any whit informing the judgment, already either satisfied of by similitudes not to be satisfied.

For my part, I do not doubt, when Antonius and Crassus, the great forefathers of Cicero in eloquence, the one (as Cicero testifieth of them) pretended not to know art, the other not to set by it, because with a plain sensibleness they might win credit of popular ears, which credit is the nearest step to persuasion, which persuasion is the chief mark of oratory,—I do not doubt, I say, but that they used these knacks, very sparingly; which who doth generally use any man may see doth dance to his own music, and so be noted by the audience more careful to speak curiously than truly. Undoubtedly (at least to my opinion undoubtedly) I have found in divers small-learned courtiers a more sound style than in some professors of learning; of which I can guess no other cause, but that the courtier following that which by practice he findeth fittest to nature, therein, though he know it not, doth according to art—though not by art; where the other, using art to show art and not to hide art as in these cases he should do—flieth from nature, and indeed abuseth art.

But what! me thinks I deserve to be pounded for straying from poetry to oratory. But both have such an affinity in the wordish consideration, that I think this digression will make my meaning receive the fuller understanding:—which is not to take upon me to teach poets how they should do, but only, finding myself sick among the rest, to show some one or two spots of the common infection grown among the most part of writers; that, acknowledging ourselves somewhat awry, we may bend to the right use both of matter and manner: whereto our language giveth us great occasion, being, indeed, capable of any excellent exercising of it.

I know some will say it is a mingled language. And why not so much the better, taking the best of both the other? Another will say it wanteth grammar. Nay, truly, it hath that praise that it wanteth not grammar. For grammar it might have, but it needs it not; being so easy in itself, and so void of those cumbersome differences of cases, genders, moods, and tenses, which, I think, was a piece of the Tower of Babylon's curse, that a man should be put to school to learn his mother-tongue. But for the uttering sweetly and properly the conceits of the mind, which is the end of speech, that hath it equally with any other tongue in the world; and is particularly happy in compositions of two or three words together, near the Greek, far beyond the Latin,—which is one of the greatest beauties that can be in a language.

Now of versifying there are two sorts, the one ancient, the other modern. The ancient marked the quantity of each syllable, and according to that framed his verse; the modern observing only number, with some regard of the accent, the chief life of it standeth in that like sounding of the words, which we call rime. Whether of these be the more excellent would bear many speeches; the ancient no doubt more fit for music, both words and tune observing quantity; and more fit lively to express divers passions, by the low or lofty sound of the well-weighed syllable.

The latter likewise with his rime striketh a certain music to the ear; and, in fine, since it doth delight, though by another way, it obtaineth the same purpose; there being in either, sweetness, and wanting in neither, majesty. Truly the English, before any other vulgar language I know, is fit for both sorts. For, for the ancient, the Italian is so full of vowels that it must ever be cumbered with elisions; the Dutch so, of the other side, with consonants, that they cannot yield the sweet sliding fit for a verse. The French in his whole language hath not one word that hath his accent in the last syllable saving two, called antepenultima, and little more hath the Spanish; and therefore very gracelessly may they use dactyls. The English is subject to none of these defects. Now for rime, though we do not observe quantity, yet we observe the accent very precisely, which other languages either cannot do, or will not do so absolutely. That cæsura, or breathing-place in the midst of the verse, neither Italian nor Spanish have, the French and we never almost fail of.

Lastly, even the very rime itself the Italian cannot put in the last syllable, by the French named the masculine rime, but still in the next to the last, which the French call the female, or the next before that, which the Italians term sdrucciola. The example of the former is buono: suono; of the sdrucciola is femina: semina. The French, of the other side, hath both the male, as bon: son, and the female, as plaise: taise; but the sdrucciola he hath not. Where the English hath all three, as due: true, father: rather, motion: potion; with much more which might be said, but that already I find the triflingness of this discourse is much too much enlarged.

So that since the ever praiseworthy poesy is full of virtue-breeding delightfulness, and void of no gift that ought to be in the noble name of learning; since the blames laid against it are either false or feeble; since the cause why it is not esteemed in England is the fault of poet-apes, not poets; since, lastly, our tongue is most fit to honour poesy, and to be honored by poesy; I conjure you all that have had the evil luck to read this ink-wasting toy of mine, even in the name of the Nine Muses, no more to scorn the sacred mysteries of poesy; no more to laugh at the name of poets, as though they were next inheritors to fools; no more to jest at the reverend title of "a rimer"; but to believe, with Aristotle, that they were the ancient treasurers of the Grecians' divinity; to believe, with Bembus, that they were first bringers—in of all civility; to believe, with Scaliger, that no philosopher's precepts can sooner make you an honest man than the reading of Virgil; to believe, with Clauserus, the translator of Cornutus, that it pleased the Heavenly Deity by Hesiod and Homer, under the veil of fables, to give us all knowledge, logic, rhetoric, philosophy natural and moral, and quid non? to believe, with me, that there are many mysteries contained in poetry which of purpose were written darkly, lest by profane wits it should be abused; to believe, with Landino, that they are so beloved of the gods, that whatsoever they write proceeds of a divine fury; lastly, to believe themselves, when they tell you they will make you immortal by their verses.

Thus doing, your name shall flourish in the printers' shops. Thus doing, you shall be of kin to many a poetical preface. Thus doing, you shall be most fair, most rich, most wise, most all; you shall dwell upon superlatives. Thus doing, though you be libertino patre natus, you shall suddenly grow Herculea proles, Si quid mea carmina possunt.

Thus doing, your soul shall be placed with Dante's Beatrice or Virgil's Anchises. But if—fie of such a but!—you be born so near the dull-making cataract of Nilus, that you cannot hear the planet-like music of poetry; if you have so earth-creeping a mind that it cannot lift itself up to look to the sky of poetry, or rather, by a certain rustical disdain, will become such a mome, as to be a Momus of poetry; then, though I will not wish unto you the ass' ears of Midas, nor to be driven by a poet's verses, as Bubonax was, to hang himself; nor to be rimed to death, as is said to be done in Ireland; yet thus much curse I must send you in the behalf of all poets:—that while you live in love, and never get favour for lacking skill of a sonnet; and when you die, your memory die from the earth for want of an epitaph.

Chapter 9

The Relationship of Teaching

'Poesy, therefore, is an art of imitation, for so Aristotle termeth it in the word mimesis, that is to say, a representing, counterfeiting or figuring forth - to speak metaphorically, a speaking picture - with this end: to teach and delight'.

Discuss the relationship of teaching (docere), delighting (delectare) and moving (movere) in the Defence.

Stephan Gosson's Puritan attack on poetry, and the source from which he derived a number of his complaints, Plato's Republic (X), in which Socrates banishes poetry from his idealised state, were joint forces in prompting Sir Philip Sidney's Defence of the art. Responding primarily to Plato's suggestion of fiction's morally corrupt influence on its readers (specifically incorporated into Gosson's The School of Abuse), Sidney employs a style that fuses the rhetorical and polemical with an almost conversational friendliness in order to present his argument in a persuasive manner.

Sidney's various assertions centre on poetry's positive force for inspiring its readers not, as Plato contested, towards 'sinful things', but instead towards virtuous action, through following the traditional tripartite aim of rhetoric; to teach (docere), delight (delectare) and move (movere) 'not only in furnishing the mind with knowledge, but in setting it forward to that which deserveth to be called and accounted good, which setting forward and moving to well-doing'.

The verbs Sidney uses here relate to affecting the mind into action, and it is exactly this notion of 'transforming individuals' that Dr. Gavin Alexander captures when he describes poetry as teaching not only 'what to think but what to do, and inspiring the reader with a desire to act accordingly.' The 'lynch pin' of this civilising function is undoubtedly mimesis, the Greek word more or less translating as 'imitation' or 'representation' in English, although there is no easy or exact translation due to the complexity of the concept.

In order to fully comprehend Sidney's meaning here it is necessary to contrast Plato's and Aristotle's separate understandings of mimesis. Whilst both poets undoubtedly believed in physical and ontological realities transcending the realms of the human mind, Plato's mimesis was rooted in his belief that this world and the things in it are simply imperfect versions of perfect conceits that exist only in the 'ideal,'of which everything in this world is only a copy.

When art imitates life, it is merely imitating an imitation, there being two removes between it and the original: 'the tragic poet is an imitator, and therefore, like all other imitators, he is thrice removed from the king and from the truth' (Republic X). However, Aristotolian doctrine dictated that the artist represents realistic possibilities; he redefined mimesis as the figuring forth of an idea, a fore-conceit, existing in the poet's mind. Thus, the poet takes on the almost divine persona of the creator; rather than making a mere duplication of the original, in Aristotle's view, he should attempt to capture the essence of an idea, and represent it by embodying the whole in exemplary characters and actions.

Plato's argument led him to believe that poetic mimesis was a force used by poets to misdirect and deceive, emphasising his claim that it is over-dramatic with his warning to the admirers of Homer that by accepting the 'sweetened Muse', they are accepting emotions in the place of rationality and reason, but it was the Aristotolian view of mimesis that Sidney adopted in his Defence as a basis for his view that poets 'imitate both to teach and delight, and delight to move'.

By employing the metaphor of the 'speaking picture,' Sidney eloquently conveys that without them, poetry could without much difficulty descend into either vitriolic diatribe or pointless amusements; the vivid description's appeal to the imagination evinces the general notion, and Sidney draws on the Horacian opinion that things seen make more of an impression on the mind than things heard in his explanation that poetry's metaphorical nature is not only part of its pleasure but also part of its power to move. Indeed, The Defence of Poesy is itself extremely metaphorical, and Sidney incorporates his own 'speaking pictures' in the work as a means of illustrating his point.

For example, he dramatises the argument between the figures of philosophy, history and poetry with the rhetorical prosopopoeia: 'Among whom as principal challengers step forth the moral philosophers', setting it in a metaphorical courtroom environment in order to mimetically seal the image in the mind's eye of the reader as they are 'tricked into taking the sugar-coated pill.'

It would be convenient, for the purposes of study, to be able to separate 'docere,' 'delectare' and 'movere' into three individual categories in order to deal with each respectively, but Sidney affords the reader no such pleasure. The three 'aims' are intertwined in their purpose and, more confusingly, in their meaning; Sidney at no point gives us a completely lucid and logical explanation as to the precise effect of each, but he executes his argument, despite the apparent minor vacillations, by always grounding it in the idea of mimesis.

Clearly, the function of teaching knowledge is 'to lift up the mind from the dungeon of the body to the enjoying his own divine essence', but Sidney emphasises multiple times that poetry is rhetorical in its ability to transform people not by teaching them what to think, but instead by teaching them what to do. It is not, Aristotle maintained, the knowing, but the doing that is the 'fruit' - knowledge without action on it is pointless.

In dwelling upon the steps towards virtue; 'make to imitate, and imitate both to delight and teach, and delight to move men to take that goodness in hand, which without delight they would fly as from a stranger, and teach to make them know that goodness whereunto they are moved...', Sidney stresses the meticulousness of his argument, exploiting the rhetorical climax to create the effect of theoretical, systematic processing of a methodical series of events, each one logically leading to the next.

An apposite literary illustrative example of mimesis appears in Shakespeare's Hamlet, when the protagonist dons the rÃ´le of the tragic playwright in the 'Mousetrap' and contends 'the purpose of playing, whose end, both at the first and now, was and is, to hold as 'twere the mirror up to nature: to show virtue her features, scorn her own image, and the very age and body of the time his form and pressure'. Through the medium of drama, Hamlet presents his court with the truth as a 'speaking picture,' to generate action as the 'mirror' in one relatively short sequence mimetically not only reflects the murder scene but also embodies far more about the corruption in the court.

Sidney's comparison between poetry and other disciplines spans most of his Defence, punctuating the work in a rhetorical manner, each time reverting to similar arguments as he challenges similar complaints, and in all of this drawing attention to the poet's prowess in contrast to others. He stresses the precepts of philosophy and the concrete, bound nature of history, and complains that whilst both may have knowledge to deliver, neither will be truly successful in the delivery as they do not apply the triple aim of rhetoric: 'docere,' 'delectare,' 'movere.' Unlike poetry, neither impart information using the Aristotolian 'figuring - forth' (mimesis) and since one must be 'moved to practise' by pleasure, they ultimately fail in 'winning of the mind'.

As Sidney introduces his argument against philosophers (that they teach in such an obscure way that it is indigestible for the un-learned - Sidney actually uses the metaphor of the 'tenderest stomachs', indicative of the dynamism involved in absorbing knowledge and acting upon it, just as a stomach has to actively absorb food) and historians (that they only 'recite') it is clear that he has far more of a polemic unfolding than was previously realised. Not simply is Sidney defending poetry's place in the world, but in addition, he is asserting its place over and above the other forms of learning; it is, he maintains, 'the monarch' of sciences.

Of course, as critics, it is important to interpret The Defence of Poesy as itself a piece of literature, albeit a piece of literary criticism, and to bear in mind that the Philip Sidney in the Defence is a literary rhetorical construct, designed purely to present an argument, and does not necessarily bear a great resemblance to Sidney the author. This may account for a number of discrepancies and apparent contradictions in the work, which I shall examine. Also, perhaps more importantly, it serves to remind us that as literature, it too works on a mimetic level, indicating once again that the teaching, delighting and moving that Sidney writes about in his Defence he also integrates into the main body of the work, exploiting it as an illustration of his theories.

The story of Sidney, Wooton and Pugliano serves as an introduction and reason for Sidney's apology, and his provision of a parallel (the praise of horsemanship) furthermore enhances the 'speaking picture' that is the whole of the Defence, as Sidney continues in his effort to define what the idea of poetry really is. The fact that we know the Defence to be both judicial, in defence, and epideictic, in praise, rhetoric of poetry is significant in that it tempting to think Sidney 'may therefore be more intent on winning the argument than on building a viable literary theory.' This need to convince the reader of the ability of poetry to teach, delight and move, rather than any strong conviction in the argument itself, plays itself out in the general style of the work. Sidney seems to be performing a balancing act between formal oration and wanting to have fun with the reader.

There is in this tension one sense that the conversational style functions to veil the didacticism of the work, lending the flippancy a studied edge, but the rather romantic interludes when Sidney expands on classical mythology and a number of witty ironies such as 'this ink-wasting toy of mine' denote a playfulness in the writer's approach as he treats us metaphorically as children and tries to bring us to 'take most wholesome things by hiding them in such other as have a pleasant taste' as he describes poets doing generally.

Furthermore, a number of ambiguous contradictions arise

as Sidney clutches at his argument but fails (when we look closely) to be able quite to sustain that the reader experiences 'docere,' 'delectare' and 'movere' through the process of imitation. There are various examples of this self-contradiction, but to examine only a few contradicting statements is sufficient to ascertain that in order to defend his argument that poetry is a force for teaching, Sidney has to compromise the details of his imitation argument.

In considering comedy, and defending its reputation against the charges of moral corruption, Sidney says that 'And little reason hath any man to say that men learn the evil by seeing it so set out, since... there is no man living, but, by the force truth hath in nature, no sooner seeth these men play their parts but wisheth them in pistrinum', thus maintaining that men would turn away rather than follow any 'evil' actions observed on stage. He goes on to describe the way heroic poetry 'inflameth the mind with desire to be worthy, and inform with counsel how to be worthy', but it is difficult to imply the two and still sustain the argument that imitation always moves people to virtue.

That the assumption that people are inherently good is a naÃ¯ve viewpoint is actually subsidiary (due to the fact that we are dealing not with the author Sidney but with the literary construct) to the way that it undermines Sidney's argument, as he gives no explanation for it.

Ultimately, the implications of my argument are that in bestowing the ennobling function on poetry as a force for teaching, Sidney illustrates his theory with the work itself, and sets it as its own 'speaking picture,' incorporating many other 'speaking pictures' within itself, as a rhetorical method. However, the many relationships between teaching (docere), delighting (delectare), and moving (movere) in the Defence are complex because the work in which they are set is a didactic piece, it is not just a personal opinion; the author is prepared to sacrifice minor accuracies in order that the overall argument is won by the convincing nature of his rhetoric, and this affects the authority and validity of the argument.

Sidney's various rhetorical devices influence his theory

of mimesis (and its tripartite aim), pulling it in the opposite direction to that of the several contradictions that also arise. Counterbalancing his rhetoric and formal style with witticisms and some more playful contradictions, Sidney concludes that pleasure experienced, in the imitation of ideas, is what makes poetry effective in propelling the reader towards virtuous living, and, in effect, nothing can teach and move to virtue as well as poetry can.

Chapter 10

The English Masque

HAD Ben Jonson never lived, the English masque would scarcely need to be chronicled among dramatic forms. For despite the fact that mumming, disguising, and dancing in character and costume were pastimes in England quite as old, if not older, than the drama itself, it is to Jonson that we owe the infusion of dramatic spirit into these productions, together with the crystallization of their discordant elements into artistic unity and form. Generically, the masque is one of a numerous progeny, of more or less certain dramatic affiliation. Specifically, a masque is a setting, a lyric, scenic, and dramatic framework, so to speak, for a ball. It is made up of "a combination, in variable proportions, of speech, dance, and song;" and its "essential and invariable feature is the presence of a group of dancers... called masquers." These dancers — who range in number from eight to sixteen — are commonly noble and titled people of the court. They neither speak nor sing, nor is it usual to exact of them any difficult or unusual figures, poses, or dances.

Their function is the creation of "an imposing show" by their gorgeous costumes and fine presence, enhanced by artistic grouping, and by the aids which decoration and scenic contrivance can lend to the united effect. On the other hand, the speech of the masque, whether of presentation or in dialogue, and the music, both vocal and instrumental, were from the first in the hands of the professional entertainer, and developed as other entertainments at court developed. The masque combined premeditated with unpremeditated parts. The first appearance of the masquers with their march from their "sieges" or seats of state in the scene, and their first dance — all designated the "entry" — was carefully arranged and rehearsed; so also was the return to the "sieges" or "going cut," and this preparation included sometimes the preceding dance. The "main," too, or principal dance, was commonly premeditated, as in Jonson Masque of Queens, where the masquers and their torchbearers formed in their gyrations the letters of the name of Prince Charles. Between the "main" and the "going out," two extemporal parts were interpolated, the "dance with the ladies" and the "revels," which last consisted of galliards, corantos, and la voltas. It was in the development of the "entry" and the "main" that the growth of the masque chiefly consisted.

The masque will thus be seen to be distinguished by very certain limitations. Its nucleus is always a dance, as the nucleus of the "entertainment" is a speech of welcome, and that of the "barriers" a sham tournament. Jonson employs these terms with exactitude; but it is not to be supposed that either before or after Jonson's time was the term 'masque' used with precision. To most of his predecessors and contemporaries a masque meant any revel, masking, or disguising, from a visit such as that of Henry VIII and his courtiers in mask to the palace of Wolsey, immortalized by Shakespeare, to imaginative, mythological interludes like Heywood's Love's Mistress or Dekker and Ford's Sun's Darling. Indeed, even belated moralities such as the Microcosmus of Nabbes were included among masques. In a full recognition of the precise significance of the term masque, we may deny that title, with Soergel and Brotanek, to Milton's beautiful Comus; because the dancers and actors are here probably the same persons and not divers as in the true masque. But in view of the looseness of the employment of the word as a term in its day, and the intimate relations of the masque in origin and growth with the numerous ludi, disguisings, mummings, and other like entertainments, its predecessors, the subject may be considered here with some latitude, and in no absolute neglect of the various congeners that accompanied it.

It has been customary time out of mind to regard the

masque as an exotic by-form of the court entertainment, come out of Italy and introduced to the court of Henry VIII as a choice novelty; and much dependence has been placed on a quotation from Hall, wherein we learn: "On the daie of the Epiphanie at night, the kyng with XI other went disguised, after the maner of Italie, called a maske, a thyng not seen afore in Englande." But there is little that seems novel in the description that follows, nor anything that differs in any material respect from other descriptions of like proceedings by Hall, both before and after; unless it be, as has recently been pointed out, a new element of dancing and conversation between the masquers and selected spectators. Brotanek explains that the novelty in this case was in the costume, not in the form of the entertainment.

Cunliffe finds the novelty that impressed Hall in the circumstance that the masquers "desired the ladies to daunce," and that the masquers and spectators "daunced and commoned together." As to the foreign influence suggested, these authorities likewise fall apart; Brotanek claiming that it is to France rather than to Italy that we should look for analogues to the later masque; Cunliffe offering many early Italian analogues of Tudor mumming, disguising, and dumb shows. But we need not here look so far afield.

The masque in the height of its development falls into two readily distinguishable and contrasted divisions, the first, performed by costumed but unmasked personages, in nature dramatic; while the second, presented almost wholly by the masked and professional participants, is lyrical and musical. Brotanek finds the model for the first in the costumed speeches of welcome and farewell which were offered Queen Elizabeth on her numerous progresses into the provinces of her realm. For the second he takes us back to the masked visitations and dances which had formed a popular variety of courtly amusement from the days of King Edward III downward. Nor does he deny the complex influences of riding, procession, pageantry, and holiday revels in offering models, precedents, and suggestions to this most graceful and effective of dramatic by-forms.

Interesting as is the subject, none of these origins of the true masque concerns us here, or we might assign to John Lydgate, about 1430, the credit of giving a literary bias to the mumming of his time; trace disguisings into early Tudor days, tell of the rich and elaborate pageantry which sometimes accompanied them there; and dilate on the rejoicings of Christmas, New Year, Twelfth Night, Candlemas, Shrovetide, and May Day, all regarded as naught without masking and disguising. Nor did the maskings of Elizabeth's earlier days differ so much in kind as in degree, although the queen added to the occasions for these shows by her frequent progresses into the provinces, where her nobility vied with her civic entertainers, each to outdo the other in novelty and cost.

If definite points in the development of these forerunners of the masque must be named, one was certainly the elaboration of the Earl of Leicester's devices on the famous occasion of his entertainment of Queen Elizabeth at Kenilworth in 1575. For this purpose some half dozen poets were assembled, among them Gascoigne, Hunnis, and Mulcaster, and the literary and even the dramatic elements were no less a matter of forethought than the feasts and the fireworks. Three years later, when her majesty was entertained at Norwich, we find Thomas Churchyard using comedy as a foil, interspersing amongst his songs and speeches a "dance with timbrels," and "a heavenly noyse of all kinde of musicke," besides employing the device of a canvas cave to effect the sudden appearance and disappearance of nymphs in unexpected places, all of which suggests the grand ensemble of poetry, music, dancing, and stage carpentry in which the later triumphs of Jonson and Inigo Jones were soon to consist.

Sir Philip Sidney, too, had his part in the development of dramatic elements in the entertainment and the "barriers" or tournament. In 1578, as the queen was walking in Wansted Garden, Leicester's seat in Waltham Forest, she was regaled with a lively little pastoral idyl, The Lady of May, in place of the customary formal speech of welcome. Here was dialogue in prose and contest in song, comic relief in Master Rombus, the pedant, but no dancing. The Lady of May is a pastoral, for such was the mode of the moment, and Sidney rode always on the crest of the wave of his time. No less a step in advance were the sumptuous devices accompanying the mock tournament of 1581, likewise referable to the taste and inventive talents of Sidney. The barriers and entertainment thus advanced; the development of the true masque was to come later. "Christmasing" of English annals.

A "Prince of Purpoole," as he was called, was chosen to rule over the revels, and solemnly surrounded with all the insignia of mock royalty: nobles, counselors, officers, guards, family, and followers. Proclamations, the reception of foreign embassies, the levying of taxes, reception of petitions, creation of knights, even a trial—all were sagely parodied; and this stately fooling was interlarded with feasts, dancing, masking, and at least one play. This last was "a Comedy of Errors, like to Plautus his Menechmus," played by "a company of base and common fellows," who were brought in as a last recourse when things were in confusion and going badly. Wherefore the night "was ever afterwards called the night of errors." But it is the masques of the Gesta Grayorum that claim our present attention. They are three:

The Masque of Reconciliation, wherein was represented the friendship of Graius and Templarius, come to offer sacrifice together upon the altar of the Goddess of Amity; secondly, The Masque of the Helmet, a stately allegorical device in which Prince Purpoole's Knights apprehended Envy, Malcontent, and other "monsters and miscreants;" and thirdly, The Masque of Proteus and the Rock Adamantine, the composition of Francis Davison, compiler of The Poetical Rhapsody, and Thomas Campion, the musician and lyrist. This last was performed before the queen, who graced the court of Prince Purpoole with her royal presence on Shrovetide evening, 1595. It opens with a "hymn in praise of Neptune sung by Nymphs and Tritons" attendant on Proteus, who comes to fulfill a pact with the Prince made long since. An Esquire narrates in verse how the Prince, returning along the sea from his victory over the Tartarians, surprised Proteus asleep, and though the sea god assumed various fair and loathsome shapes, succeeded in holding him fast until he promised as ransom to remove the adamantine rock that lies beneath the arctic pole and to transport it whither the Prince might will, assured that "the wild empire of the ocean would follow the rock wherever set." But this is to be fulfilled only on condition that the Prince on his part bring Proteus into the presence of a power "which in attractive virtue" shall "surpass the wonderful force of his iron-drawing rock," the Prince offering that he himself and seven of his knights shall be inclosed within the rock as hostages. The upshot is obvious. Elizabeth's is the "attractive virtue" which draws all hearts. Proteus strikes the rock, and the knights, issuing forth, dance with the ladies their "galliards and courants;" and the performance ends with a second song, "the while the masquers return into the rock."

Space has been given to the description of this masque because it constitutes the type out of which the later masque was to grow. In both productions the structural order is song, dialogue, and the entry of the masquers, followed by the dances and the closing song. The Masque of Proteus well presents, too, the moment of surprise, so effectively to be employed in later times, when the rock opens at the stroke of the "bident" of Proteus and the masquers issue forth.

The entertainments of the latter years of Queen Elizabeth exhibit little that is novel or to any extent contributory to the history of the masque. With the accession of James came a new order of things. The worn and exacting old queen was succeeded by "the British Solomon," with his known penchant for learning and poetry; and the poets and scholars accordingly burst into a chorus of adulation. Nichols lists no less than three and thirty tracts in verse and prose, inspired by the accession and coronation of the new monarch and more than a score of "miscellaneous eulogistic tributes to King James and his family," most of them of the earliest years of his reign. Daniel wasearly in the field with a lengthy Panegyric Congratulatory delivered at Burly-Harington, before James had reached London; and Jonson soon after devised the pageants of the royal welcome in the city and the "Panegyre" on the session of the king's first parliament. But neither with these nor with the devices and pageants of his coronation and his progresses, which he continued after the manner of his predecessor, are we here concerned. For with the reign of James begins the speedy development of the masque, which soon outstripped in elegance, elaboration, and artistic value all other entertainments at court. The masques of the reign of King James are no less remarkable for their learned ingenuity than for their originality and splendor; for if the frivolous nature of Queen Anne of Denmark lent them vogue, the pedantry of her royal spouse often determined their character.

In A Particular Entertainment of the Queen and Prince Henry at Althrope on their way to join King James, Ben Jonson struck, for the first time, that rich vein of poetic fancy which was to distinguish his more regular masques. His material, a satyr surprised in his haunts by the royal train and a dancing bevy of fairies, contained nothing new. But the dramatic humour of the satyr's altercation with the fairies and their turning on him presaged the antimasque to come. The second masque on this occasion was a slighter affair, in which the old satirical figure of Nobody with the popular morris dance was utilized.The first true masque of the reign was Samuel Daniel's Vision of the Twelve Goddesses, presented at court by the queen and her ladies, January 8, 1604.

One end of the presence chamber was fitted to represent a mountain on which was "the Temple of Peace, erected upon four pillars, representing the four virtues, that supported a globe of the earth." About this temple and on the mountain were grouped twelve goddesses and graces from "Juno, in a skycolor mantle embroidered with gold and figured with peacock's feathers," to Tethys, "in a mantle of sea-green, with a silver embroidery of waves and a dressing of reeds," presenting a trident. After an introduction in which Night awakens her son, Somnus, who is sleeping in a cave at the foot of the mountain, Iris descends, delivers a message and a "prospective" (surely a crystal rather than a telescope) to Sibylla, "decked as a nun in black upon white;" and Sibylla, viewing the goddesses as they successively descend in her glass, describes each in fitting verse. All having reached the floor, move in procession to the upper end of the hall before the throne, sing a song, and the dances, alternating with other songs, follow. The masque ends with a return of the masquers to their first position on the mountain. In this masque of Daniel's we have not, as has been maintained, the earliest regular masque, for none of the elements that constitute it are wanting to the two masques of the Gesta Grayorum already described. And, besides, with all its allegory, classical lore, costume, tableaux, music, and dancing, the production is void of the least vestige of drama. It was the author of the Alchemist, not the author of Philotas, who raised the masque to a place in dramatic literature, as it had been those tuneful lyrists, Campion and Davison, who first wrote an English masque in regular form.

Jonson's career as an entertainer at court began, as we have seen, in the year of the accession of King James. It lasted until 1631, within a few years of the time of his death. During a period of some thirty years Jonson composed no less than nine entertainments, three "barriers," two antimasques, and three and twenty masques proper, these latter constituting more than twice as many as were written by all his competitors and imitators combined. Jonson contributed more than twenty masques to the thirty-seven of James' reign; Campion, Daniel, and perhaps Marston alone, writing more than one each among his rivals. Nor was Jonson's primacy in the masque grounded alone in the quantity of his work. His masques are what Daniel's never were—dramatic,—what Chapman's failed to be—genuinely inventive,—what Townsend and Davenant strove for in vain, that is, supereminently poetic. In short, they were rivaled but once by Campion, and by Francis Beaumont, and once again by William Browne.

Several classifications of the masque are possible. We might consider its form, with the growth and degeneracy of the antimasque. We might treat of the masque mainly with reference to its costly and gorgeous performance and the august occasions to which it lent its novel splendors; or we might turn our attention to its material and divide it, with Brotanek, into groups, mythological, astronomical, mythological-allegorical, allegorical-romantic, and allegorical-historical, did not the saving grace of humour forbid. It is safest to tell the story of the Jacobean masque in simple chronological order. On January 6, 1605, the first of Jonson's masques, The Masque of Blackness, was acted at Whitehall. It formed part of Queen Anne's entertainment of the Duke of Holstein, her brother, and on the same day Prince Charles was created Duke of York. Moreover, the queen was herself one of the masquers, and had suggested to Jonson his subject, a masque of blackmoors.

On this hint the poet conceived the idea of twelve "negrotes" (the masquers), who appear in mid-ocean, ranged "in an extravagant order" on a floating concave shell, and attended by Oceaniæ (the light bearers), by Niger, Oceanus, tritons, and other sea monsters. They are seeking a land, foretold by prophecy, wherein their darkened skins shall be changed to fairness. Britannia is that land, and the miracle is wrought. Here for the first time is disclosed the scenic art of Inigo Jones, long to be associated with Jonson in such devices. In The Masque of Blackness, unlike what had gone before, a regular scene was set at one end of the hall representing "a landscape consisting of small woods," and this "falling," an artificial sea flowed in, "raised with waves which seemed to move.... The masquers were placed in a great concave shell like mother of pearl, curiously made to move.... and rise with the billows," and the horizon, on a level with the stage, was drawn by the lines of perspective. Here was a step in scenic representation, the greatest of its time. Yet be it remembered that Jonson had already alluded familiarly to "a piece of prospective" in Cynthia's Revels, acted by the Children of Paul's at least three years before.

Jonson's next effort was Hymenæi, or the Solemnities of Masque and Barriers at a Marriage, that of the young Earl of Essex to Lady Frances, daughter of the Earl of Suffolk. This is one of the most gorgeous and elaborate of entertainments and a departure from precedent in presenting a double set of masquers, the men as Humors and Affections, the ladies as attendants on Juno. In his prefatory words Jonson notes how "royal princes and greatest persons... [are in these shows] not only studious of riches and magnificence in outward celebration,... but curious after the most high and hearty inventions to furnish the inward parts: and those grounded on antiquity and solid learning." And accordingly he embroiders his page with an elaborately learned commentary on the suggestions which he has gleaned from the classics, a practice which fell in alike with his own taste and that of his learned sovereign, and one which his rivals failed not to mark for the shafts of their wit. Hymenœi is an allegory in which the Humors and Affections issuing from a microcosm or globe figuring a man, offer to disturb the rites at Hymen's altar, whereat Reason interferes.

Thereupon Juno appears seated in state and splendor above the "rack" of the clouds, Iris and her rainbow beneath with the eight lady masquers, Juno's "powers," as they are termed. These descend from either side of the stage on floating clouds and, joining the Humors and Affections, are reconciled and the rites proceed. Features of this masque were the exceeding richness of the costumes, all described in Jonson's account; the gigantic golden figures of Atlas and Hercules, supporters of the scene; and the surprising mechanism which managed the drifting and descending clouds, and caused the golden globe or microcosm to appear to hang in mid-air and turn on an invisible axle. Elaborate, too, were the music and the dances; and the lyrical excellence of the many songs rises to all but Jonson's highest level in the exquisite Epithalamion with which the whole masque concludes. The barriers of the next night included a novel device by which "a mist of delicate perfumes," that is of steam, obscured a part of the stage.

In the following January, Campion's Masque at Lord Hayes' Marriage, no unworthy successor to Hymenæi, was acted before the king. As might be expected from a musician, Campion gives much attention in his description to the placing of instruments and voices with a view to the musical effect. "On the right hand of 'the skreene' were consorted ten musicians with base and mean lutes, a bandora, a double sackbote, and an harpsichord, with two treble violins; on the other side somewhat nearer the screen were placed nine violins and three lutes, and to answer both consorts (as it were in a triangle) six cornets and six chapel-voices in a place raised higher in respect to the piercing sound of those instruments." Forty-two instruments and voices supplied the music for this masque. The masque is of Phœbus' Knights turned to golden trees through the wrath of Cynthia. They are freed at last by Night, at the behest of Hesperus, and the trees sink out of sight, a knight clad in green taffety cut into leaves emerging out of each. But, proceeding to the Temple of Night, this habit is plucked off and all appear in resplendent caparison of carnation satin and silver lace. Jones apparently was not the "architect" in this masque. The poetry of Campion is very tuneful and lyrical. The other masque of this year, presented at the Earl of Huntingdon's house of Ashby in honour of his mother, the Countess of Darby, is a composite performance by John Marston, and none of it notable.

To 1608 belong two works of Jonson, The Second Queen's Masque of Beauty and that which celebrated Lord Haddington's marriage at court, called by Gifford The Hue and Cry after Cupid. The latter is a charming adaptation of the well-known Idyl of Moschus, so often amplified by the poets, and contains, besides a happy suggestion of the antimasque in "the Sports and pretty Lightnesses that accompany Love," a superb Epithalamion. In February, 1609, was acted The Masque of Queens, and in it we note a new departure. "And because her majesty (best knowing that a principal part of life, in these spectacles, lay in their variety) had commanded me to think on some dance, or shew, that might precede hers, and have the place of a foil, or false masque; I was careful," says Jonson, "to decline, not only from others, but mine own steps, in that kind; since the last year, I had an antimasque of boys; and therefore, now devised that twelve women in habit of hags or witches... should fill that part... as a spectacle of strangeness, producing multiplicity of gesture and not unaptly sorting with the current and whole fall of the device." Accordingly the scene was set, once more with the help of Jones, to represent "an ugly hell, which flaming beneath, smoked unto the top of the roof," and out of this came forth eleven hags "all differently attired," singing their incantations, followed by "a magical dance full of preposterous change and gesticulation." This scene, the first true antimasque, is filled to overflowing with Jonson's recondite and curious learning, and strong with grotesque and virile poetry. For ingenious diablerie with all the horrid appurtenances of their wicked craft, these witches of Jonson are without comparison. Their relation to the witches of Macbeth and Middleton might be more difficult to trace than their diverse sources in the classics and in contemporary books on the black art. In the heart of the witches' dance the scene changes to a magnificent building, figuring the House of Fame, wherein were discovered the twelve masquers seated on a triumphal throne. And after a speech from "one in the furniture of Perseus expressing heroic virtue," the throne wherein they sat, "being machina versatilis, suddenly changed," and in place of it appeared "Fame, attired in white, with white wings, having a collar of gold about her neck," and described each masquer as she descended, arrayed as a famous queen of history, Penthesilea, Thomyris, Boadicea, and the rest, the last and most glorious being BelAnna (royal spouse of James), "of whose dignity and person the whole scope of the invention doth speak throughout."

We have seen already above how Jonson, followed by other playwrights, had singled out Samuel Daniel, the accepted poet of the court, as the type of literary affectation, unoriginality, and coxcombry, and how that fastidious scholar and courtier had been satirized again and again on the London stage. We have also noticed both Daniel and Jonson as early rivals for the patronage of the new court. The ten or a dozen years that had elapsed since Jonson first represented Daniel as Master Matthew and Fastidious Brisk had wrought a change in the relative positions of the two poets. Daniel, now one of the grooms of her majesty's privy chamber, had continued his epical and lyrical activity, had been chosen to write, as we have also seen, the first of the royal masques at court, and had reached his greatest success in his pastoral, The Queen's

Arcadia, acted during the royal visit to Oxford in the summer of 1605. But Jonson within the same period had become one of the foremost of the popular dramatists, and had supplanted Daniel as the accepted entertainer at court. Now in the very year of Jonson's popular triumph, The Alchemist, Daniel made a final attempt to regain his lost prestige at court, and elected to try to excel his younger rival in that rival's own chosen field. Jonson had never been unconscious of his own merit, nor loath to explain to the world how all his work "was grounded upon antiquity and solid learning," so that when he received a gracious command from Prince Henry "to retrieve the particular authorities to those things which I writ out of fulness and memory of my former readings," the delighted poet did not hesitate to embroider the margin of his Masque of Queens with an erudite and most elaborate commentary. To this weakness of his rival Daniel alludes somewhat splenetically in the Preface to his Tethys' Festival, calling the makers of masques "ingeners for shadows" who "frame only images of no result," and deprecating the conduct of those who "fly to an army of authors as idle as themselves." And he thanks God that he labors not "with that disease of ostentation."

Tethys' Festival or the Queen's Wake was celebrated June 5, 1610, on the occasion of Prince Henry's creation Prince of Wales. It was the concluding solemnity of several days of royal ceremonial in which Jonson took his part as the author of the allegorical entertainment at the Barriers, where the Lady of the Lake, Prince Arthur, and Merlin all welcomed the heir to the British crown to the honors of the tilt and of knighthood. For Daniel's masque Inigo Jones devised three changes of scene, a haven and castle with ships moving at sea, the golden and gem-studded caverns of Tethys and her nymphs, and lastly an artificial grove. Novel features were the rich golden settings for the scenes, the first made up of figures of Neptune and Nereus, on pedestals twelve feet high, embossed with other figures of silver and gold; the use of artificial fountains and the employment of a device of circles of moving lights which "so occupied the eyes of the spectators that the manner of altering the scenes was scarcely observed." Daniel's own invention included what he called an "ante-maske or first scene," the appearance of Zepherus and eight tiny naiads of the fountain, acted by the young Duke of York (later Charles I), then ten years of age, and eight little maids of the court; and "the main appearance of Tethys and her nymphs of the several rivers," who make offering to a tree of Victory. A novel departure was the later appearance of the queen and her ladies, this time in their own shapes.

The incidental poetry is graceful and adequate, as was to be expected of the author of Delia, but the design is uncertain and the allegory incoherent. With a last thrust at Jonson and the professional aid which The Masque of Queens must have required, Daniel prides himself on the circumstance that "there were none of inferior sort mixed amongst these great personages of state and honour (as usually there have been), but all was performed by themselves with a due reservation of their dignity." As may be supposed, the cost of these entertainments was often very great.

Two contemporaries declare that Jonson's Masque of Blackness drew £3000 out of the Exchequer. His Masque at the marriage of Viscount Haddington cost twelve gentlemen contributors each the sum of £300. But it seems that in both these estimates the cost of the entire entertainment, supper, and wines must have been included. The total cost of Jonson Love Freed from Ignorance amounted to £719 1s. 3d. Jonson received £40 of this sum "for his invention," Inigo Jones as much "for his paynes and invention," while Mr. Confesse, "for teaching all the dances," was paid £50. Boys who acted Cupid and the Graces received each two pounds; mere "fooles that danced, one pound." If cost, then, be evidence of splendor, Daniel Tethys, reckoned at £1600, exceeded the cost of its immediate successor, just mentioned, by more than as much again. From a contemporary letter it appears that the court was not without its difficulties in raising the requisite ready money for these expensive revels; and the mention that the queen would spend but some £600 on two masques that year (1610-1611) seems to indicate an intention to retrench in this direction. Whatever the facts, the next three masques of Jonson contain no such elaborate descriptions as to scene and costume, though each develops the dramatic possibilities of the antimasque. In Love Freed from Ignorance (December 15, 1610), Cupid, bound by Sphynx, is beset by the Follies and She-Fools and rescued by the Muses, who supply his bewildered godship with the answer to the Sphynx's riddle. Oberon, the Fairy Prince (January 1, 1611), opens with a vivacious antimasque between Sylvanus and several satyrs who gibe the sleeping Sylvans, guards of Oberon's temple; but less is made of fairy-lore than might have been expected of the author of The Sad Shepherd.

Lastly, in Love Restored (January 6, 1612), Jonson boldly opens with a lively little piece of realistic farce in which Robin Goodfellow satirically recounts the difficulties of a plain man's access to a masque. We have here a picture, doubtless only too true to the life, of the confusion and petty intrigues that attended a royal masque at Whitehall. Masquerado, who would "make them a show himself," is not impossibly Daniel once more; but the sketch is much too slight to make the identification at all certain. But one other masque belongs to this immediate period, the anonymous Masque of the Twelve Months, acted doubtless in January, 1612. Here, after a humorous dialogue between Pigwiggen, a fairy, and Madge Howlet, the twelve spheres descend and call Beauty from her fortress, represented as a huge heart. From this, opening, there issues forth not only Beauty, but Aglaia attended by "the two Pulses." An antimasque of pages follows, a second "of moones like huntresses with torches in their hands," and a species of grotesque pas de seul by a personage called Prognostication. At length the masquers descend, arrayed to signify the twelve months, and "Somnus, hovering in the air," sings the final song. The variety of this masque, though it is not badly written, is its chief claim to consideration.

On November 6, 1612, Prince Henry died, and the makers of masques had cause to lament the loss of a liberal patron. Jones lost his surveyorship of the Prince's works, and went once more to Italy to pursue the wider study of art and architecture; and Jonson, despairing of immediate employment at court, accepted the post of tutor to the son of Sir Walter Raleigh and traveled with his charge into France. But the sorrow of James' court was shortlived.Before two months had expired the court was agog with flutter and expectation of the marriage of the Princess Elizabeth to the Palsgrave, and masques were once more preparing and practicing.

This is not the place in which to recount the extraordinary celebrations—the sea fights and fireworks, the royal passages, triumphs, and ceremonials —that accompanied this august event. Among them were three notable masques, not furnished by queen or prince as customary heretofore, but by lords of the court and gentlemen of the several inns of court, and vying in elaboration, if not in expense, with the royal masques themselves. On the evening of the marriage, February 14, The Lords' Masque of Thomas Campion was given, and the talents of Jones were once more enlisted. The scene was changed no less than four times, the last representing "a prospective with porticoes on each side which seemed to go in a great way." Two antimasques appeared, the first of "franticks," the second of "fierie spirits," the torchbearers, and the masquers were stars and golden statues called to life. Campion's masque is full of graceful poetry, and must have been especially rich and novel in its music.

On the following evening the gentlemen of the Middle Temple and Lincoln's Inn assembled at the house of Sir Edward Philips, Master of the Rolls, and proceeded in mask in a grand procession of horsemen and cars triumphal, attended by two hundred halberdiers in a show, "novel, conceitful and glorious," to the court at Whitehall.

There they presented a rich and ponderous allegorical masque, "blind and deformed Plutus, made sightly, ingenious and liberal by the love of Honour," the composition of George Chapman, "Homeri Metaphrastes." Chapman's antimasques were of baboons and torchbearers, their torches lighted at each end. His masquers were clothed as "Virginian priests," called the "Phœbades," and the scene represented the heart of "a refulgent mine of gold," and again a vast and hollowed tree, "the bare receptacle of the baboonerie." Chapman is very indignant, in his Description, concerning "certain insolent objections made against the length of my speeches and narrations." Yet, with every esteem for Chapman's art, we cannot but sympathize, on the perusal of his masque, with the "vulgarly-esteemed upstarts" who appear to have dared thus "to break the dreadful dignity of antient and autenticall Poesie."

The Masque of the Middle Temple and Lincoln's Inn had come to Whitehall by land; it was planned that the Masque of the Inner Temple and Gray's Inn should move up the Thames from Winchester House in a gallant flotilla, with lights, music, and peals of ordnance on the following evening. And this was partly carried out, though by reason of the crowd (albeit farthingales were forbidden the feminine spectators), and the fagged condition of the court, this masque was postponed until Saturday, February 20. An unusual interest attaches to this production, as it was the composition of Francis Beau mont, and was aided and abetted in chief by Sir Francis Bacon, then King James' solicitor-general. Bacon's interest in such entertainments was of long standing, and we have seen him as far back as 1587, a student of Gray's Inn, devising "dumbe shewes" for a Senecan tragedy, while his familiar essay, Of Masques and Triumphs, from its allusions doubtless written soon after the events on which we are now engaged, is a complete epitome in little of the lore as to "these toys," as wisdom must ever term them.

As to Beaumont, it may be remarked that he wrote this masque as a member of the Inner Temple and about the time of his retirement from writing for the popular stage, a retirement not improbably due to his marriage with a lady of station. The Masque begins with an altercation between Mercury and Iris, messengers of Jupiter and Juno, in which each presents a rival antimasque; the main masque introduces the Olympian Knights to do honour to these nuptials on their way to revive the ancient Olympian games. A new departure is the habiting of both the antimasques, not "in one kind of livery (because that had been so much in use heretofore), but, as it were, in consort [that is diversely], like to broken music."

The setting presented nothing novel. Beaumont's lines are full of life and beauty. Nor is the dramatist wholly lost in the occasional poet. This was Beaumont's only masque.

In Jonson's absence Campion gained a brief vogue. He was called on by Lord Knowles to entertain the queen in the following April, on her progress, at Cawsome House, and joined a simple masque to many speeches and songs of welcome and praise. And he furnished, too, the nuptial masque for the ill-starred union of Robert Carr, Earl of Somerset, with the divorced wife of the Earl of Essex, December 26, 1613. Here, again, the antimasque is made up of a variety of vices, winds, elements, countries, and other abstractions, and a grotesque dance of twelve skippers is inserted just before the conclusion. A feature of the setting, which was the work not of Jones, but of one Constantine de Servi, was a scene of London with the Thames, and the masquers departed on four "barges" that apparently floated away. "I hear little or no commendation of the masque made by the Lords that night, either for device or dancing," says the Lord Chamberlain, "only it was rich and costly." But Jonson had already returned, and furnished the sprightly little Challenge at Tilt for a further celebration of this marriage next day. Two days later, he furnished The Irish Masque, which is no more than a humorous dialogue between four Irish footmen in broken English followed by songs in praise of the king, sung by Irish bards. But it pleased the king and was ordered again for January 3.

The final solemnity of Somerset's marriage was The Masque of Flowers, the work of three gentlemen of Gray's Inn, acted by their fellows and discharged as to cost by Sir Francis Bacon, who was said to have expended thereon no less a sum than £2000, The antimasque is a duel between Silenus and Kawasha (who appears to be the god of smoke) as to the superior worthiness of wine or tobacco, "to be tried at two weapons, at song and at dance," followed by the now customary dance of various characters, here realistically transplanted from the streets of London. The masque unites Winter and Spring in the celebration of this union, and a charm transforms a gorgeous garden laden with bloom into the group of masquers. "The masque ended, it pleased his Majesty to call for the anticke-mask of song and daunce, which was again presented; and then the maskers, [all of them gentlemen of the Inn,] uncovered their faces, and came up to the state, and kissed the King's and Queen's and Prince's hands with a great deal of grace and favour, and so were invited to the banquet."

With the coming of the next New Year we find Jonson once more firmly established as the accepted writer of masques for the court; and for four succeeding years (1615 to 1618 inclusive) each January witnessed a masque of his at Whitehall; whilst one private masque and two independent antimasques (all within the same period) attest alike his activity and his inventiveness. Mercury Vindicated from the Alchemists (1615) opens with a humorous scene in which that lithe deity escapes from the furnace of Vulcan. The antimasques are of "thread-bare alchemists" and "imperfect creatures with helms of limbecks on their heads." The Golden Age Restored (1616) is a beautiful fancy in which Pallas turns the Iron Age and his attendant evils to statues which sink out of sight. It is one of the most poetical of Jonson's masques.

The [Anti] Masque of Christmas (1616) is a piece of drollery in which that jolly personage introduces his sons and daughters, among them Carol, Wassel, and Minced-pie. In it Cupid (who forgets his part) and his mother Venus, a deaf tire-woman, also figure. In The Vision of Delight and in Lovers Made Men (both 1617), Jonson returned to more normal forms. Pleasure Reconciled to Virtue (1618) is of interest alike for the extraordinary scene in which Altas is represented "in the figure of an old man, his head and beard all hoary and frost as if his shoulders were covered with snow;" and from the opening entry of Comus, "the god of cheer or the belly," a personage who may well have conveyed a hint to an impressionable child of ten named John Miltcn. King James was so pleased with this masque that he ordered it repeated, like each of its three predecessors; and for the second performance Jonson wrote an additional antimasque which he called For the Honour of Wales. But it was not alone at court that the masque continued to flourish. In January, 1615, William Browne of Tavistock, the tuneful pastoralist and lyric poet, furnished the Inner Temple with one of the most exquisite works of this kind, and the only masque from his pen. Aside from the beauty of its poetry, Browne's masque is distinguished by a coherence of plot almost unexampled among masques. The fable is that of Ulysses and Circe. The first scene—so Browne calls it—is the Sirens' rock, the second a grove on Circe's Island. One antimasque is appropriately the beast-men of Circe's transformation, another the maids that gather Circe's "simples." But it is not the beast-men that Ulysses transforms to their human shape with the wand of the enchantress, but his companions, the masquers, whom he arouses, asleep in a glorious enchanted arbor.

Even metaphorically, Browne could not call his fellow Templars beasts, so the fable was sacrificed. Another private masque of this period was that presented on Candlemas night, February 8, 1618, at Coleoverton, by the Earl of Essex and his friends. The verse of this masque is fluent and not wanting in poetry. It was written under Jonson's influence, if indeed he is not the author of it himself, as Brotanek thinks. Cupid's Banishment by Robert White was a ladies' masque presented to the queen at Greenwich in May, 1617; a like production, in which Lady Hay with eight others were to have appeared as Amazons, was "disliked and disallowed by the queen" in the following year. On February 2, 1618, The Mountebank's Masque was acted at Gray's Inn and repeated before the king a few days later at court. This masque contains the lengthy drollery of a mountebank and one Dr. Paradox, but is not otherwise conspicuous.

Fleay seems conclusively to have answered Collier's ascription of it to Marston by showing that the masque forms part of the Gesta Grayorum of 1617, and that Marston belonged to the Temple. So, too, Middleton's one Masque of the Inner-Middle Temple (otherwise The Masque of Heroes, January 1, 1619) offers nothing unusual save a coarse, if well-written, scene between Doctor Almanac and various Days of the year, fantastically set forth. A novel feature of the contemporary edition is a table of five principal professional actors, among which number are the playwright, William Rowley, and Joseph Taylor, successor to Burbage as the most important actor of the King's company.

Late in 1615 Inigo Jones had returned from abroad to enjoy the reversion of the office of surveyor of the king's works, which he had long been promised and which had lately fallen in; and for some years we hear little of his employment in connection with the masque. He was busy with more important projects, building and designing for the king. Moreover, after the gorgeous heights which masking reached at the marriage of the Princess Elizabeth, there was a perceptible falling off in the expense and elaboration of these entertainments. To this period, too, belongs the breach between Jonson and Jones, which was certainly complete as early as 1619, in which year Jonson reported to Drummond that "when he wanted to express the greatest villaine in the world, he would call him an Inigo." The causes of this quarrrel are not clear, and it was certainly patched up for a time, as Jonson and Jones collaborated in the masques of the last years of King James. Queen Anne died in March, 1619, and masques at court were intermitted for a time. But after his return from Scotland, whither he had gone afoot on his well-known pilgrimage in the summer of this year, Jonson took up once more his avocation as maker of court masques.

Brotanek has assigned Pan's Anniversary or The Shepherds' Holiday to the king's birthday, June 19, 1620. It is distinguished by its many beautiful lyrics, abiding proofs of the vital poetical spark in "old Ben." The New Year of 1621 was celebrated with a return to masking in the slight and fanciful performance, News from the New World Discovered in the Moon; and in August came one of the greatest of Ben Jonson's triumphs, The [Anti] Masque of Gypsies, celebrated at Burley-on-the Hill, the seat of the favourite Buckingham, at Belvoir and at Windsor, each time to the exceeding delight of the king, and to the enrichment of Jonson by £100 and an increased pension. This masque is vulgar and ribald to a degree beyond any product of its class; but it is admirably vivacious and humorous as well. Like Ignoramus, and for a similar reason, it exactly fitted the royal taste, and is said even to have inspired the long dormant muse of his Majesty to the composition of certain verses. In The Masque of Augures, acted in January and May, 1622, Jonson again made much of the vulgar, realistic present in antimasques of "neighbors from St. Katherens," and Urson and his bears. Time Vindicated, of the next January, was given with unusual splendor, but one of the antimasques had degenerated into a dance of tumblers and jugglers. Neptune's Triumph for the Return of Albion, projected for January 6, 1624, to celebrate the return of Prince Charles and Buckingham from their futile and vainglorious trip into Spain for a royal spouse, was postponed again and again, and finally abandoned; although much of its material was worked over into The Fortunate Isles, presented on Twelfth Night, 1624, to celebrate the betrothal of Prince Charles to Henrietta Maria.

From the foregoing sketch of the masque in the reign of King James several things are derivable. We have, first, the stubborn persistence of allegory, seldom well sustained, it is true, but none the less pervading. The allegorical nature of the masque is its oldest inheritance, one that comes direct from the time-honored practices of the morality. When we consider the stern grip of allegory on the literature of generations that had gone before, how its coloring of the drama was only one manifestation of a tincture that dyed in its vivid colors the religion, the architecture, and pictorial art of the time, the masque assumes a new interest as the last flicker of expiring medieval art. The allegory of the morality was didactic; that of the masque eulogistic and artistic.

The allegory of the morality was often intellectually subtile. That of the masque was simpler and appealed—sometimes grossly—to the senses. The allegory of the Jacobean masque is rarely over-ingenious, and the use of the allegory of double relation,—like that of the Faery Queen and the dramas of Lyly,—in which a given story has alike a reference to abstract qualities and their concrete embodiment in certain well-known personages, had become practically a matter of the past. In a word, the ponderous and complete allegory of the middle ages, in which every item is figured forth with keen and tireless ingenuity, has been replaced by the delicate art of poetical suggestion, wherein allusion, hidden significance, and the force of subtle similitude are plain to the cultivated gentleman, an intimate in the charmed circle of the court, but a blank to ignorance and outside impertinence.

It was the recognition of this that prompted Jonson's words in the Masque of Queens, where, excusing himself for not making certain of his personages "their own decipherers," he says: "To have made... each one to have told upon their entrance what they were and whither they would, had been a most piteous hearing, and utterly unworthy every quality of a poem: wherein a writer should trust somewhat to the capacity of the spectator, especially in these spectacles; where men, beside inquiring eyes, are understood to bring quick ears, and not those sluggish ones of porters and mechanics, that must be bored through with narrations."

A second characteristic of the masque is a profuse employment of classical material in its personages, its imagery, and allusion. This it shared with many other species of the drama, thus falling in with an all but universal mannerism of the age. Nor did the masque, despite the classical learning of its authors, hesitate to follow the popular drama in mingling satire, abstraction, and the personages of every-day life with the stately gods of ancient Greece and Rome. Jonson and Chapman are deep in their show of classical learning. Yet it was Browne who achieved the one thoroughly successful masque on classical story, his masque of Ulysses and Circe. And this is explained by a third characteristic of the Jacobean masque, its general lack of definite plot or design; and outside of Browne and Jonson, once more, its common want even of any certain central idea.

The scenic effects and contrivances with which these amusements of the court were staged have already been indicated by reference and example in the preceding paragraphs. It is notable that this outburst of display and ingenuity is referable to one man, Inigo Jones, and is only one of several activities in which he was famous in his time. On the other hand, as already made plain, the lyric and dramatic development of the masque was almost as solely Jonson's. The antimasque, as we have seen, was his invention, and he, nearly alone, attempted to preserve this feature from degeneracy into mere buffoonery and nonsense. From a foil to the masque which followed it, the antimasque became almost any light or farcical preceding scene and was actually described by Daniel as an "ante-masque." The later confusion of the word with "anticke-masque" further illustrates the degeneracy already alluded to.

When the idea of contrast was lost in the antimasque and that of mere diversion substituted, three changes soon took place: the introduction of a second — in the next reign, even of a third and fourth — antimasque; secondly, a change from the group of characters of one kind, such as Jonson's witches or his satyrs or cyclops, to the medley of personages which we meet in Beaumont; and lastly the development of scenes of drollery in dialogue and the infusion into the antimasque of the element of satire.

For this last Jonson and the taste of his master must be held largely responsible. But in The Masque of Mountebanks and in Middleton's Masque of Heroes as well as in Jonson's Love Restored, Augures, and News from the New World, the interest is chiefly of this kind; though Jonson alone wrote productions such as Christmas and The Gypsies' Metamorphosis, in which the antimasque has usurped all.

Lastly, as to the Jacobean masque, it should be remembered that it remained, as earlier, only one form—though the most sumptuous—of the many entertainments in which the age abounded. The royal progresses continued, though more serious addresses had taken much of the function of the old allegorical welcome; and complete dramas, in Latin and English, pastoral or other, often supplied the place formerly occupied by the "entertainment." Prince Charles, like his brother, had his celebrations, though the tournament was becoming more and more a thing of the past. It was in civic ceremonial that the entertainment, with its pageantry and allegory, its songs and speeches, still preserved the customs of old time. Of the Lord Mayors' Pageants, which were held yearly between 1580 and 1639, more than thirty remain extant and in print, the work of such well-known poets as Peele, Munday, Dekker, Middleton, and Heywood, nearly all of whom with Webster, Marston, and Shirley were the authors likewise of other monologues, dialogues, and speeches of welcome. Indeed, Jonson's own little monologue, The Masque of Owls, discloses that his poetical activity in this kind was by no means confined to the statelier productions of the court. Besides this, the masque came more and more to influence the general drama, not only in setting and staging, but dramas enlivened with masque-like features became the favorites of the hour.

A recent authority states that there are "distinct masque elements in sixteen" of Beaumont and Fletcher's plays. Middleton, Field, Tourneur, and others used the masque more or less organically in their dramas. In Shakespeare's comedies masking may be said to be almost a favourite device, from the Muscovite disguises, the pageant of the nine worthies, and the dialogue of Winter and Summer, all contained in Love's Labour's Lost, to the elves and fays of The Merry Wives, Hymen's Masque in As You Like It, and the more striking examples of the later plays. Thus, besides the scene representing the historical masking of Henry VIII, this entire play was sumptuously staged to represent the ceremonials and pomp of court.

The Winter's Tale contains an antic-dance of twelve satyrs; The Tempest a betrothal masque in which the familiar classical goddesses figure, besides an antimasque of "strange shapes." Cymbeline has thrust into its final act a dream (composite of ghosts and Jupiter, who "descends on an eagle") which nothing but a degenerate taste for such stage devices could justify or excuse. An instance of direct borrowing from a masque has been alleged in the case of The Two Noble Kinsmen, in which a motley group of masquers, including a taborer, a bavian, and five wenches,—somewhat like the antimasque of Beaumont's Masque of 1613,—dance a morris. But neither this identification nor the theory which credits Shakespeare with borrowing the idea of the antic-dance of satyrs in The Winter's Tale from Jonson's Oberon, the Fairy Prince, seems altogether warranted to those whose sensitiveness as to the eternal likeness of things is not developed into too serious a disproportion with their faith in the resources of genius.

There seems no reason to suppose that Jonson was superseded as the entertainer at court in the earliest years of King Charles' reign. Masking was dropped for a season; but on its resumption, in 1631, Jonson is found once more in his familiar place. He had been ill meanwhile, and his years were pressing upon him. Charles had sent the old poet a gift of £100 in 1629, and in the next year employed him on Love's Triumph through Callipolis, which was performed with great splendor, January 9, 1631, the king himself heading the masquers in the rôle of Heroick Love. So successful was this masque that a queen's masque, Chloridia, was ordered to follow, and was acted by her majesty and her ladies late in the succeeding month. But this was the last of Jonson's masques. In both Inigo Jones had assisted. But the quarrel between Jones and Jonson, both of them now old and irascible, broke out anew, and, in the next year, Aurelian Townsend, a small poet and one time "son of Ben," was invited to supply the words to two inventions of Jones.

These were Albion's Triumph, allegorically representing London and the English court, presented January 8, 1632, and Tempe Restored, relating the story of Circe and her lovers, February 14, following. Townsend's verses are graceful and far from devoid of merit, and Jonson's unhappy attacks on Inigo did not include his coadjutor. Jonson's quarrel need not concern us. He was ill, "confined to bed and board," deprived by his rival of his chiefest means of a livelihood. But the old lion was not yet dead, nor had all his patrons deserted him. On the royal progress into Scotland in 1633, Charles was sumptuously entertained by the literary Duke and Duchess of Newcastle at Welbeck in Nottinghamshire, and again in the summer of 1634, by the same hosts at Bolsover; and for both Jonson prepared the devices of Love's Welcome. In the latter the persistent old satirist dared to gibbet his foe once more as Coronel Vitruvius. And although both king and court must have wearied of this petty quarrel of two testy old men, there seems no reason to doubt that Charles was both forbearing and kind to the infirmities of his broken old poet.

As for Jones, he proceeded on to his greatest triumphs of scenic ingenuity, marked in the two court masques of the year 1634. The first of these was Shirley's Triumph of Peace, given February 3, the most magnificent pageant ever perhaps exhibited in England,"a procession and masque in which the four inns of court united to honour their king and to show their detestation of the tenets of Prynne and such as thought with him, recently set forth in notorious diatribe, Histriomastix. The Triumph of Peace is a monster masque, like for its size and the incongruous elements which its designers, in their search after novelty, saw fit to unite in it. The main idea seems no more than the descent of Peace and Law and Justice to do honour to King Charles and his queen. But about this are clustered no less than seven changes of scene from street, tavern, and forest to the sinking of the moon in an open landscape and the rise of Amphiluche, the harbinger of morning. There were eight antimasques, a rapid succession of character dances, of abstractions, birds, thieves, huntsmen, projectors, beggars, and what not.

There were little scenes of humour and folly, a knight tilting at a windmill, four dotterels captured by mimicry, nymphs beset by satyrs; and at one point the carpenter, tailor, painter, and tire-women invade the scene in an unexpected bit of pleasantry. Shirley names more than twenty principal characters in a list prefixed as taking part, but the text discloses at least sixty more, besides musicians, torchbearers, and chorus. Shirley's verse and prose is abundantly adequate to the slender demands of such a performance. The scene, costume, and ornament was Inigo Jones', the music that of William Lawes, the famous composer. A contemporary estimate gives the total cost of the masque to the four societies as "above twenty thousand pounds."

In less than a week the court gave a return masque to this

of the inns of court, and Thomas Carew, the king's "sewer in ordinary" or cup-bearer, in association with Lawes and Jones, contrived Cœlum Britannicum, with eight changes of scene and as many antimasques. A feature of Carew's masque is the carping, cynical Momus, who speaks always in prose with a wit both searching and risqué. One of the antimasques represented a battle, marking a complete degeneracy from Jonson's conception of contrast, while "a prospect of Windsor Castle" was amongst the novelties of scene. Carew's masque is often poetic in the lyrical parts; as compared with Shirley's it is lacking in dramatic instinct. As to form, Shirley's masque is chaos in activity; Carew's, chaos inert.

To this year 1634 (September 29) belongs, too, the performance of Milton's Comus, an entertainment, masque-like in form, presented at Ludlow Castle before the Earl of Bridgewater, Lord President of Wales. This was not Milton's first venture in this kind. He had already furnished part of an entertainment presented to the Countess Dowager of Derby at Harefield a year or two before and now known as Arcades. It appears to have been Lawes' friendship that procured for Milton both of these opportunities to display his lyrical talent, as Lawes wrote music for both and personally superintended the performance of Comus. Milton's part in Arcades includes three lovely lyrics and a speech of the Genius of the Wood. Comus is a far more elaborate production, and, even if not in strict parlance a masque (from the circum stance that it does not clearly involve a ball nor contains masquers), marks in more than one respect a return to the simpler and purer conception of such entertainments in earlier time. Comus presents a coherent situation expressed in an obvious and well sustained allegory.

Comus is not dramatic, as those who have seen it in revival must confess; but the beauty and pure elevation of its thought, its lyrical music combined with "a certain Doric delicacy, "give force to the words of its earliest eulogist when he declares, "I must plainly confess to have seen yet nothing parallel in our language: Ipsa mollities." Although staged with no such pomp as that which distinguished the masques at court in this year, Comus exhibits three changes of scene, a wild wood, a stately palace, and the exterior of Ludlow Castle, in the great hall of which the masque was given. The participants were by no means all new to such devices, for not only was Lawes the guiding spirit, but Viscount Brackley and Thomas Egerton, sons of the Earl of Bridgewater (who with their sister the Lady Alice acted the chief parts of Comus), had already appeared as actors in Cœlum Britannicum. Similar productions to Milton's in kind if not in degree of excellence are The Spring's Glory, a dainty and poetical trifle intended for the prince's birthday, May 29, 1638, by Thomas Nabbes, and A Masque at Bretbie, on Twelfh Night, 1639, by Sir Aston Cockayne, presented to his kinsman, the Earl of Chesterfield. Spring's Glory is no more or less a masque than Comus. Cockayne's is in no wise notable, and probably represents the average of many a private masque which wise if envious Time has suffered to perish or lie buried in those ungarnered fields, the muniment rooms of many an English ancient family.

It was in 1635 that William Davenant offered the court his first masque, The Temple of Love. Davenant had already made a reputation as a dramatist of promise, and was destined to carry the traditions of the earlier theatrical age into the post-Restoration period. The Temple of Love is Davenant's best masque, and seems an honest attempt to restore this much-abused and deformed variety of composition to coherence and reasonable limits. The theme touches on the affectation of the hour, Platonic love; and tells how Divine Poesie has obscured from the unworthy the temple of chaste Love to reëstablish it in all pristine glory through the influence of Indamora's (the queen's) beauty.

The scenery, though reduced in variety and number of changes, was novel from its Eastern and Indian setting and costuming. The other masques of Davenant are not comparable to this. Prince D' Amour (February 24, 1636) was presented by the gentlemen of the Middle Temple in honour of Charles and Rupert, Princes Palatine, the nephews of the king. It is swift and direct in movement; and whilst the scenery was very sumptuous, the antimasques were reduced to two. Britannia

Triumphans (January 7, 1638), presenting the glory of Britanocles, not without its slurs against his enemies, the Puritans, contains the original feature of "a mock romanza," with giant, dwarf, knight, and damsel, occupying the place of one of the antimasques, while the others were furnished by the ever popular humors of the street-folk of London. Lastly, Salmacida Spolia (January 21, 1640) a double masque, in which both Charles and Henrietta Maria took part, discloses the malicious fury of Discord, none too prophetically calmed by the wisdom of Philogenes, impersonated by the king. The antimasque contained twenty "entries," as they were now styled, some of them danced by three or two, or even by a single character.

Brotanek has assigned to Davenant's another masque entitled Luminalia, presented by the queen and her ladies, February 6, 1638. This is a production of no little fancy; nor does it fall below the graceful mediocrity of Davenant. Be Luminalia whose it may, Davenant's work in the masque is direct, not particularly original, and decidedly unlyrical; though, with the ever-fertile and ingenious devices of Jones, evidently sufficient to please the none too exacting demands of a time in which serious-minded men, whether Cavalier or Puritan, were busied with affairs other than "toys."

This enumeration of English masques might be materially lengthened by stretching our period to include a few true masques that fall without it; by the identification of some few manuscripts recorded as masques in the lists and dictionaries of the drama and by a looser employment of the term to include the dialogues and belated moralities which show direct influence of the masque in their inception or staging. The sum total of all these productions is by no means small; and they range from dramas such as A Midsummer Night's Dream, or Dekker's Old Fortunatus, into which the masque-like quality has entered only in part, to complete mythological or allegorical plays such as Lyly's Woman in the Moon, Nash's Summer's Last Will and Testament, Dekker and Ford's exquisite Sun's Darling (1623), and Heywood's beautiful Love's Mistress (1634). More composite in its make-up is

Rowley and Middleton's The World Well Tost at Tennis (1620), whilst pure allegory rules in Shirley's Honour and Riches (about 1631), and in the curious Microcosmus (1634) of Thomas Nabbes. Some of these productions, such as Heywood Pleasant Dialogues and Dramas, "selected out of Lucan, Erasmus, Textor, and Ovid," and published in 1637, could not possibly have been intended for acting. Others were performed privately, and even in public, on occasions which demanded neither the restrictions of "the entertainment" nor the elaboration of the masque.

Aside from Love's Mistress and The Sun's Darling, just mentioned, none of these quasi-dramatic productions are more beautiful or poetic than those of James Shirley, his Triumph of Beauty (1939), "a spirited and elegant presentation of the old theme, the judgment of Paris,"and his Contention of Ajax and Ulysses (1640), immortal for the magnificent lyric, "The glories of our blood and state," with which it concludes. Finally, it seems altogether probable that a larger proportion of masques has perished than of some classes of the more regular drama. For masques were for the most part devised for private entertainment and by poets who lived less in the public eye, ephemeral productions of occasional literature which the world could well spare.

Apologizing for Pleasure in Sidney's 'Apology for Poetry': the Nurse of Abuse Meets the Tudor Grammar School

As one of its major strategies for defending poetry, Sidney's Apology describes poetry's capacity simultaneously to teach and to delight, to instruct effectively by appealing to pleasure. According to the Apology, it is pleasure which creates poetry as superior to history and philosophy, for poetry's ability to delight moves readers to virtue, rather than subjecting them to tedious discussions or ambiguous examples. Even in the initial stages of civilization, it was the "sweet delights" of poetry which prepared early peoples to exercise their minds for the reception of knowledge. But on the other side of the Apology's claim that poetry's delight enlivens its teaching lies the inference that the experience of delight must be justified by instruction. This inference becomes explicit in the Apology's limitation of its defence to a definition of poetry as "feigning notable images of virtues, vices, or what else, with... delightful teaching". When separated from its moral function, poetry's pleasure renders it a "nurse of abuse," dangerously capable of eliciting the wrong sort of pleasure to infect its readers with "pestilent desires". By exploring the "nurse of abuse" image, together with other highly gendered figures, this essay advances the following argument: to the explicit charges against which Sidney's Apology defends poetry—that it lies, it promotes immorality, it was banished from Plato's ideal republic, and that it serves no useful purpose—can be added an implicit charge, that the pleasures offered by poetry rendered it dangerously effeminizing.

A reading of Sidney's Apology as defending poetry against charges of effeminacy was perhaps first performed in a passing comment by Walter Ong, who suggested that the anxiety, common among Renaissance humanists, that "literature, and poetry in particular, was actually soft or effeminate" motivated Sidney's claim that the Amadis de Gaule moved men to courage.

More recently, M. J. Doherty's gendered reading of the Apology has also linked Sidney's poet and femininity. Interpreting the Apology's Lady Poesy in terms of the ancient figure of Sophia or Wisdom, Doherty's work represents Sidney's poet as appropriating a feminine self-knowledge which poses no threat, however, to his masculinity. Fran Dolan's essay on the dichotomies between art and nature, on the other hand, locates Sidney's Apology within a tradition representing poetry as an erotic threat precisely because of a long-standing association between poetry's "pleasure and desire with the feminine."

Dolan claims that, like Puttenham and Montaigne, Sidney uses a "gendered and eroticized" construction of poetry to "convey the vulnerability and impairment of the masculine poet." While much remains to be done with the gendered metaphors and concepts in the Apology, these discussions of the inextricable entanglement of poetry in gender issues provide a radically new approach which promises to recover ideological operations working deeply within the early modern culture and its texts.

Any full-scale rereading of the Apology in terms of gender must first, however, take into account recent work representing a crisis in early modern gender ideology. Since Laqueur uncovered the one-sex model of early modern gender, scholars have newly understood that in this period, in a more literal sense than in modern times, gender was a question of performance—of costume, of gesture, of status—rather than of ontological being. In her study of Gosson's Schoole of Abuse, a work dedicated to Sidney and convincingly claimed as a major impetus for his Apology, Laura Levine describes how this one-sex model created "an unmanageable anxiety that there is no such thing as a masculine self." Thus, for Gosson and others, the spectacle of boys on stage in women's clothing embodied the culture's worst fantasy concerning the reversability of male gender, as adopting the costume and gestures of femininity, the boy actor became in some sense the part he played.

Extending Levine's argument, Stephen Orgel discovers an early modern anxiety that heterosexual love can turn men not only into women, but "back into women," for "in the medical literature we all started as women, and the culture confirmed this by dressing all children in skirts until the age of seven or so." Laqueur's performative version of masculinity further explains Orgel's perception of the essential femininity of early modern boys: in his dependence upon women who dominated him, a boy was not yet able to enact his masculinity. But these essays do not account for the source of this threat of infantilization. What within the nature of heterosexual love was understood to propel boys (or men) helplessly back to this degraded, effeminate state?

Sidney's Apology provides an ideal vehicle through which to study this fear of regression in its representation of the wrong sort of poetry as a "nurse of abuse." Enacting a sort of demonic pieta reducing grown men to the passivity of sleeping infants, this nightmare figure recurs in various texts to embody a widespread anxiety that the pleasures of poetry somehow unleashed the most infantilizing effects of female domination on adult males. In Spenser's Faerie Queene, she appears as Acrasia, cradling the limp Verdant who has left his "suspended instruments" hanging in a nearby tree to sink into a helpless (and seemingly permanent) post-coital lethargy; critics have noted that Acrasia's Bower of Bliss is described in the same terms used by contemporary defenders of poetry.

On a lighter note, Shakespeare's comic artist-figure Bottom takes the place of the changeling child to be pleasured and dominated in the arms of the fairy queen in A Midsummer Night's Dream before he attempts to write a "ballad of this dream." In the Schoole of Abuse, Gosson's scorn for men who choose "wallowing in ladies lappes" over "wrastling at arms" includes a warning against "all suche delights as may winne us to pleasure." Gosson's description of how such delights may "rocke us in sleep" enacts this same merger of adult lust with regressive infantilism.

While Sidney may have been directly influenced by Gosson, the presence of this figure in the works of Shakespeare and Spenser shows that the fear of this regressive process, elicited by the pleasures of poetry, was widespread in the early modern culture. These anxieties, and their link to poetry, are expressed with special clarity in Sidney's "nurse of abuse" passage: " is the nurse of abuse, infecting us with many pestilent desires; with a siren's sweetness drawing the mind to the serpent's tail of sinful fancies... both in other nations and in ours, before poets did soften us, we were full of courage, given to martial exercises, the pillars of warlike liberty, and not lulled asleep in shady idleness with poet's pastimes.". This splitting of the male self between the warrior of the past and the infant-like reader, nursed and "lulled asleep" in the present controls much of the argument and the imagery of the Apology. Like rabbits and ducks, warriors and infants perform a mental trompe d'oeil as they vie for the prominent position in the Apology which will render the loser invisible. Any victory is only temporary. They repeatedly exchange places because in the binary oppositions which construct them, the existence of each depends upon the absence/presence of the other. The effeminacy of the infantilized readers of poetry is necessary to define the highly phallic masculinity of the warrior: hard (not softened by poetry), strengthened by continual effort (not weakened by idle pleasure), oriented towards war (not towards sexual desire). But like most alien Others, this effeminate infant lies not outside but within the warrior. Following Theweleit's depiction of the soldier-male, the phallic depiction of men as pillars connotes the hard body surface—the armor—of the warrior male, which sharply differentiates him from others and from the desiring "female" (or the effeminate child) which remains within the self.

Pleasure plays a central role in this process. Theweleit describes the conversion of pleasure into anxiety in this splitting of the self between female (or childish) interior and male exterior: for the warrior male, pleasure evokes a fear that "dissolution may occur along the borders of the body" (1:414), that the defined male self might become lost in the "desiring-production of the unconscious" (1:432). The worst fears described in Theweleit's paradigm are realized abundantly in this passage. Dramatizing poetry's irresistible power, the merging of nurse's lullaby with siren's song enacts a destructive female engulfment of readers who are simultaneously infants and adult males. Readers once "full of courage" now have no more will to resist the pleasures of poetry than infants who cannot resist a lullaby or refuse disease-laden nurses' milk. Equating nurses with sirens recasts the narrative pleasures of lullabies, and the closeness with dominant women they enact, as a seductive desire which draws men to their death. Lured by an irresistible pleasure in poetry which dissolves the boundaries between adult love and infantile passivity, readers of love poetry helplessly regress to the time of female dominance when they were not yet male.

If the reader is infantilized, the poet is cross-dressed. It is one matter for poetry to be represented as a woman; it is another to represent even the wrong sort of poetry as nurses' milk and sirens' songs. The lullaby function of "poet's pastimes" which lulls readers' (moral) selves asleep not only blurs the distinctions between adult poetry and the songs and nursery rhymes of childhood; it also blurs the boundaries between the poet's voice and the voices of nurses. Feminizing the poet even more radically, the image of siren acts out the reversibility of gender inherent in the one sex gender system. The homonym of "tail" and "tale" in the description of the "siren's sweetness drawing the mind to the serpent's tail of sinful fancies" locates the wrong kind of poetry within the tails or genitalia of women. This homonym measures the extent to which textual pleasures, even the textual pleasures offered by poems written by adult males, were perceived as sexual pleasures, and both were encoded as female.

It might be argued that the Apology presents the "nurse of abuse" passage as one of various attacks against which Sidney defends poetry. But Sidney's counter-argument does not deny the role of poetry in this regressive process. In his impassioned claim "not that poetry abuses man's wit, but that man's wit abuses poetry", Sidney defends moral kinds of poetry by distinguishing them from love poetry. But, as Helgerson notes, against the wrong kind of poetry which "trains man's wit to wanton sinfulness and lustful love," the charges still stand. Moreover, the very terms of Sidney's counter-argument confirm the gender anxieties elicited by the "nurse of abuse" passage: "I yield that Poesy may not only be abused, but that being abused, by reason of his sweet charming force, it can do more hurt than any other army of words" (125; my italics). Explicity countering the effeminizing force of nurse-sirens in the imagery of poetry as an "army of words," the Apology personifies poetry as masculine for the first time in this text. But the stereotypically feminine adjectives "sweet charming" suggest that even as a military force, poetry's masculinity is vulnerable to the reverses imagined within a one sex gender system.

Anxieties elicited by this reversability of gender identity similarly underlie the rigid polarities contrasting poetry and needlecraft in the counter-argument: "Truly a needle cannot do much hurt, and as truly (with leave of ladies be it spoken) it cannot do much good. With a sword thou mayest kill thy father, and with a sword thou mayest defend thy prince and country. So that, as in calling poets the fathers of lies they say nothing, so in this their agument of abuse they prove the commendation". The silent emendation of the original accusation leveled against poetry as the "mother of lies" to call poets the "father of lies" suggests the extent to which gender has become a sensitive issue in this passage. The phallocentric anxiety revealed by the contrast between the man's large sword to the woman's small needle has pushed the Apology's argument into a false position. Instead of defending poetry's morality, as this passage purports to do, it presents the ability to kill fathers as a necessary, if regrettable, aspect of poetry's virility. This morally dubious assertion of the poet's masculinity is further undercut by the terms it employs. In size, the poet's pen resembles a woman's needle more than a warrior's sword; and like needles, poet's pens mark a flat surface within a private, domestic space. The inherent instability of this comparison of pens to swords calls into question an entire line of martial representations of poetry in the Apology. But to understand the wider cultural context which gives meaning to these representations, it is necessary to return to the "nurse of abuse," this time to consider the social formations by which middle- or upper-class males were installed into a prominent form of early modern masculinity.

Like most nightmare figures, Sidney's "nurse of abuse" embodies both a fear and a wish; it enacts both the desire and the threat of that desire to regress to female nurturance and domination. At this time, when according to Aries, "the effeminization of little boys" "had reached its height," a natural nostalgia for childhood posed a threat to gender identity. Yet while a desire for a release from masculinity was rendered unspeakable within this highly patriarchal culture, it was also an almost inevitable result of an abrupt childhood transition commonly experienced by privileged males. Sometime between seven and ten years of age, most upper class boys were suddenly separated from a relatively easy-going environment dominated by women to learn Latin from tutors or schoolmasters. A significant force in shaping the elite male subject was not only this abupt separation of seven-year-old boys from their extended families, but the meanings invested in this transition by the culture. One primary meaning was the conferral of a dominant early modern version of masculinity. William Kerrigan has eloquently represented the project of the early modern grammar school as the rebirth of the students' "linguistic ego" into a masculine world of Latin. For Walter Ong, the learning of Latin, and the severe methods through which it was taught, formed a "male puberty rite."

The learning of Latin functioned not only to mark gender, but to justify it as a means of transforming young boys into men worthy of assuming power. This process left little time for play. As T. W. Baldwin put it, Elizabethans "did not found schools to let boys play; in fact, invented all kinds of sinister devices to attempt to thwart that natural instinct.... They wanted taught to be men." The discipline required for a boy to spend most of his waking hours memorzing Latin grammar, translating from Latin and then back to English, and reciting lessons from rote, installed him within the prevailing grammar school ethic of "instinctual renunciation." This considerable mental discipline, reinforced at most schools with whippings and canings, was to be internalized to create a student population "'broken and bridled'" into strict control of the passions. The theory advanced for this submission appealed to the elite nature of its population: training in obedience enabled children better to claim their proper positions of authority over others as adults. This rationalization is, in fact, explicitly stated in a letter to Philip Sidney from his father: "Be humble and obedient to your masters, for, unless your frame yourself to obey others—yea, and feel in yourself what obedience is, you shall never be able to teach others how to obey you." This obedience was to be internal as well as external, as stated in, for example, the common schooltext Erasmus's Adages: "Nemo bene imperat": "A man must fyrst rule his own lustes, and be himselfe obedient to ryght reason, ere he can well governe other."

Central to the grammar school project was the forceful assertion of the difference of boys both from women and from androgynous children they had been under their charge. Richard Halperin's general argument, that the Tudor education and culture were shaped by a troubling awareness of a vagrant class of the new poor which it could not quite "banish from its unconscious", is even more true for the determinative influence of the women and "effeminate" children of childhood. In the schoolroom culture where reason and self-control were constructed as masculine, the intensely desiring body had no legitimate space. For Vives, physical pleasures decrease virility and even threaten penetration: "Therefore our inner judgement must discover this inclination toward the love of our body, and the desire of things here in this life, which is customarily called our self-love. Such self-love enervates the strength and virility of our minds to such a degree that nothing can be so minute but that it is easily able to penetrate therein" (italics mine). The simple, sensual pleasures of early childhood became something that, by and large, schoolboys were to give up. Not to give up the pleasures of the maternal environment meant not to enter the arena where male adulthood was achieved, according to a "learned man," a friend of Vives, who thanked God for the death of his mother, for "if she had lyved, I had never come to Paris to lerne: but had syt styll at home all my lyfe, among dicying, drabbes, delycates, and pleasures, as I begonne."

The immense power given by Vives's friend to his mother, who had to die before he could attend school in Paris, resembles the power given to the mothers, nurses, and other women of childhood, who formed a silent binary term shaping (and threatening) the projects and even the curriculum of the early modern grammar school. One sign of their power appears in pedagogical writings which endow the vernacular fictions or nursery rhymes first heard in childhood with a dangerously effeminizing power. As Halperin has mentioned, one function of this educational system was to alienate boys from a popular and a specifically female culture whose influence was embodied in its stories. Erasmus's advice reveals the extent to which these tales were contaminated by the gender of their female narrators: "A boy learn a pretty story from the ancient poets, or a memorable tale from history, just as readily as the stupid and vulgar ballad, or the old wives' fairy rubbish such as most children are steeped in nowadays by nurses and serving women."

As an enactment of an affectionate bond between children and women, the vernacular tales of childhood were rendered almost unspeakable. But scattered evidence—a childhood reminiscence, warnings in books on childrearing, histories of nursery rhymes—strongly suggests that these seldom-mentioned stories—of fairies, ghosts, and goblins—told by women to children remained widespread.

While the few remaining references to this oral tradition identify (and usually disparage) the narrators as women, sometimes narrators could, of course, be male. The Apology's allusion to a domestic scene of narration draws on this possibility in its argument that poetry teaches morality more effectively than philosophy. Enticing readers with delight rather than boring them with definitions, the poet begins "with a tale which holdeth children from play, and old men from the chimney corner". Conflating the pleasure offered by simple domestic narratives with that offered by all poetry, the Apology insists upon the childishness of literary response, a childishness which most adults never outgrow: "So it is in men (most of which are childish in the best things, till they be cradled in their graves): glad they will be to hear the tales of Hercules, Achilles, Cyrus, Aeneas".

The contrast between the childishness of this delight to direct instruction in morality which most readers resist, swearing "they be brought to school again," stresses its incompatibility with schoolroom experience. This contrast merges this childish delight, essential to the effectiveness of poetry, with the narrative pleasures later so infantilizing to readers of love poetry. The threat of this identification accounts for a troubling discrepancy in this passage. What is the significance of the fact that the heroes claimed for these tales—Hercules, Achilles, Cyrus, and Aeneas—were, in fact, the heroes of texts universally taught in schools? Were tales of Hercules prominent among the tales "which holdeth children from play," or were the more common "old wives' fairy rubbish" indefensible within the argument of the Apology?

The actual gender of Sidney's narrators of vernacular tales is less important than the ambiguous gendering of the boys who heard them; it was their childhood effeminacy which created fictions as a threat to later masculinity. Still, the Apology's substitution of a male narrator of tales of Hercules for the more usual narrators of "old wives' tales" participates in a wider silence within the culture. The erasure of the influence of the women known in childhood could never be complete: abjected from the schoolroom, they returned as spectres inhabiting the psyches of early modern males and the texts they produced.

Sidney's famous evocation of the poet's golden world is one such text haunted by the ghosts of childhood. As set apart from astronomers, mathemeticians, musicians, and other intellectual professionals, poets alone attain true masculinity through the creativity of their minds:

Only the poet, disdaining to be tied to any such subjection, lifted up with the vigour of his own invention, doth grow in effect another nature, in making things either better than Nature bringeth forth, or, quite anew, forms such as were never in Nature, as the Heroes, Demigods, Cyclops, Chimeras, Furies, and such like: so as he goeth hand in hand with

Nature, not enclosed within the narrow warrant of her gifts, but freely ranging only within the zodiac of his own wit... her world is brazen, the poets only deliver a golden. In her exploration of early modern distinctions between nature and art, Dolan has aptly read this passage as the poet's attempt to create "a world that surpasses nature and bypasses the female role in reproduction," to ally his art with the "masculine and the divine". Dolan's interpretation of this passage can be pressed further, as an expression of the project of the early modern grammar school to provide the "rebirth" of the male subject into "another nature," where masculinity is constructed through the constant exercise of the intellect, with an ensuing disregard for the "natural" pleasures associated with the body and women.

Through the study of Latin, and the process through which that study was conducted, the male subject moved beyond the "old" nature now perceived as a confinement "within the narrow warrant" of Nature's "gifts." Through the sheer effort of intellectual endeavor, "lifted up with the vigour of his own invention, "the schoolboy learned to participate in a new subjectivity centered on the mind, taking precedence over the former subjectivity centered on the body.

Especially resonant of the early modern grammar school is the Apology's peopling of this new nature of the mind with figures encountered in a standard classical education. Besides revealing an educated familiarity with classical texts, the figures themselves embody in exaggerated from the privileges of class and gender forming the basis for the early modern grammar school.

Through military deeds or the privilege of birth, male figures can be elevated to heroes or even (following Aeneas and Caesar) demigods. They can also be degraded to the stupidity of the despised Cyclops, the strong but clod-dish wooer of Galathea so easily outwitted by Ulysses. (Indeed Erasmus used the Cyclops figure to warn his students to study by comparing him to a person "who has great strength of body, but not of mind.")

Within this new and misogynistic nature, women can only appear as monsters. Their depiction as furies embodies the anger projected upon women and the guilt they elicit, the "painful remorse and gnawing of conscience, horribly tormenting wicked mindes" in hell. Their representation as chimeras, or "unreal creatures of the imagination" (OED), points to their elision from the misogynistic discourses informing the grammar schools.

Constructed within yet outside language, women are yet present in this wholly male environment as dangerous illusions. This chimera image may also refer to women's narratives. According to Puttenham, chimeras were bred only by "distempered imaginations" rather than the fantasies of "good poets." In its resemblance to the serpent's tail of the chimera, Sidney's image of poetry with a serpent's tail/tale of "sinful fancies" enacts the denigration of women's fictions within the humanist culture of the schoolroom.

This rejection of the brazen world of sensual pleasures for a golden world of intellectual accomplishments created a problem within an institution designed to transform androgynous boys into virile leaders of men. Poetry remained essential to students as a repository of eloquence, but because of its pleasures, poetry became a site of conflict, or at least of suspicion, in the grammar school curriculum. Helgerson points out that among humanists, whose ideas were so formative for early modern schools, poetry was "soft and effeminate, weakening boys and leading them to lascivious pleasure rather than manly and courageous accomplishment". The dangers posed by poetry to the establishment of the disciplined schoolboy were eloquently expressed in Gosson's passage describing their progress from the lower to the upper forms in the Schoole of Abuse:

You are no soner entred but libertie looseth the reynes and geves you head, placing you with poetrie in the lowest forme, when his skill is showne too make his scholer as good as ever twangde: he preferres to pyping, from pyping to playing, from play to pleasure, from pleasure to slouth, from slouth to sleepe, from sleepe to sinne, from sinne to death, from death too the Divil, if you take your learning apace, and passe through every forme without revolting. Richard Halperin has argued that this crisis posed by poetry to humanist teaching derived from its subject matter, which was "pleasure itself" without reference to "social utility or seriousness"; poetry offered the possibility of "detaching language's pleasing or persuasive force from its ideological anchor." But a startling contrast in gendered metaphors describing poetry's role in education reveals the extent to which the pleasure of poetry brought on a crisis of gender as well as of meaning. Simultaneously representing poetry as a nurse and a military agent, works such as Thomas Elyot's The Book Named the Governor signal radically unstable gender assignments for boys as (effeminate) infants and (masculine) warriors. The presence of both of these contradictory identities corresponds to the uneasy splitting of the self between the effeminate child of the nursery and the masculine youth of the schoolroom.

These radically opposed metaphors for poetry, and the unresolved gender identities for students they imply, enter the Tudor grammar school curriculum in its two contrasting strategies for dealing with the effeminizing potential of poetry. On the one hand, the emphasis on epic poetry, and especially the martial episodes of epic poems by Homer and Virgil, in the curriculum was to promote not only morality but martial courage. Ong's claim that the "masculine" appeal of epic was responsible for its privileging in grammar schools and in the culture generally is well substantiated by, for example, Thomas Elyot's recommendation of the reading of "noble poets," particularly Virgil and Homer, to teach boys the "marciall and discipline of armes" as well as to inflame their "courage" (fols. 31v, 35). The second strategy presented the pleasures of poetry as especially appropriate for younger students, who needed to be "nursed" or enticed into learning Latin at this early stage of their education. Any effeminizing effects of the pleasure offered by poetry in the lower forms were then to be counteracted by dispensing a healthy antidote of history and moral philosophy in the upper forms.

The prominence of both of these strategies in Sidney's Apology creates the Tudor grammar school as an important cultural context through which to read Sidney's defence of poetry. By moving readers to martial rather than purely moral ends, military representations of poetry in the Apology attempt to recuperate poetry's pleasure as "courage." The Amadis de Gaule, for example, has moved readers' hearts to the exercise of "courtesy, liberality, and especially courage". For the citizens of Hungary, songs of their "ancestor's valour" were the "chiefest kindlers of brave courage" in that "soldier-like nation". Sidney attests to the power of that "the old song of Percy and Douglas" to move his own heart "more than with a trumpet". Alexander's admiration for the "pattern of Achilles" stirred up his courage on the battlefield.

Edward Berry has analyzed these and other military allusions as Sidney's attempt to transform the "marginal figure of the poet's vocation into the leader of a militant aristocracy." But surely both Sideney's metaphors and his military aspirations participate in a wider project: to assert the masculinity of poets (including himself) and their readers. More than the actual utility claimed for fictional works, the claim that "Orlando Furioso, or the honest King Arthur will never displease a solider" attests to the masculinity of the pleasure taken by soldier-readers in these texts.

The Apology does not adopt this strategy for defending poetry uncritically; it also tests it to reveal its limitations and the limitations of the version of masculinity it constructs. As in the comparison of swords to needles, a disturbing gender instability lurks within the representation of poetry as the "companion of the camps": the phrase could as easily apply to the male and female prostitutes commonly following the troops. In the emphasis on poetry as a warrior-art, the Apology's argument shows more signs of strain. As Katherine Duncan Jones has succinctly put it, Sidney's own poems were "hardly the stuff to give the troops."

With what "seriousness" was this military use for poetry advanced? Was it part of an intellectual experiment to see how strongly a position could be defended, according to oratorical practice in schoolrooms and law courts? As Peter Herman has recently noted, at the time he wrote the Apology, Sidney also directed a letter to Edward Denny to recommend books to further his knowledge of "soldiery"; all mention of poetry is conspicuously absent. Within the Apology itself, the representation of the warrior-reader is most undercut by its portrait of John Pietro Pugliano in its opening frame.

The admiration for soldiers expressed in the Apology is exaggerated to absurdity in Pugliano's overly enthusiastic defence of soldiers as the "noblest estate of mankind, and horsemen the noblest of soldiers". The "strong affections and weak arguments" of this soldier, whose very name means "fighter," cast into doubt the plausibility of the soldier/reader who reads Homer before battle. Pugliano's unthinking fervor validates, by contrast, Sidney's delicate irony; Sidney's wit makes the martial form of masculinity look obtuse so that poets, even effeminate ones, seem attractive by contrast. But Pugliano presents too broad a target. Despite Sidney's own death from battlewounds, the feudal warrior was fast becoming an anachronism in this proto-capitalistic society; the majority of grammar school graduates finally entered the professions or the court's bureaucracy rather than the military. The primary function of the warrior-reader within the grammar school was not, then, so much to improve courage in battle, as to cast a mystique over a less glamorous masculinity better adapted to the hierarchical social structures of early modern England. This masculinity of the disciplined subject revived a model dating from classical times by which (male) passion was to exert mastery over (female) passions within the self. Pleasure threatened these gender boundaries; for yielding to a pleasure, especially a sensual pleasure, strong enough to overturn reason's control transformed otherwise rational men to not-men: to women or, I would argue, to children, dominated by passions. This hierarchical model of masculinity enacted a defence not only against the desiring female within the self, but also against the androgynous child, whose traces it records.

The Apology contests the effeminizing threat posed by poetry by appropriating its power to inculcate a disciplined form of masculinity delineated especially well in its portratis of Cyrus and Aeneas. The Apology's treatment of these two denizens of the poet's golden world of intellect may well reflect the way the Cyropedia and Aeneid were read at Sidney's own grammar school; for both works figured prominently as required texts at Shrewsbury. In praising Xenophon for his "effigiem justi imperii, 'the portraiture of a just empire'" under the name of Cyrus, the Apology alludes not so much to Cyrus' skill in battle as to his ability to create order both in his realm and within himself by exerting rigorous control over his passions and sensual desires. The ascetic Cyrus presents an especially good example of a disciplined subject; his contempt for physical pleasures may well have contributed a military panache to grammar school discipline, as he addresses his soldiers, for example: "yt becometh a ruler to excede hys subjectes, not in easines of lyfe, but in the care of provision, and prest courage of travell." Thus, by bestowing the Idea of Cyrus "upon the world to make many Cyruses", the poet was imitating not only his heavenly Maker but also the project of the grammar school curriculum.

In its depiction of how Virgil's Aeneid "stirreth and instructeth the mind... with desire to be worthy, and informs with counsel how to be worthy", the Apology explicitly argues poetry's power to produce within its readers the ideal of the disciplined subject, who like Aeneas excels both in his "inward self" and his "outward government." These traits are revealed in Aeneas' reverence to patriarchal values shown in "preserving his old father, and carrying away his religious ceremonies." They are revealed in his obedience to duty, including "god's commandment" to leave Dido to fulfill his epic destiny.

Obedience to hard patriarchal duty, the suppression of soft emotions emerging from relationships with women, the choice of a future destiny over a present pleasure: each of these triumphs of (masculine) reason over the(effeminate) desiring body was as essential to the creation of the disciplined grammar school subject as to the founding of Rome. Suzuki's recent reading of the Dido episode as representing "Aeneas' passage from a dependence on a maternal figure to a position of leadership in a society of male comrades" suggests an apt analogy to the similarly difficult passage experienced by grammar school boys. The protest expressed in Sidney's description of Aeneas's abandonment of Dido despite "all passionate kindness," against even "the human consideration of virtuous gratefulness", suggests a conflict in Sidney's own loyalties to patriarchal values. Like his subversion of the warrior-reader in his portrait of Pugliano, this empathy with Dido suggests that Sidney's interpellation as a disciplined subject was not complete.

The instability in Sidney's loyalties is symptomatic of a larger instability within the early modern culture which proceeds from the splitting of the male self between effeminate child and masculine adult. This splitting is reflected in the widespread metaphor of poetry as nurse, which makes visible the effeminate child it was precisely the function of the warrior imagery to conceal. Within grammar school pedagogy, nurse imagery permitted the pleasure of poetry as appropriate to an early stage in what Kerrigan has aptly termed a "rebirth" of the pedagogical subject into the masculine world of intellect. Thus, William Kempe's ideal schoolmaster acts as a "paineful nurse" to beginning students as, reducing Latin to its simplest elements, he "cheweth it all in small pieces, and thrusteth it into the childs mouth." Elyot recommends Virgil as a nurse to young students: "this noble Virgile like to a good norise/ giveth to a childe if he will take it/ every thing apte for his witte and capacities" (fol. 34v).

Robertello, an Italian scholar, revived Strabo's representation of poems as functioning as nurses to entire cultures, for their "fables gradually suckled and nurtured men until the time they would be more capable of understanding matters in philosophy which are most difficult." The representation of poetry and the schoolmasters who taught it as "nurses" in this early stage of the educational process appropriated the formative pleasures of the child's earlier experience with female nurses even as it attempted to erase the traces of their influence.

In its own use of nurse imagery, the Apology draws on the grammar school strategy of justifying the pleasures of poetry as part of a longer process. The Apology's description of "the poet as food for the tenderest stomachs" presents literature as uniquely qualified to teach because of the pleasure it offers to those who are very young in intellect. Its specific reference to Aesop's tales as an example of pleasureable teaching draws upon current educational practice, for these fables (in Latin or Greek) were commonly recommended for beginning students precisely for the charm of their arguments in which "children moche do delite." The Apology extends the range of grammar school practice in its representation of poetry as a necessary preliminary for more difficult subjects, not only for students but for nations: even for the "noblest nations and languages," poetry acted as the "first nurse, whose milke by little and little enabled them to feed afterwards of tougher knowledges". The Apology represents poetry as operating for Indians the same way it was to operate for boys in grammar schools, to prepare their minds for more difficult studies ahead: "Until they find a pleasure in the exercises of the mind, great promises of much knowledge will little persuade them that know not the fruits of knowledge".

This strategy for justifying poetry as a stage in learning depended on the introduction of more serious subjects—especially history and moral philosophy—later in the curriculum. To some extent, this pattern prevailed in the grammar schools, although it was no means absolute, for it competed with the pressure to begin with the easier Latin texts before moving on to more difficult ones. Thus, Philip Sidney would have read some moral philosophy in the relatively simple Latin of Vives and Cato in his early years at Shrewsbury before he advanced to the sophisticated Latin poetry of Ovid and Virgil. But Sidney's own general sense that history and moral philosophy were appropriate for older students emerges in his recommendations to Edmund Denny for a course of study. If Denny were younger, Sideny would have directed him to study Latin, Greek, and logic.

Since Denny is older, however, he recommends history and moral philosophy. Sidney's recommendations to Denny lend credence to Sidney's own deprecatory representations of the Arcadia as a "toyfull book" and an "ink-wasting toy" as more than simple modesty. As Ong has noted, "literary studies in the Renaissance were for youngsters". This perception of poetry sheds insight on Joseph Loewenstein's findings, drawn from the many references in the Astrophel and Stella to the schoolroom and the nursery, that poetry was perceived as essentially childish.

What, then, can be made of the Apology's claim that pleasure creates poetry as a more efficient teacher of morality than history or philosophy? Not only does this argument run counter to Sidney's advice to Denny, but within the context of the grammar school curriculum, the Apology's advocacy of poetry's pleasure was no less than revolutionary. The privileging of history and moral philosophy in grammar schools was more than a curricular choice; this hierarchy of studies was to replicate itself within the subjectivities of schoolboys. Read according to grammar school dieologies, the Apology's defence of poetry subverted not only the early modern curriculum but also the pedagogical subject it attempted to shape. The very desire for pleasure which history and philosophy were to "bridle" as schoolboys advanced in discipline became, in the Apology, the standard of judgment by which these later studies are found wanting. In the Apology, pleasure becomes equated with, rather than opposed to, morality; for without offering pleasure, texts can have no effect upon the minds and actions of their readers.

The seriousness of Sidney's argument hinges on whether the representations of philosophers and historians are read as portraits or as caricatures. Read as portraits, they further subvert the grammar school project by questioning the ability of philosophers and historians to inculcate virtues they obviously do not possess. Moral philosophers are unable even to follow their own teaching that "passion... must be mastered," for the passions dominating their own souls are only too apparent as they approach "with a sullen gravity," "angry with any man in whom they see the foul fault of anger". A very "tyrant in table talk," the historian is no better. The very "great chafe" with which he denies that "any man for teaching of virtue, and virtuous actions is comparable to him" in fact reveals the falsity of his position. But these representations can also be read as caricatures, as vicious as they are hilarious. Read this way, the presence of these morally dubious pleasures undercuts the Apology's defence of pleasure as a moral force.

In this section of the Apology, any pretense of reasonable fairmindedness has begun to slip. In its passionate defence of its own highly self-interested argument, the Apology employs the unfair tactic of contrasting the worst traits of historians and philosophers to the best traits of poets: only the "peerless poet" appears as a model of rationality as he combines moral teachings and uplifting examples to "entice any man to enter" upon the path of a virtuous life. The exclusion of the amoral poets who offer pleasure without instruction—the writers of love poetry or (even worse) the lower-class, female narrators of fairy tales—finally grants to them the considerable power of very bad dreams. Hovering in the moonlit spaces around and between the words of the text, these ghostly presences assume silent control of the central arguments of the Apology.

More than poetry, and even more than pleasure, is at stake in Sidney's Apology for Poetry. Sidney's text marks a transitional stage in the history of the bourgeois subject; it traces the process through which anxiety became installed in the very experience of pleasure.

The stringent civilizing process shaping the privileged male subject provides a context through which to read the Apology, which recapitulates its figures, its experiences, and its ideologies in its imagery and its argument. Like the Cartesian subject described by Francis Barker, the early modern privileged male had begun to harbor a "profound and corporeal guilt," to internalize a "self-disciplinary fixation predicated on the outlawing of the body and its passions." The stirrings of the Cartesian splitting of the self, with the location of subjectivity securely in the cogito, were already present in the early modern grammar school, where the desiring body was tainted with effeminacy. Unable to reject absolutely this emerging gender ideology, Sidney strains logic to clear a legitimate space for the pleasure offered by poetry. While Sidney records his own interpellation as an early modern masculine subject, he also contests it, casting a lingering look backward to the androgynous subjectivity of childhood.

Bibliography

Craig, D. H. "*A Hybrid Growth: Sidney's Theory of Poetry in An Apology for Poetry.*" Essential Articles for the Study of Sir Philip Sidney. Ed. Arthur F. Kinney. Hamden: Archon Books, 1986.

Davies, Norman. Europe: A History. London: Pimlico, 1997.

Frye, Northrup. Words With Power: Being a Second Study of the Bible and Literature. Toronto: Penguin Books, 1992.

Garrett, *Martin. Ed*. Sidney: the Critical Heritage. London: Routledge, 1996.

Greville, Fulke.Life of the Renowned Sir Philip Sidney. London, 1652.

Hale, John. The Civilization of Europe in the Renaissance. New York: Atheeum, 1994.

Jasinski, James. Sourcebook on Rhetoric: Key Concepts in Contemporary Rhetorical Studies. Thousand Oaks: Sage Publications, 2001.

Kimbrough, Robert. Sir Philip Sidney. New York: Twayne Publishers, Inc., 1971.

Leitch, Vincent B., Ed. The Norton Anthology of Theory and Criticism. New York: W. W. Norton & Company, Inc., 2001.

Lewis, C. S. English Literature in the Sixteenth Century, Excluding Drama. Oxford: Oxford University Press, 1954.

Robertson, Jean. "*Philip Sidney.*" In The Spenser Encyclopedia. eds. A. C. Hamilton et al. Toronto: University of Toronto Press, 1990.